Satyric and Heroic Mimes

SATYRIC AND HEROIC MIMES

ATTITUDE AS THE WAY OF THE MIME IN RITUAL AND BEYOND

by KATHRYN WYLIE

McFarland & Company, Inc., Publishers
Jefferson, North Carolina, and London

British Library Cataloguing-in-Publication data are available

Library of Congress Cataloguing-in-Publication Data

Wylie, Kathryn, 1948–
    Satyric and heroic mimes : attitude as the way of the mime in
ritual and beyond / by Kathryn Wylie.
        p.   cm.
    Includes bibliographical references and index.
    ISBN 0-89950-897-9 (lib. bdg. : 50# alk. paper) ∞
    1. Mime.   2. Pantomime.   I. Title.
PN2071.G4W95   1994
792.3 — dc20   92-51103
                                                                    CIP

Manufactured in the United States of America

McFarland & Company, Inc., Publishers
    Box 611, Jefferson, North Carolina 28640

For Antonio, Sofia, and Gabriel

TABLE OF CONTENTS

ACKNOWLEDGMENTS

I owe the inspiration for this book to two important teachers and mentors: the late Etienne Decroux and Benito Ortolani. Etienne Decroux imparted to me both his passion for the sources of the mime and the spirit of inquiry that has lead to the completion of this book. Dr. Benito Ortolani transmitted to me his love for the No drama and his interest in the shamanic roots of the No. Special thanks are also owed Dr. Stanley Waren, Charles Gattnig, Sahomi Tashibana, Claude Kipnis, Janie Abe, and the PSC-CUNY Research Foundation. Finally, a fond thank you to my parents, husband, and children for their support and understanding throughout this project.

INTRODUCTION

Numerous histories and descriptive works have detailed the diverse genres of mime that have existed in the West. The enigma, however, remains unsolved: What is mime? Is it an art in its own right? The prevalence in mime of adjunct performance arts such as juggling, acrobatics, and dance has hindered critics' attempts to ascertain the "pure" elements that form the core of mimetic representation.

The general consensus is that mime is a hybrid art which employs denotative gesture as its primary constituent feature. While denotation is certainly a key element of mime, it cannot be applied as the main defining criterion to modern abstract and nonrepresentational forms of mime.

Essays that probe the mime's generic elements have touched upon important properties such as identification, metamorphosis, illusion, and the mask, but they rarely tie them together into a coherent aesthetic. The lack of clear articulation of the means proper to the mime has contributed to muddied discussions that attempt to establish mime as an art. The end result is that mime today is still viewed by many as a type of popular performance genre with secondary status, hovering on the edge of dance and theatre.

Compounding the definition problem is the fact that mime performance is generally considered to exist in two distinct types: mime and pantomime. The term mime, which has historically referred to group performances involving improvisation, spoken dialogue and a variety of other elements such as dancing, acrobatics, and juggling, is largely preferred by twentieth century performers in talking about their art.

Pantomime, which is viewed as a specialized development of mime, refers to the silent, solo art of gestural storytelling. Originating in the classical dance of the Greeks, pantomime appears as a distinct genre most notably with the Greco-Roman pantomimes and the nineteenth century *pantomime blanche*. Today, the general consensus among performers is that it is an outmoded style because of its tendency towards mutism in which gestures replace words with codified corporeal signs. As a result of these pejorative connotations, not only has little serious attention been paid to this form, but performers who are in essence pantomimes insist on calling themselves mimes. Indeed, much of

1

what passes under the rubric of mime today actually uses many elements drawn from pantomime such as the solo performer, silence, illusion, and narrative.

Mime obviously has something to do with *mimesis,* which is the "act of imitating" that Aristotle more than two millennia ago set forth as the basis of all the arts. In the sixth century B.C. when the *mimeisthai* word group first arose to denote the act of imitating through mimesis, the secular art of mime came into being. In the fifth century B.C. the root sense of *mimos* "was a miming or mimicking of the external appearance, utterances, and or movements of an animal or human being by a human being; in short, precisely the kind of mimetic performance we associate with the Sicilian mime."[1] The mimes were so named in ancient Greece because the essence of their performance was to portray corporeally and or vocally traits of phenomena, animate or inanimate, in order that they could be linked in the viewer's mind with what was being imitated. The other elements that mimes employed in their performances — juggling, acrobatics, tightrope walking, nonmimetic dance, etc. — were not mime per se, but corollary skills that the mime employed, in addition to imitation, to amuse their audience. These performers did not merely copy objects of mimetic representation detail for detail. They were artists who selected, limited, and arranged movements taken from everyday life to create highly stylized representations.

From its first mention in ancient Greece, mime has been closely allied to the art of the actor. Both the mime performer and the actor use vocal and corporeal imitation as the basis for their representations. However, the actor relies on speech as his primary means of expression and uses vocal and corporeal mimesis as a secondary mode of communication. The art of acting is a special development of mimesis which finds its source in speech and literary drama. The literary script builds indirectly upon the primary corporeal expression that underlies language formulation. Aristotle and other Greek and Roman philosophers viewed the mime as "low life" entertainment and did little more than give passing reference to these performances. However, the theory of mimesis set forth by Aristotle for tragedy and comedy is firmly grounded in a discussion of many of the elements that are properly the domain of mime as applied to literary theory.

Historically, mime has also been linked with the art of dance. While dance historians and critics have largely glossed over the role of mime in the dance, much of what was originally termed dance in classical antiquity was in actuality pantomime with dance elements. Today, modern abstract mime in the West seems to broach the hazy borderline between mime and dance, presenting an apparent rupture with earlier forms of pantomime in which gesture was linked in the viewer's mind with concrete denotata.

The tendency towards abstraction which characterizes all art meets a curious paradox with the mime. While highly abstract forms of mime tend to be viewed as dance rather than mime, dance with a predominance of mimetic elements is still termed dance. Yet mime, even highly abstract mime, is not dance although it may contain dance elements. Those who have studied mime and are versed in its principles know that they are witnessing a mime performance despite its abstract nature.

There must be some other constituent element that has largely been overlooked in analyzing mime that delineates it from dance proper. Mime artists, theoreticians, and critics begin to touch on this element when they talk about mime performers' unique "boundness" to gravity. Unlike the dance which is most often characterized by freedom from gravity, mime performance tends to be high in the Effort factor of "bound flow." Mimes are rooted creatures whose primary means of locomotion is the walk and whose gestures are clearly articulated in terms of withheld and channeled energy.

The quality of boundness is closely linked to another commonly recurring term in the field of mime performance — attitude. Today's statements by critics and mime performers are essentially representative of the historical usage of this term:

• One may conceive of a movement as a succession of attitudes. — Etienne Decroux

• Whoever studies the idiom of a mime will be struck by the multiplicity of attitudes and by their nature.... Attitude is the original method of the mime and the essence of mime. — Jean Dorcy

• [Mime is] the art of gesture and attitude. — Tony Montanaro

• Mime is the art of attitude. — Marcel Marceau

• The attitudes which many mimes consider to be the result and quintessence of the mimodrama, crystallize the whole sequence and form the armature of the story. — Patrice Pavis

Historically, critics who have attempted to define the nature of mime performance focus their analysis on the terms gesture and movement. Most would agree that movement is an important aspect of mime. Yet attention given to mime's motional qualities tends to obscure the equal, if not greater importance, of the bodily attitude as a basis for mime. As one looks at the many mime genres throughout history, one is struck by the "sculptural" or "pictorial" nature of their styles. Like sculpture, mime gesture often appears to unfold from and culminate in a stationary bodily attitude. While many mime performers have attested to the importance of attitude in their work, few have made any attempt to explain their usage of the term. Nor have they sensed that in the element of attitude might be found the key defining feature of both the unique creative process of the mime performer and the key stylistic element of this art form.

The term attitude has been used with a variety of meanings. Tracking the term historically reveals that it was originally employed in the fine arts to indicate "the posture of a figure in sculpture or painting." This usage which has continued to the present, refers to a pose of the body resulting from the arrangement of its various parts into a fixed and stationary formal composition. The poses or postures of painted and sculpted figures have frequently served as models for the depiction of attitudes in the various performance arts which employ gesture. In dance, attitude and posture have been used for centuries to denote "any position held momentarily." Gloria Strauss states, "Like the rest in music with which it shares several functions, a posture or pose [in the dance] may literally stop or interrupt the process of movement."[2]

An attitude is more than a discrete shape that appears to be at rest in space; it serves the purpose of conveying information. Attitude also means "a posture of the body proper to or implying some action or mental state." In recent years the term attitude has also come to refer to the mental state of the individual and is defined in psychology as "a complex of feelings, desires, fears, convictions, prejudices or other tendencies that have given a set or readiness to act to a person because of varied experiences."[3] According to attitude psychologists, the mental state of an individual tends to manifest itself in movement "held up from going into action" or in a dynamically charged posture of the body, which expresses emotion and or readiness for action. Individuals' attitudes towards external stimuli or internal imagery cause them to assume a pose which reflects their psychic state.

Mental attitudes form the basis of individuals' thoughts, dreams and memories, and hence, their language. The bodily attitude is not merely a stylistic device of the mime but the result of a psychophysical process bound up with the expression of mental attitudes. Attitudes or postures of the body function as corporeal linguistic signs which articulate the inner world of the individual.

Mental states of thought, emotion, desire, fear, etc., as expressed through held positions of the body, form a part of our everyday expression. Each individual has a particular bodily attitude that expresses their personality. They also perform movements based on postural freezing of the body or parts of the body. Is attitude, then, any more than just one of the many elements that make up the arts involving corporeal expression? Moreover, if attitude is also a feature of the dance, how then can it be claimed as the unique ingredient of the mime? Further, it could be argued that attitude was predominant in dance and mime before the twentieth century and thus, is more a stylistic element than a primary constituent feature of these genres. The old arts of posing and posturing in acting, dance, and mime seem to have given way to a concern with the qualities of dynamism and motion that characterize the arts of the twentieth century.

In order to answer the questions "What is mime?" and "Is it an art?", the question of mime's importance in ritual must be broached. Corporeal mimesis in sacred rituals involving possession is the crucible in which the mimetic instinct is transmuted into art. It is the *a priori* root of mime as a performance art.

Possession trance and shamanic ecstasy provide an example of how attitude is conveyed by means of role playing and posturally based gesture. Only by reconnecting mime with its sacred origins in ritual performance can there begin to be an understanding of what mime is, its uniqueness as an art form, and its value for society.

Scholarship in the West until recently has occupied itself with postritual mime, creating the erroneous impression that mime first established itself as a viable performance art in the West with the Greeks and Romans and that it bears little relation to earlier ritual forms. Anthropologists have long noted, however, that mime is an essential element of ritual performance. Indeed some, such as Jane Ellen Harrison, have argued that it forms the trunk of a large tree whose branches include not only the art of mime, but those of dance, drama, art and poetic language, as well: "We shall find in these [pantomimic] dances the meeting-point between art and ritual.... Moreover, we shall find in pantomimic dancing a ritual bridge, as it were, between actual life and those representations of life which we call art."[4]

While mime is an essential element of many types of ritual manifestations, from hunting dances to various kinds of ceremonies, possession trance and shamanic ecstasy provide a paradigm for the creative process and postural style of mime as a performance art. The dramatic enactment engaged in by possessed devotees and shamans is not dance nor is it acting; it is mimesis pure and simple. Its primary function is to express and release emotion (attitudes) through corporeal enactment based in imitation of phenomena in which the body of the possessed individual is literally sculpted internally by attitudes which are expressed externally through held body postures. Attitudes are in a sense articulated by the muscles and joints of the possessed individual's body, in a manner analogous to spoken diction.

Ritual mimesis is based in abstraction and metaphor. The essentialized traits of concrete objects of imitation serve as metaphors for the ritual performers inner world of thought and emotion. The secular art of mime, which grew out of ritual, continues the use of highly abstract and symbolic gesture. Denotation serves as evocation. Corporeal signs in both ritual and secular mime move on a continuum from direct mimesis of phenomenon to a highly charged and evocative formulation of signs as the original impulse is codified, purified, and abstracted. With time, the original denotative reference may be all but effaced, but the essence of the underlying attitude remains in the articulated postures and gestures of the mime.

An examination of ritual mimesis assists in resolving the problematic question of the difference between mime and pantomime that continues to puzzle critics. There is a precedence for these two distinct mime genres in possession trance and shamanic ecstasy which are two diametrically opposed forms of trance. Anthropological and historical evidence establishes that the largely solo and silent pantomimes are shamanic in origin and technique, while the group revelry and role playing of the mimes originates in possession trance.

An understanding of ritual mimesis in rites of shamanism and possession not only provides a set of defining criteria for the mime and pantomime, it also assists in determining how performers use aspects of one or the other of these genres in creating their unique styles of mime. In addition, it provides a way of looking at the diversity of mime genres by revealing them to be branches of twin modes of mimetic representation that have not vanished but live on in the psyche of the viewer. A discussion of ritual origins can reveal why some types of mime have wide popular appeal and others seem to be only for an initiated few. It also provides a way of talking about the diverse blends that constitute the work of so many mime artists. The success of their performances so often depends on truth to one of these two models. While mime is often a hybrid art, it has achieved its highest expression with those performers who have distinctly manifested either the satyric impulse of possession trance mimesis or the heroic impulse of shamanic pantomime.

This book is divided into two parts. Part I, entitled Satyric Mimes, deals with the elaboration of the satyric impulse of possession trance mimesis into the secular art of mime in the West. Chapter One examines the psychophysical principles of attitude expression that are found in possession trance mimesis, i.e., identification, metamorphosis, role playing by means of mask and posturally based gesture. It concludes with an analysis of the improvisational and comic behavior of the most common forms of possession trance and sets forth the hypothesis that ritual mime is primarily grounded in comic catharsis.

In Chapter Two, the origin of mime in the West is traced to the masked role playing and comic subject matter of Dionysian possession trance. Greek mimes and their descendants have frequently been accused of possessing "low life" and profane subject matter. However, if we consider the ritual roots of the Dorian mime, it becomes clear that mime carried over many of the sacred elements of ritual into the secular realm. Its basic impulse was satyric and its style was that of grotesque realism.

The apotheosis of the mime was achieved in the comic improvisations of the *Commedia dell'Arte* masks. An examination of commedia in Chapter Three confirms the basic elements that comprise the mime established in the preceding chapters. Commedia dell'Arte has been a primary source for the renewal of the twentieth century art of mime in the West precisely because it provides one of the best extant examples of how the root satyric impulse can be elaborated into a highly codified performance genre.

The training program of Jacques Lecoq in mime, mask and theatre, which is the subject matter of Chapter Four, grew out of his search for the primal roots of theatre in corporeal and vocal mimesis. Lecoq's training method, which essentially initiates the student in many of the ritual techniques of attitude expression through the use of various types of masks, corroborates the psychophysical laws of attitude expression and the satyric essence of the mime.

Part II, Heroic Mimes, traces the secular art of pantomime to the solo performances of the shaman. Chapter Five establishes in shamanic corporeal technique the fundamental elements of the secular art of pantomime. The shaman is a solo performer who undertakes the paradigmatic voyage of the mythical hero for the purpose of divination, exorcism, and curing. The events of the shaman's sacred voyage are frequently narrated gesturally in which corporeal images serve as metaphorical equivalents to the spoken or sung narration. Like modern day pantomimes who employ illusion, the shaman must make invisible presences palpable for the audience by sleight-of-hand and manipulation of the laws of time and space.

A discussion of the *No* mime-dance in Chapter Six is included because it marks a clear ritual bridge between shamanic performance and theatrical performance. The central character *shite* and the mime-dance of the No are direct descendants of ritual mime performed at ancient Shinto ceremonies by spirit mediums and shamans. In looking at the art of the No actor, one can clearly see that it is grounded in attitude expression by means of immobility and body attitudes. The mime of the shite serves to corporeally narrate the spoken and sung performance text. It is basically a form of pantomime dance that uses denotational signs as well as abstract, choreographed, and rhythmically repeated dance movement as an element of its style. The No is important because, along with the Commedia dell'Arte, it has been a primary source to which twentieth century theatre practitioners such as Jacques Copeau and Etienne Decroux have returned to rediscover the roots of mimetic expression.

The Greco-Roman pantomime, which is the subject of Chapter Seven, can also be traced indirectly to the shaman through the art of the Greek bards or story tellers (*rhapsoidoi*). The early Greek dance which was performed in conjunction with chanted, sung, and recited Greek epics was basically pantomime, with elements of choreography and rhythm. This genre was adopted by the Romans and developed into a separate art known as the Greco-Roman pantomime. The discourse of the pantomimes was narration of heroic myth and legend; its vocabulary consisted primarily of codified postures, gestures, and hand-signs which could be linked in the viewer's minds with verbal equivalents. However, there is evidence that the best of these performers also employed highly symbolic, noncodified signs as a basis for their representations.

Chapter Eight deals with the romantic pantomime blanche of Deburau and the modern pantomime of Marceau. The nineteenth century pantomime blanche was a blend of mime and pantomime elements. It incorporated characters and subject matter from the Commedia dell'Arte but was founded on the silent and narrative elements of the pantomime in which gestures replace speech. The performance style of Jean Gaspard Deburau, who embodied the ideal of the Romantic antihero in the role of white-faced Pierrot, was characterized by silence, absence, and a codified pantomime vocabulary. The twentieth century mime of Marcel Marceau was inspired by classical pantomime, silent cinema stars, and the "objective" or illusionary mime techniques developed by Etienne Decroux. Marceau's performance style continues and deepens the art of pantomime by replacing the system of codified gesture with the techniques of illusion.

Some will wonder why I have placed Etienne Decroux, the subject of Chapter Eight, at the end of a line of continuity that begins with shamanism, passes by way of the No, the Greco-Roman pantomime, and Deburau and Marceau. Decroux, they will argue, has nothing to do with pantomime. He averred the nineteenth century pantomime blanche and turned away from his earliest work on objective mime in which he created many of the illusions that Marceau uses as the basis of his style. However, Decroux marks a continuation and deepening of trends apparent in the shamanic mime of the Romans and the No. While corporeal mime does not have a codified vocabulary or use hand signs of the classical pantomime, it is, nevertheless, built upon the dictional elements that underlie spoken poetic narrative. Decroux is unique because he, more than any other modern performer, critic, or theoretician, has realized that attitude is the origin and essence of the art of mime.

PART I
Satyric Mimes

Chapter One

Sacred Mimes and Buffoons

Imitation is natural to man from childhood, . . . he is the most
imitative creature in the world, and learns at first by imitation.[1]
                                                    — Aristotle

We are all born mimes. Perception of the world which surrounds us and
our knowledge of being in the world cannot be divorced from the body which
is our condition of being in the world. A mimetic dialogue with nature forms
our first intelligence out of which a consciousness of self develops. At the root
of human intelligence — the mind that perceives, knows, feels and remembers — are "automatisms" or kinaesthetic motor responses based in the imitation of nature.

The cosmos performs an immense "mimodrama," according to the French
anthropologist Marcel Jousse, in which each phenomenon or "agent" possesses
a "characteristic gesture" which sets it apart from other classes of phenomenon.[2] The gesture characterizing an agent causes it to appear to be "taking an
attitude."[3] This attitude is none other than the stable identifying action of the
phenomenon — its gestural "name." Agents in turn perform "transitory gestures" upon other phenomena (agents) and so on in a myriad of triphased actions of "agent–acting upon–agent" (*Agent-Agissant-Agi*).[4] Jousse gives the
example of "the owl grips the tree." Here the characteristic gesture of the owl
is a "wide-eyed stare." The owl, in turn, performs a transitory gesture of "grip-
ping" upon the tree whose characteristic gesture is "that which sways." Written
mimographically it appears as follows[5]:

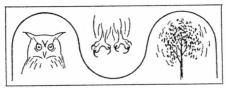

Man, the most mimetic of all animals, records these gestic traits that
characterize agents and their actions in the form of gestural images which

11

serve as metaphors for his internal life.[6] The popular term for the inward play of the gestures of phenomena within the individual's memory is "image." However, this term is misleading as it tends to imply a type of mental picture. In the West we tend to think of phenomenon as fixed and static snapshots of arrested motion. According to Jousse, however, the images which make up our mental life are primarily gestic in content.

The child discovers in the gestic reenactment of phenomena a mirror of his internal world. In the mime of the bird in flight, he is borne aloft and experiences a sense of exhilaration and freedom. As a tree buffeted by the wind, he experiences passion and the turbulence of being. In the mime of the owl, he discovers the idea of fixity, singleness of vision, and immobility. The child also mimes the anthropomorphic world of his storybook and cartoon characters, along with the adults who he depends upon for his nurturing. These too are "powers" whose behavior provides a map of social discourse. Through identification with and countless repetitions of the essential vocal and gestural attributes of model-images the child tries out and constructs his social roles. These gestural images which the child incorporates through play form the basis of his adult attitudes as revealed in his thoughts, dreams and memories.

Identification and role playing not only comprise the powerful learning reflexes of the child, they are the primary mechanisms of ritual enactment as well. Possession trance, in which a devotee is "mounted" by a spirit and acts out its behavior, is the *a priori* root of the art of mime. An examination of the psychophysical techniques of spirit possession reveals that they are based in a fundamental human need to express attitudes through posture and gesture. These same techniques underlie the creative process and the distinct corporeal style of that diverse group of secular performers loosely termed mimes.

RITUAL AND ATTITUDE

A "rite is a ceremonial act or action or series of such acts. Its purpose is to reestablish a connection with the sacred."[7] In the terminology of comparative religion, the sacred is commonly referred to as the Illud Tempus. It denotes a mythical period of beginnings when the ritual was performed by a god, ancestor, or hero. The Illud Tempus is really a metaphor for the ceaseless replaying of paradigmatic images within the memories of archaic peoples. These images are based in the expression or outward propulsion of the most deeply felt archetypal attitudes of the individual and the society as a whole. Carl Jung defines archetype (which he also terms "the primary image") as "a memory deposit, an engram, derived from a condensation of innumerable similar experiences ... the psychic expression of an anatomically, physiologically determined natural tendency."[8] The body of the self is in synecdoche with nature.[9] Archetypes are inscribed in the individual as corporeal images which constellate psychophysical tendencies in terms of agents and their actions from the phenomenal world. These images are most commonly expressed

Chantal Regnault. "Haitian Voodoo in Brooklyn, NY. 'Guédé' ceremony (spirits of the dead)," November 1985. Photograph by Chantal Regnault.

in the dreams and myths of archaic peoples and are recorded in their ritual performances and sacred artifacts.

Ritual is not concerned with the crude mimesis of phenomenal events, but with the reproduction of primordial agents and their actions which are the figurative embodiments of archetypal attitudes. A rite contains man's response to the supreme realities of generation, achievement, and death:

> it is primarily an *articulation* of feelings. The ultimate product of such articulation is not a simple emotion, but a complex, permanent *attitude*. This attitude, which is the worshipers' response to the insight given by the sacred symbols, is an emotional pattern, which governs all individual lives. It cannot be recognized through any clearer medium than that of formalized gesture.[10]

Archaic peoples tend to view the world animistically. It is often the movement associated with a phenomenon that suggests it is imbued with life. Because the source of movement remains a mystery, it is often attributed to the presence of a supernatural power, spirit or god. Thus the swaying motion of a tree might be seen as a result of an invisible, inhabiting force rather than the action of the wind.[11] The figurative mimesis of the motional qualities of phenomenon in terms of spiritual agents and their actions forms the core of mimetic representation in ritual.

Rituals are inherently dramatic and tend to involve mimetic enactment of a society's myths. Myth is essentially a map for human behavior. It reinforces group cohesion by providing models for social interaction.

> Myth involves explication of psychic tensions which activate archetypes and dreams, but are now expressed in the ordinary state of consciousness in terms of images. . . . Psychic tensions exist in a society as well as in individuals. The parataxic outlet for these tensions in the individual is art; in society it is myth and ritual.[12]

Myths are seen as "responses to the problems of social disequilibrium — to the tensions at the interior of the social structures — like screens on which the group projects its collective anguish, and its problems of being."[13]

Through the portrayal of agents acting upon one another, the ritual performer reenacts the great conflicts of the psyche. The tripartite structure of the image (agent–acting upon–agent) is mirrored in the overall rhythm of the mimetic enactment, which depicts the confrontation of the dynamic forces in the universe. The energy patterns involved in the confrontation of protagonist and antagonist are a reflection of the archetypal conflicts involved in the individual's own struggle for psychic and social equilibrium.

POSSESSION TRANCE

The secular art of mime originates in sacred rites of possession in which individuals believe they can actually become gods, spirits, and human or animal incarnations. Spirit possession may be defined as "any altered state of consciousness indigenously interpreted in terms of the influence of an alien spirit."[14] Possession generally involves the "mounting" of an individual by a god during a trance phase induced by drumming, chanting, and rhythmic dancing. Once possessed, the individual enacts behavior associated with the deity through the use of mimetic gesture and spoken dialogue. The parallels between the possessed devotee and the actor have been amply explored by David Cole and others.[15]

Possession cults exist in most areas of the world. Chief among these is Africa, particularly the west coast, and those parts of the New World that have retained African forms of worship, as the West Indies and parts of South America. The most well known possession cults are the Zar cult of Ethiopia, the Vodou in Haiti, and the Candomblé of Bahia. Possession cult rituals generally involve a group of individuals whose mounting by one or more divinities is orchestrated by a priest. In such rites, the individual may enact roles associated with sacred events — mythology, secular history, or individual impulsions — all in the guise of possessing deities, as in the Vodou cult of Haiti. However, these three types of enactment are generally mixed.

Possession trance is a phenomenon of agrarian societies in which the power of the group — its cohesion and well-being — supersedes that of the individual.

The highest concern of all the mythologies, ceremonial, ethical systems, and social organizations of the agriculturally based societies has been that of suppressing the manifestations of individualism; and this has been generally achieved by compelling or persuading people to identify themselves not with their own interests, intuitions, or modes of experience, but with the archetypes of behavior and systems of sentiment developed and maintained in the public domain.[16]

Possession trance is characterized by group performances in which devotees incarnate one of more roles in either highly structured reenactment of mythology or more loosely ordered sociodramas.

TECHNIQUES OF DISSOCIATION /
IDENTIFICATION / METAMORPHOSIS

Possession trance generally involves two distinct phases. The first is characterized by dissociation or "loss of self," frequently achieved through one or more aids such as intense drumming, music, dancing, and the use of hallucinogens. The most frequent means of achieving dissociation is through rhythmic and repetitive dance that is not grounded in the mimesis of concrete phenomena. This type of dance is termed "imageless dance" by Curt Sachs: "The purpose of its movement is to lift the body out of its accustomed corporeality" and to deaden the senses' connection with the external world, opening the way for possession by a god. In short, the individual "dances to lose his body and to become spirit."[17]

The verb form of trance stems from the old French *transir*, which means "to pass away, to die."[18] Possession is generally characterized by dispossession of the self; that is, individuals must first free themselves from the habitual mental attitudes that make up their personalities in everyday life. These attitudes constitute a complex of needs, wants, fears, and desires. While they may be attributed partly to the individual's genetic make-up, they are determined to a greater degree by the complex of attitudes that comprise the cultural milieu which the individual inhabits.

The second phase of the trance is what Sachs terms "image dance." In this phase, the individual "is constantly tempted to give himself up to an object and to assimilate with the object."[19] The god who has been "called forth" by the desire of the devotee "mounts" him, as the expression goes, like a rider mounts his horse. The individual becomes totally identified with the possessing deity and undergoes a radical physical and psychological metamorphosis. In actuality, he or she becomes possessed by the culturally sanctioned images that embody latent personal and social attitudes striving for expression. The identification with these images in the guise of possessing deities is expressed outwardly through vocal and gestural mimicry, which has all the attributes of role playing.

The possession phase is purely a motor phase in which the individual is literally moved by the spirit, like a puppet on a string. "Trance is a condition of dissociation, characterized by lack of voluntary movement, and frequently by automatism in act and thought, illustrated by hypnotic and mediumistic conditions."[20] It is typified by a loss of control by the devotee, who is then manipulated by the possessing spirit. On coming out of the trance, the individual often remembers nothing of what has occurred. However, there are various degrees of trance, from complete loss of consciousness by the devotee to partial or total consciousness and control, which seems to differ according to whether it is a matter of a novice, new initiate, a confirmed adept, or an officiant in full control of the trance.[21]

Some individuals eventually gain mastery over their possession and eventually may reach a point in which they achieve a permanent doubling of consciousness, making them wisepersons. Michel Leiris describes a devotee of the Zar cult named Malkam-Ayyahou who was able to put on and take off various "roles" in daily life while remaining fully lucid and aware of what she was doing.[22] In Haitian possession cults the houngans and mambos (priests and priestesses who direct the rites) are able to maintain a partial or total consciousness during possession. This is called *la prise des yeux* and refers to an adept who can see on two levels simultaneously.[23] Moreover, in daily life the houngan and mambo may be able to call down the spirits for assistance without dissociation.

ROLE PLAYING

Possession is clearly a learned behavior in terms of prescribed roles available in a particular culture. Individuals often experience an initial crisis of possession spontaneously during a possession rite, or exhibit an illness or uncontrolled, anarchic behavior in the course of daily life which is symptomatic of a latent attitude seeking expression. However, this initial crisis must be articulated muscularly according to prescribed patterns of behavior in order for the individual to achieve communication with the sacred.

During an initiation period novices are instructed by priests in the sacred knowledge of the group. In this process, they learn how to model their behavior in accordance with a pantheon of deities who each have a certain aspect and history. They undergo intensive corporeal training in which the original anarchic expression is given order through deliberate and conscious imitation of the dances, comportment, and gestures of the gods.

Sheila Walker differentiates three varieties of possession trance on the basis of their possession roles: "predominantly cultural," "cultural and psychological," and "predominantly psychological."[24] Type one, predominantly cultural, is typified by the original Haitian *loa* who are part of a coherent mythological structure. The possession roles are based on "powerful nature deities concerned with the functioning of the universe and the life of the whole community."[25] Rituals involve the reenactment of scenes from the lives of gods or primal ancestors by means of highly stylized gesture. Since type one gods embody universal human attributes, the devotee must undergo a long training in order to learn ritual dissociation and actual possession. Walker suggests that because the devotee is not expressing his own latent attitudes in the guise of the possessing deity, the trance is very light and involvement is similar to that of an actor who plays a role.

Type two, mixed cultural and psychological, is the most common form of possession trance. The deities are minor gods, spirits or human personages that reflect the structure and values of society. New deities and spirits are added to the repertoire of available roles to reflect the development of new needs within the society. In Haiti, the gods in this type of trance have been integrated into secular history and portrayed as secular heroes. For example, Toussaint has become a loa in the Vodou pantheon. The Ethiopian Zar are spirits who are not in control of nature and who are involved with man's everyday behavior. The focus of type two rituals is on the enactment of the attributes of the gods as they express profane social tensions rather than a coherent mythology. They are more in the nature of ethnodramas in which, "the human social interaction determines the interaction of the deities when they come to the ceremonies. The possessed individuals, rather than re-enacting the lives and acts of the deities, are actually re-enacting on a sacred level their ordinary profane social interactions and tensions."[26] Devotees may enact a deity who is similar to their everyday personality or a deity which allows them to exhibit latent attributes of themselves that are normally hidden. On mastering the external attributes of various roles, devotees in type two possession rituals are generally able to achieve real internal identification with the attitudes embodied by the role; in other words, they are able to become possessed by it.

Type three, predominantly psychological, is found where the cult is in a state of disorganization and decline. In this type of ritual there is little social structure or control and the devotees are largely uninitiated. The possessing deities are expressions of the individual's own "libidinous attitudes" or are people that they know.[27] They constitute the invention of personal roles by the individual which serve to vent their private psychic conflicts and tensions rather than the social tensions within the group. In Haiti, these are new loa with no definite place in the traditional pantheon.

ROLE PLAYING AND ATTITUDE EXPRESSION

The possessed is then a subject hypnotized by a mythological figure, and if this figure can reveal itself in taking "possession" of the body of the subject, it is because it has already been inscribed within the person in an invisible manner....[28] — France Schott-Billman

The "re-presenting" of psychic images by means of role playing in ritual enactment is based in the expression of attitudes. In rites of possession a devotee becomes identified with images in the form of possessing deities that represent their own latent attitudes as well as the attitudes of the group. Images are interpreted as part of reality. In the Dinka religion, the world is filled with powers or supernatural entities "which represent images of the Dinkas' reactions to and interpretations of their experiences in their physical and social environment. They see these images not as memories of the past existing only in their minds and influencing them, as would be the case in the Western world, but rather as part of objective reality, which can act upon them at any time as outside agents."[29]

In Haitian Vodou, the loa represent a constellation of needs, desires, and fears. In possession trance the devotee projects images of his desire into the personalities of the possessing deities and then embodies them and acts them out. "Projection and articulation by means of spirits are both essentially *metaphorical* processes. In projection, the other is the vehicle for the qualities, feelings, and desires . . . that are within the self."[30]

Possession trance is sought when the individual and the group feel a need to change the course of events in the world around them and feel powerless to do so on their own. Psychic tension builds up from the inability to fulfill their needs. According to Walter Abell, these tensions resulting from delayed gratification are translated into tension imagery, which lies at the bases of individual fantasy, ritual expression, and the various forms of cultural expression: "these tensions stimulate our imagination to form images embodying their emotional essence. The mental activity through which psychic tensions are thus translated into equivalent forms of mental imagery, we shall call the *tension imagery process*."[31]

The collective needs and fears of the group engender emotions from which imagery is derived. This imagery is figuratively embodied in ritual mimodramas, based on myth, in which possessed devotees become gods and act out their own tensions and desires as well as those of the group. The enactment of psychic tensions under the guise of possessing gods serves to generate and release emotion. "Ritual then involves *imitation*; but does not arise out of it. It desires to recreate an emotion, not to reproduce an object."[32]

In the language of modern psychology, the psychic tensions that lie at the core of imagery may be defined as "attitude," that is "a complex of feelings, desires, fears, convictions, prejudices or other tendencies that have given a set or readiness to act to a person because of varied experiences."[33] Emotions are essentially motor attitudes that the individual holds within his body and which constitute his personal stance or response towards his inner and outer worlds. According to Ida Rubinstein, human feelings "express not the attributes of the objects but the state of the subject, the modifications of the internal states of the individual, and his relation to what surrounds him. Human feeling is a person's attitude to the world."[34]

ROLE PLAYING, ATTITUDE AND "EFFORT"

A person's ability to change the quality of effort, that is, the way in which nervous energy is released, by varying the composition and sequence of its components, together with the reactions of others to these changes, are the very essence of mime.[35] — Rudolf Laban

The energies contained in agents and their actions in the phenomenal world serve as metaphors for the ritual performer's latent attitudes. The possessed is able to identify with the energies of the possessor because these energies mirror energies arising from conflicting impulses in the form of latent attitudes within his own body. In his book *Power of Myth*, Joseph Campbell asks, "What is a God? God is a personification of a motivating power or a value system that functions in human life and in the universe — the powers of your own body and of nature. The myths are metaphorical of spiritual potentiality in the human being, and the same powers that animate our life animate the life of the world."[36]

The gods, as previously mentioned, are figurative embodiments of the important powers residing in natural phenomena. Beneath the gestures that characterize agents and their actions in the phenomenal world lie basic tensions or energies that fill out the agent's form and give sense and significance to its gestures. The possessed individual essentially identifies with the agents' energies; the energies mirror the psychic tensions contained in the attitude which gave rise to the enacted image. The possessed is then able to act out latent tensions in ritual through mimetic postures and gestures.

Rudolf Laban's theories of "Effort/Shape" provide an insight into what is meant by the tension or energy that underlies the gestic content of imagery. Effort is a system developed by Laban in the twentieth century to describe a person's inner attitude (conscious or unconscious) towards the movement factors of "time, weight, space and flow."[37] Effort is a translation of the German word *antrieb* which means "motor." The individual reveals his own basic "Effort attitudes" by a preference for either an "indulgence in" (yielding to) the basic Effort factors or a "fighting against" them. Briefly, the motion factors which comprise Effort can be described qualitatively as the moving person's attitude towards space (the flexibility of directness of attention), weight (the sensitivity or forcefulness of attention), time (the leisureliness or urgency of decision) and flow (the ease or restraint of the action).[38] Quantitatively, the motion factors can be described as: the amount of *space* (the measurable degree of angles or movement), *weight* (the measurable degree of strength used in an action), *time* (the measurable length of time taken to make a movement), and *flow* (the measurable degree of continuity or pausing in the movement).

Each phenomenon in the universe presents a combination of the four Effort factors which are apparent in the special material qualities of the phenomenon but are most clearly seen in its characteristic gestures or actions.

For example in the tripartite action of "the owl grips the tree," the owl is "that which stares wide-eyed" (*l'ocularisant*). The Efforts are direct (space), forceful (weight), slow (time), and restrained (flow). That is, the owl stares fixedly in space. The eyes seem to be constantly expanding as their orbs push outward on space. Because there are few blinks to give a sense of duration, the stare seems timeless. Coupled with the immobility of the owl's body there is a constant tension present in the bound energy of the fixed and staring eyes. In representing an owl, the body remains immobile and the eyes become the locus of the image. The tree, on the other hand, "that which sways," has a very different energy combination, characterized by a predominance of free flow and indirectness.

The enactment of roles in possession trance is essentially based on the portrayal of the motion factors underlying the gestic content of imagery — those which cause it to appear to be "taking an attitude." Possession roles are metaphorical embodiments of psychic tensions that animate the individual and or his group. One aspect of this process involves a reaction to images. "Images can revive and even produce emotions and corresponding emotional expressions.... Thus emotional images have a direct influence on the organism."[39] In addition to reacting to images, the devotee can become the image and enact its characteristic Efforts or tensions through posture and gesture. Effort is, therefore, that form of energy that underlies the postures and gestures of the possessed devotee and which imparts to them their sense and significance.

CHARACTERISTIC GESTURES OF THE GODS AND EFFORT

The gods, according to Laban, are perceived by primitive peoples as "the initiators and instigators of Effort in all its configurations; and the ritual mimesis of agents symbolically embodied by their effort actions is an embodiment of these people's 'effort thinking.'"[40] In rites of possession, the incarnated deities are distinguished by their basic Effort attitudes. Often, as in the case of Haitian Vodou, the gods are figurative embodiments of animal powers. For example, Damballah is portrayed as a slithering snake. In the Nâgo-Yoruba cult

> *Orun*, god of blacksmiths, warriors, hunters, and all who use iron, is characterized by coarse and energetic manners; *Shango,* god of thunder, by manly and jolly dances; *Orishala,* the creator god, by calm and serene behavior; *Shapana,* god of smallpox and contagious diseases, by restless agitation; *Eshu Elegba,* messenger of the other gods, by cynical and abusive attitudes.[41]

The Effort attitude characterizing each god manifests itself in a signature action or behavior. This can be seen in the mimesis of gods in the reenactment of myth during the Kwakiutl ceremonies in northern Vancouver Island. The highest order of the winter ceremonial is that of the *hamatsa* or cannibal dancer.[42] The reenactment of the myth among the Kwakiutl signals the entrance of young men, who have undergone a lengthy initiation period, into the hamatsa society. This is a highly structured type one possession ritual which involves spirit possession by powerful nature deities, masks, costume, spoken dialogue and mimetic gesture. The following are some examples of the characteristic gestures of the gods performed in the mimetic hamatsa dances. The performer incarnating the Cannibal Bird "hops sideways, moves the beak [of his mask] through sweeping arcs and shakes his head. The motions are reminiscent of the movements of ravens scavenging for food on the beach."[43] The god *Bookwus* or "Man-of-the-Ground," who is the chief of the dead, wears a skeletal, grimacing mask, has a bent over posture and possesses the characteristic gesture of shielding his face with the back of his hand because he is essentially very shy.[44] The performer portraying the sea monster *Iakim*

> circles the floor in an extended undulation which represents the creature as diving under a kelp bed and rising on the other side. At the top of each crest, the dancer pauses slightly and peers around as if scanning the horizon. The articulated lower jaw is opened at this point and the dancer emits a gasp as a sea mammal would when surfacing for air.[45]

In type two Haitian possession rituals, *Asaka*, loa of mountain and field in the Rada-Dahomey cult, and *Agwe*, loa of the sea and water, are portrayed by characteristic gestures in dances representative of their domains. The devotees of Asaka will bend low while dancing, in movements of planting and hoeing with the crude, awkward movements of mountain people. Agwe dances with the flowing movements of waves representative of the sea or swimming.[46]

ATTITUDE AND POSTURE

> Whoever studies the idiom of a mime will be struck by the multiplicity of attitudes and by their nature.... Attitude is the original method of the mime and the essence of mime.[47] —Jean Dorcy

Dynamic postures of the body which discharge emotion through gesture are the essence of mime. Gestures are the active expression of energy and emotion held in bodily-attitudes. They are symptoms of latent attitudes which have restructured the muscular configuration of the body, causing it to assume the outward shape and form of the deity.

Attitude is a term that is used to denote either a mental state or a bodily posture, or both. Attitudes affect the muscular configuration of the body, manifesting themselves in characteristic postures. Posture is "the relative arrangement of the different parts, especially of the body: the characteristic position of the body or that assumed for a special purpose."[48] The representative posture of an attitude is generally an immobile or held form that interrupts the flow of movement. Emotion always indicates the presence of tension in the body. It is this tension that causes a restructuring of the muscular configuration to produce a posture and its corresponding gesture.

Lowen describes some typical emotions as reflected in the outward appearance of the body: "We can recognize the angry person by his flushed face, clenched fists and snarling mouth.... Affection or love produces a softening of all the features.... Sadness has a melting look, as if the person were about to break down in tears."[49] These are clearly preparatory postures in which the thought or emotion is "constructed" in the musculature of the body. In this process there is a tendency to restrain the impulse toward movement by immobilizing the body or parts of it. It would appear that the maintenance of the posture involves a kind of internal struggle in which the emotions connected with it are realized. "Emotion originates from suspense and conflict. It does not function when an inner situation finds a direct and satisfactory solution."[50]

In possession, the posture associated with an incarnating deity is an expression of emotions that modify the postural tonus of the body. In Haitian Vodou, the possessing god's personality generally corresponds to some latent aspect of the possessed individual's personality probably not expressed in his normal everyday behavior. These contradictory, latent attitudes remain locked within the musculature of the body until they are permitted expression in the context of ritual: "every pattern of muscular tension betrays some hidden psychological attitude, and every attitude which is allowed to act out its emotional life to the full is a loa."[51] Ritual possession serves to provide a socially sanctioned and structured outlet for emotions that might otherwise be damaging to the individual or society.

ATTITUDE AND THE SPINAL COLUMN

According to Francis Huxley, if emotions are grounded in the awareness of physical states, then when certain emotional experiences are repressed from consciousness, the physical sensations associated with them are also repressed.[52] Repression of strong emotion is effected by bracing the body—that is, by tensing muscles in the immediate area where those sensations are experienced. This creates other, stronger, but more neutral sensations which block the original feeling. That these blocked emotions cause back tensions which affect the entire postural tonus of the body has been borne out by Mathais Alexander and others. Ritual mimetic enactment is characterized by a predominance of posturally based movement in which the bones of the individual—most notably the spinal column—become the locus of dramatic enactment.

The whole of the posture and balance mechanism centers in the nape of the neck. In Vodou during the initial stages of the trance, dissociation or loss of the habitual attitudes associated with the ego begins in the neck, where the possessing spirit is believed to enter. In the trance the devotee achieves loss of self—his habitual posture and the blocking tensions associated with the ego. The loss of the habitual posture and the expression of latent ones in the form of possession deities is often described by archaic peoples with the image of a tree. The tree is a metaphor for the spinal column—the center of posture through which one senses one's self.

ROLE PLAYING, ATTITUDE, AND POSTURE

Character portrayal has typically been the major vehicle for attitude expression in possession trance. Lowen has noted that "character" or "personality" is "a psychic attitude" which is conveyed outwardly through the maintenance of a bodily posture.[53] Character is essentially a constellation of dominant emotions whose tensions affect the muscular tonus of the body and which manifest themselves in characteristic postures. In Laban terminology, this posture is referred to as a "body attitude": "It is concerned with what qualities are *maintained* in the body, which spatial emphases, body part relationships and tensions are held in the body as a kind of baseline from which the mover operates."[54]

Character is expressed outwardly as a "mask" of the body. In ritual possession, the psychic tensions or emotions that are metaphorically embodied in the particular energies of the possessing deity alter the postural tonus of the body, transforming the devotee into the simulacre of the god. According to Francis Huxley:

> There is good reason to believe that character is a number of attitudes summed up physically in posture, or the way a man carries himself; just as neurosis, or nervousness, is another name for the accumulation of tension in the musculature. These tensions, we may say, are the half-acted attitudes that a man stores within himself—attitudes towards other persons which he has learnt over his life. They are, it must be stressed, bodily attitudes.[55]

It is these "half-acted attitudes" which tend to be enacted under the guise of gods in possession rites. The devotee's habitual posture is displaced at the moment of possession and is altered by the possessing spirit. This transformation may be seen in a description of Tanti, a woman in the Trinidadian Shango cult who is possessed by Ogun–St. Michael.

> When the "spirit begins to manifest on" or "catch" Tanti, a dramatic physical transformation takes place. If in a standing position, she staggers, appears to lose her balance, begins to sway (bending her body forward and backward rhythmically), and may fall either to the ground or into the arms of bystanders. Her entire body begins to vibrate, while her arms are either rigid at her sides or stretched out above her. Her feet are planted widely apart and she may lurch back and forth from toe to heel.

The vibrations increase in intensity, and somewhat resemble the convulsions of a seizure state. At the same time, she deep grunts and groans. Her jaw begins to protrude, her lips pout and turn down sharply at the corners, her eyes dilate and stare fixedly ahead. An expression of masculinity and fierceness envelopes her face. She rises from the ground or breaks away from her supporters.... In the standing position her stomach and pelvis are thrust forward, her head and shoulders are thrown back, legs wide apart, hands on hips. The entire posture is quite rigid. At this point the spectators recognize that full possession by a particular power has occurred.[56]

The crisis of possession appears to manifest itself in an internal struggle between the devotee's habitual mental attitudes (as manifested in her everyday postural tonus) and the mental attitudes of the possessing deity. The rigidity of the body and eyes, which are apparent in the bound quality of the posture and accompanying movements, may well be the result of a struggle between opposing forces in the individual's psyche. The opposing nature of the balancing forces, caught between two extreme postural tensions in the individual, creates the blocking mechanisms associated with the loss of self.

The function of possession trance is primarily curative. It is a means by which individuals restore balance within themselves and their society. The universe is recorded and interpreted by individuals in terms of their own bilateralism: above/below, front/back, good/bad, etc. By acting out deities in possession ritual the devotee is reenacting a drama of precarious balance in order to effect change in the dynamics that unite the self, society and the universe.

In the ultimate union of opposites that is the aim of all human religious rituals is the union of contingent and vulnerable man with a powerful, possibly omniscient force. Man and a personified power or powers represent the ultimate poles of much mythic structure, and polarity is the basic problem that myth and ritual must solve..... [S]uch polar opposites include heaven/hell, sky/earth, good/bad, left/right, strong/weak, as well as an almost endless series of other polarities that recur in human myths.[57]

In Haiti, individuals are possessed by spirits representative of their innermost nature or its opposite; that is, either their positive emotions or antagonistic attitudes. In addition, individuals may be possessed by a number of different loa each representing distinct attitudes, "some of them energetic and outgoing, others withdrawn; some again fierce and tormented, others minatory and censorious. During possession, it seems, neuroses are dissociated into their positive and negative elements, and either of them can then emerge into physical action."[58]

In Haitian Vodou there seems to be a correlation between the character of the god and that of the devotee who represents him. Vodou adepts say that spirits prefer to come down into people who resemble them. Gentle people are often inhabited by calm and friendly gods, while the violent harbor fiery and brutal spirits. Often, however, devotees are possessed by loa whose character is the very opposite of their own.

The possessed individual not only imitates the characteristic posture of a possession agent, but also conveys its essential energies or Efforts through the dynamic tensions that animate its postures and are contained in its characteristic gestures. The representative attitude of an agent manifests itself in a fixed pattern of behavior and often by a characteristic means of locomotion or distinct manner of walking. In Tanti's possession by Ogun–St. Michael in the Trinidadian Shango cult:

> The particular gait and/or dance, as well as other elements of behavior which follow, are to some degree prescribed for the particular power who is manifesting, and vary considerably both for the different powers and within the varying interpretations given by different individuals to the same powers. In Tanti's behavior as Ogun, the gait is slow; as each leg is extended there is a momentary rest on the toes or ball of the foot, a swaying of the leg, and finally a heavy step as the weight is placed on the heel.[59]

MASK AND METAMORPHOSIS

"Possession could best be defined as a transformation of the personality. The face metamorphoses and the entire body becomes the simulacre of the god."[60] The release of repressed attitudes during ritual incarnation affects the outward appearance of the body, triggering mechanisms of imitation similar to mimicry. Mimicry involves mechanisms of camouflage or transformation which operate on the forms and colors of insects and animals, causing that which is present (the animal) to appear to be absent and that which is absent (the phenomenon that is mimicked) to appear to be present. The possessed individual undergoes an "inner transformation" of his mental state, expressed externally in the assumption of the postures and gestures of the incarnating deity, as well as through costume and a mask or mask-like face.

The transformation of the individual's posture into that of the possessing deity is emblemized by the wearing of a mask or the formation of the facial muscles into a mask of the god. As Bourguignon points out, masks are commonly used in ritual for the purpose of disguise. It hides the identity of the wearer, making that which is present (the wearer) appear absent. However, in the case of possession trance the identity of the impersonator is known to all: "Instead of covering the face and body with a mask or disguise, the body itself, so to speak, becomes the 'mask' that clothes the identity of the spirit who now inhabits the body."[61]

THE NEUTRAL MASK

The trance state itself is often signified by the neutral or blank expression of one in deep sleep. The word mask, according to Leuner, is derived from the Langobardic masca, meaning the net in which a corpse was shrouded and later by extension, it meant the dead man himself on his return as an evil spirit.[62] The face during trance and at the moment of dispossession often assumes a blank or neutral expression. Schott-Billmann recounts his impression of a group of African trancers: "I was struck by their expressions. Their eyes were vague, the eyelids rarely blinked. They appeared to me to be hypnotized and they moved like sleep walkers."[63] It appears that the blank facial expression is bound up with the loss of the attitudes normally associated with the ego.

THE CHARACTER MASK

Once possessed, the individual's face takes on the expression of the incarnating god. According to Schott-Billmann:

> The crisis of possession properly speaking manifests itself by an important modification of the face.... The expression and features of the face are unrecognizable, it appears as if the possessed devotee has put on a mask. This mask corresponds naturally to the characteristics of the incarnated god; masks of wrinkled old men (*Legba*, Haiti), (*Sofo*, Haoussa), grimacing individuals (*Guédé*, Haiti),... beautiful women....[64]

The metamorphosis of the facial expression is supported by a global modification of the individual's posture, motor behavior and voice into a mask of the god. Schott-Billmann relates how a toothless old woman was transformed into a beautiful young princess with graceful carriage and a lovely voice, all in the space of a few minutes.

Often a devotee is possessed by many gods over the course of a ceremony giving rise to a series of metamorphosis. Alfred Métraux writes:

> They can, like a *hungan* I saw one evening, become successively *Ogu-balindjo*, a shrill god who sprinkles his head with well water, and then on the spur of the moment turn into *Guédé-fatras* and carry out an acrobatic dance which in its turn gives place to transformation into Petit-Pierre—a gluttonous and quarrelsome spirit who, to the joy of the gallery, tries to pick a quarrel with the audience.[65]

THE MASK, IMMOBILITY, AND ATTITUDE ARTICULATION

Possession in the initial stages of the trance is generally accompanied by a violent seizure, signaling a rupture with the everyday personality and a radical identification with the deity. This stage of total identification is similar to catalepsy. In catalepsy, which is clinically induced through hypnosis, the subject mimes the gestures and attitudes of the hypnotist. Pierre Janet, who studied this phenomenon in depth, states that "the first and most striking characteristic [of catalepsy] is the subject's absolute immobility."[66] The subject is literally dead to his everyday self and is totally open to suggestion and external "modeling" by the hypnotist. The hypnotist, as it were, sculpts the subject as though he were clay. Janet writes, "If one touches his members, one perceives that they are extremely mobile and, one might say, light, that they offer no resistance so that one can move them very easily. If one leaves them in a new position, they do not fall back according to the laws of gravity, but remain absolutely immobile exactly where one left them. . . . The face, like a wax mask, lets itself be modeled and keeps its new expression."[67] In addition, Janet notes that the subject mirrors perfectly any gesture or attitude that hypnotist assumes.

Moreover, placing the cataleptic's body or part of the body (i.e., arm and fist) in an posture of defiance, for example, the subject's members are effected internally by the attitude encapsuled in posture, the rest of the body and facial expression outwardly conforming to the attitude.

Possession trance is almost identical to cataleptic behavior with the exception that in the case of the possessed devotee, the model has been internalized in terms of roles available in the society. The deity-model serves the function of a mask which suggests the comportment and gestural behavior to the possessed devotee. In the inner dissociation produced by possession the body becomes rigid but is sculpted or manipulated by internal impulsions modeled on the mask of the incarnating god.

The body, as we have seen, is immobilized both by dissociation and by the struggle between habitual attitudes and latent attitudes. Many descriptions of possession trance behavior (such as that of Tanti's possession by Ogun–St. Michael) refer to the rigidity of the body. The modification of the posture and facial expression are the first symptoms of the hardening of the body into a mask of the god. The ensuing gestures also partake of the resistance and immobility that characterize the individual's internal struggle with precarious balance as he seeks to articulate latent attitudes.

Gesture always unfolds from the "fixing" of the body or parts of the body. The original definition of gesture as "a position or attitude" indicates that gesture originates in a pose of the body or its various organs. Today, gesture refers to all voluntary or involuntary movements of the human body, the aim of which is to signify thought or emotion. Gesture is the active expression of the emotion encapsuled in the posture. It is characterized by the articulation of a thought or emotion through the localization of segments of the body, allowing for isolated movements of body parts. Gestures tend to have literal associative meanings which relate to the attitude from which they evolve.

Aristotle in his famous "Movement of Animals" was one of the first scholars to indicate the postural basis of emotion and action. He states that the relationship of posture to action is primarily mechanical. In order for an animal to move any part of its body, some other parts have to be fixed, like fulcrums from which movement can take place as when the shoulder is fixed in order to permit the measured movement of the forearm.[68] There is a temporal sequence in which the fixing of the muscle groups must come first. He speaks of the fixing as the origin of movement and thus lays down a mechanical law in which posture (the fixing) is prior to and leads to an action.

Twentieth century research in attitude psychology lends support to the notion that posture is the origin of movement and prepares for action. "The preliminary stage in every kind of action is attitudinal, by which we mean *postural* with orienting tensions. Some portion of the organism has to be stabilized and oriented before movement can take place, and this is true even when the movement is spontaneous, with no delay between the attitude and action stages."[69]

An attitude is reflected in a bodily posture characterized by a frozen preparation for an action. "Much of the reflex reaction expressed by the skeletal musculature is not motile but postural, and has as its result not a movement, but the steady maintenance of an attitude."[70]

Nina Bull has advanced a theory of attitude in which prohibiting the immediate action prepared for by the postural inner adjustments of the skeletal structure results in an emotion which in turn can lead to an action. Contemporary psychologists, such as Feldenkrais, also support this view: "Which comes first; the motor pattern or the feeling? I would like to stress the idea that they are basically the same thing. We cannot become conscious of a feeling before it is expressed by a motor mobilization, and therefore *there is no feeling so long as there is no body attitude.*"[71]

Abell, in his discussion of the tension imagery process, states that dreams, fantasies, myth, and artistic expression are a result of psychic tensions or emotions that are *delayed* fulfillment. In ritual the participants embody this tension in various forms, one of which may be mimetic enactment. In the process of reenactment the psychic tensions manifested in postural freezing find release through action.

The Attitude theory of emotion, according to Bull, is a modification and extension of the James-Lange theory, which postulates that action produces an emotional response. Feelings of sorrow come because we cry, feelings of fear are produced because we run away, feelings of anger come because we strike, etc. Bull's theory states that bodily changes that lead to feelings in emotion are due to the initial step in a response, "that is, to a preparatory motor attitude — *held up from going into action;* and not to the action itself," as in the James theory.[72] Thus, feelings come from a readiness to cry, anger is the feeling of readiness to strike. According to this more recent theory, the action phase of the response (crying, sorriness, escape) is not only unnecessary for feeling an emotion, but if carried out intensively results in the extinction of the emotion.

ATTITUDE ARTICULATION AND
THE AESTHETICS OF THE MARIONETTE

The release of latent attitude-images throughout the body manifests itself in a style of movement similar to that of the marionette. In the initial throes of possession when the devotee is "mounted" by the god, he is often jerked and propelled like a marionette that has been picked up by its manipulator. In the calmer mimetic phase of the trance the devotee is literally moved by the spirit—his body, like a large marionette, propelled by his inner attitudes.

The bodily attitude, gestures and walk of the possessed devotee accentuate the postural aspects of movement. They are a means by which he articulates attitudes. The language of this articulation is purely mimetic, and corporeal expression is marked by a tendency towards immobility rather than movement. The possessed individual appears to have a predominance of the Effort quality of "bound flow." Cecily Dell describes flow as follows: "As you watch a person moving, you may notice that he either holds back, restricts, binds the flow of his movement, or that he goes with the flow, his body moving freely and easily with the motion. The 'going with' the flow of the movement we call free; the restriction of the flow we call bound."[73]

She explains that bound flow is similar to what we often call very tense; free flow similar to relaxed; however, both require muscular tension, and it is the relationship among the muscles tensed rather than the presence of tension in the body which determines the quality of flow. The element of bound flow is most clearly seen in the elements of posture and immobility in ritual possession in which the movement becomes totally bound or frozen.

Huxley has noted that the incarnation of loa through behavioral and postural changes represents "a mask of the entire body, not of the face alone."[74] The transformation of the individual into the possessing deity essentially constitutes a mask of the body which clothes the identity of the spirit. The etymology of the word person is in fact "mask." The Latin term *persono*, meaning "to sound through," indicates the mask worn by actors in the classical theatre which amplified the voice by means of a built-in megaphone. The performer's body in ritual trance becomes a mask or an articulated marionette through which latent attitudes are communicated by means of posturally based gesture.

Marionettes, puppets, masks and mime play important roles in ritual ceremonies in which ancestor-spirits are brought to life. The custom of portraying the dead not only through masks, but also through larger or smaller figures whose limbs can be made to move, seems to have been widely practiced in the past and still exists in some regions. The mask and the marionette are paradoxical emblems for dead matter animated by a living spirit, and as such they are a paradigm for the mime. The immobility of the mask or mask-like body moved by an unseen force creates a striking aesthetic that is typical of ritual mimesis.

It is precisely in the performer's struggle against the stasis imposed by the mask in order to articulate the attitudes that the mask demands that mimesis is born. While the limbs may be more or less free, the spinal column, which originates the movement of the extremities, is bound and from it radiates the essentially marionette like quality of articulated immobility.

Possession and puppetry are closely interwoven in rites of possession and shamanism. Jane Belo has identified what she terms a "puppet complex" in the possession rituals of Java and Bali, in which the dancers are trained to emulate the gestures of the *wayang kulit* (shadow puppets). Belo says of the Javanese *wayang wong* (human puppets):

> Anyone who has ever seen one of these performances given by the highly trained actors cannot doubt that their every action was modeled upon that of the puppets, and the stylization of the gesture, the position of the figure in profile to the audience, the absolute immobility of the face, recalled the puppets' representation of the mythological characters, and not any human rendering.[75]

Belo sums up the puppet complex by stating that "actors and dancers are like puppets, for they behave in accordance with a spirit which is not their own."[76] The word *boroek* is used by the Balinese to describe a corpse which is falling to pieces with decay. It is also used to epitomize the fantasy of the body as made of separate independent parts. This fantasy takes many forms — among others, that the body, like a puppet, is pinned together at the joints. This idea is closely linked with the postural release involved in possession whereby energy, tension or the sensation of self tends to be experienced in the joints. Milton Erickson describes trance gesture as "unitary movement" in which the arm, for example, tends to be moved from a stationary shoulder joint as a single unit and as "economy of movement," that is, the use of only that part of the body necessary for the action.[77] The isolation and independence of segments of the body which move as units imparts to the performer the aura of an articulated marionette. It appears that the emotion that lies at the base of the enacted attitude is "held up" in the joints of the body which serve as a kind of "platform" for the unfolding of gesture.

COMIC BURLESQUE AND IMPROVISATION

Possession trance, whether it involves enactment of myth or the social tensions of the group, is "structured" ritual that verges on theatrical performance. The enactment of group myth in the predominantly cultural possession trance (type one) is more like a scripted performance, following rigid guidelines in which the gestures and comportment of the gods are highly codified and formalized. The personalities of the devotees are distant from those of the gods and there is less leeway for personal expression and improvisation.

Type two, cultural and psychological, which is the most common form of possession trance, is less highly structured than the predominantly cultural type and tends to be largely improvised. The gods have human attributes closely allied with the personalities of the devotees. Rather than enacting mythology, the devotees in these rituals are more concerned with the attributes of the gods — their likes and dislikes, activities, and personal quirks. In the Haitian Vodou and Ethiopian Zar cults these performances are termed ethno-dramas by anthropologists and involve a high degree of comedy, spontaneity, free play, and improvisation among the participants.

Like the Commedia dell'Arte, to which they are frequently compared, type two rites exhibit a group of stock character types. Devotees behave according to a clearly defined set of rules that are embedded in the attributes of the roles and the structure of the ritual occasion. The Zar may be looked upon as a group of dramatic characters who

> are not just types but give dramatic color to the actions accomplished in their name — and these figures properly belong to the domain of theatre, like those which the Roman actors incarnated in the ancient Atellanes or in more recent times, their Italian successors of the commedia dell'arte; characters modeled by tradition, who guard a certain fixity throughout the diverse intrigues in which they are inserted, to each of them corresponds a particular range of behaviors which the actor draws upon at his pleasure.[78]

Performers in these types of ritual are expert improvisors because they are thoroughly versed in the mythology and behavior of the gods and often have years of experience performing their roles. As individuals are mounted by a god and enter into the performance, they know how to "pick up the action" and carry it forward because it is inscribed in the milieu — much like a commedia scenario tacked on the wall outside the performance space. The priest plays an important role in "directing" the rite by inducing possession among participants and orchestrating the behavior of those involved. Members of the audience also play minor roles in the ensuing action. They greet the arrival of the gods, help them change into their costumes, bring food, drink and tobacco, make comments on the action, question the gods and seek their advice.

Rites of possession serve an important function as entertainment for performers and audience. They are not only a means of venting tensions and anxieties through role playing, they are also an opportunity for relaxation and enjoyment. This is especially true of type two rituals which are less structured and offer more freedom for humor and play. In ritual, according to Mahadeve Apte, "Humor plays a significant role in dramatization and is often the primary mode of entertainment, especially in preliterate societies."[79] As in the Commedia dell'Arte, performances often entail burlesque of religious and social behavior, and comic and obscene subject matter. Improvisations involve comic bits (similar to the *commedia lazzi*) that are associated with characteristic behavior of the various possessing gods.

Many societies in which possession trance operate have ritual clowns or buffoons who create humor through burlesque of rituals and comic play. The American Indian tribes of North and South American have ceremonial buffoons. In Bali, comic scenes enacted by ritual clowns Penasar and Kartala provide a counterpoint to the character of the hero and they perform parodies of the sacred ritual.[80] The behavior of the clowns provides a counterbalance to the seriousness of the ritual; in mocking it, they reaffirm its importance and also provide comic catharsis through laughter.

In the Haiti, there are spirits of the dead called *guédé* which play the role of buffoons. Métraux describes a typical "impromptu" Haitian possession rite, involving *guédé* and a buffoonish peasant *zaka*, which has all the appearances of a Commedia dell'Arte performance, including stock characters, improvisation, dialogue and a repertoire of tricks:

> someone possessed by Zaka appears under the peristyle in the get-up of a peasant. By canny movements he mimes the anxiety of a countryman come to town, and who fears to be robbed. Now another possessed person joins him, one might almost say "comes one." It is Guédé-nibo, of the Guédé Family, which watches over the dead. Zaka is clearly terrified by the presence of his gloomy colleague and tries to propitiate him, inviting him to have something to eat and to drink some rum. Guédé who is making a show as a townsman exchanges courtesies with him, trying to tease him. He asks him: "What have you got in your bag?"; he searches it and examines the contents. Alarmed, Zaka cries "Stop. Stop." The bag is returned to him only to be surreptitiously lifted off him while he is examining one of the sick....[81]

Burlesque and comic parody of social and religious customs also plays an important part in the Zar cult. Leiris describes one such improvised comic burlesque of the punishing of a participant for the transgression of ritual behavior:

> prohibitions constitute the pretexts for mockery, the adept who incarnate subordinate zar ... pretend to take the erring assistants and submit the matter to an improvised court of justice constituted of the adept incarnating the grand zar and the other important adepts. The result is a burlesque process during which the guilty are judged and condemned to fines which serve to pay for drinks....[82]

Despite the prevalence of comic elements, possession rites are generally seen as very serious business, especially in predominantly cultural (type one) rites. The burlesque of sacred ritual serves to reinforce the power of the gods. As faith declines, however, the elements of comedy and parody increase. The lived theatre of possession becomes the theatre performed, "the serious part diminishes in rapport to that of the frivolous...."[83] The diminishing seriousness of ritual is especially prevalent where the rites are held as a part of carnivals or festivals.

Possession rites are not generally public in nature. They are most often held secretly, as in Haiti, and include a select group of individuals. As tourism and other pressures of the modern world gradually intervene the rites are held for a wider audience. In these performances, which are of a more theatrical and spectacular nature, comic elements tend to predominate.

The following chapter on the Greek mime supports the findings that as possession trance moves away from its ritual function towards secular performance, it tends to manifest itself in comic behavior. The Dionysian herd of satyrs and sileni mark a bridge between possession trance and the art of the satyric Dorian mimes. The mimes carry over the sacred release and renewal of the Dionysian fertility rituals into festival entertainments based in parody and burlesque or myth. The satyric mask is the vehicle that effected the transformation of sacred mimesis into secular mimesis.

Chapter Two

The Greek Mimes

DORIAN ORIGINS

Mime existed as a part of ancient fertility rites and ancestor worship centuries before it evolved into a secular performance art in Greece in the sixth century B.C. As early as 2000 B.C., mimetic performances based on the myth of Isis and Astarte were performed in Egypt. In the Peloponnesian peninsula, from ancient times, mimetic dances formed the core of various seasonal agrarian rites celebrating the death of winter and the triumphant rebirth of spring, which was associated with a primitive goddess of fertility who later became identified with Artemis. Dance drama, mainly in the Dorian parts of Greece, flourished in the century preceding the founding of the city Dionysia in Athens in 534 B.C. At some point mime evolved from these dances to become a secular art.

Aristotle, in chapter three of the *Poetics,* states that mime first arose in Dorian Megara (just outside of Athens) and then Sicily after 581 B.C. Its origin coincides with the first mention of the mimeisthai (mimesis) word group by authors in the sixth century B.C.[1] An examination of the ancient usage of mimos and related terms reveals a root sense of "a miming or mimicking of the external appearance, utterances, and or movements of an animal or a human being by a human being; in short, precisely the kind of mimetic performance we associate with the Sicilian mime."[2]

Mime, which flourished in Dorian communities of the Peloponnesus, Sicily, and southern Italy, was an improvisational form of vulgar comedy consisting primarily of short sketches involving satiric treatment of everyday domestic situations or burlesque of myth. These playlets were part of vaudeville-like performances (that included, among other things, juggling, tightrope walking, singing, and dancing) and were mounted by troupes of traveling entertainers at folk festivals, carnivals, fairs, and wealthy men's banquets. While the term mime was also broadly applied to these variety performers as well as their acts, its root meaning makes it clear that the essence of mime was to be found in the short playlets.

The birth of Greek mime in ancient Doria is coincidental with the arrival

"Schauspielergruppe" (masked comic actors miming a scene of drunkenness).
Greek fourth century, B.C. at Staatliche Museum, Berlin.

of the cult of Dionysus from Thrace in sixth century B.C. The singular element
the cult of Dionysus brought with it that contributed to the emergence of the
secular art of mime was the phenomenon of spirit possession. Dionysus was the
god of death and rebirth. Cult behavior was essentially collective and orgiastic.
Its aim was *ecstasis*—which "could mean anything from 'taking you out of
yourself' to a profound alteration of personality."[3]

Initially, the devotees of Dionysus were primarily women called *maenads*.
Women in Greek society had little personal freedom or power. Dionysus was
known as the "great liberator." Cult practice, which included intoxication,
ecstatic dance, and possession by the god, offered release from constricting
social codes and the possibility of joyous renewal. In Euripides' *Bacchae* the

maenads are repeatedly referred to as having upward and flung-back heads. Upward and flung-back heads, which appear as a popular motif on many ancient Greek vases, are associated with Dionysian ecstacy. They signify the moment of possession when the god "mounts" the individual—displacing the center of the ego at the base of the neck.

The semi-nude and maskless maenads are frequently shown on sixth century vase paintings accompanied by masked and padded satyrs wearing phalli. It seems that in certain Dionysian cults the devotees of the god would cross-dress, disguising themselves as satyrs and other mythical creatures and beings, which were incorporated from preexisting fertility worship. As the Dionysian rituals grew in popularity, men as well as women appeared masked and costumed as satyrs and sileni, birds, fish, horses and riders, giants on stilts, ugly women, and men wrapped in cloaks. These theriomorphic deities probably played a part in primitive animal worship in which animal disguises represented spirits of ancestors whose incarnation helped with the promotion of fertility.

MIME, DIONYSIAN POSSESSION, AND SATYRIC ATTITUDES

> The initial step towards mimesis was taken when the dancer-singer was changed, through ecstasy and a corresponding disguise, into a mime, one who represents someone other than himself."[4]—Margarete Bieber

The mimetic impulse that lies at the core of mime and the drama was present in the Dionysian devotee's conviction that he or she could not only worship, but could become the god in possession trance.[5] In the worship of Dionysus, individuals could step out of their everyday personality and through divine ecstasy become transformed into one of the Dionysian herd.

The satyrs, sileni and other half man–half beast creatures of the Dionysian *thais* (crowd of worshipers) represent a release from inhibitions in pursuit of the senses. They are a celebration of the instinctual side of life. Their behavior, which emphasizes gluttony, sexual license, and drunkenness, is typical of fertility worship whose aim is the celebration of nature's abundance and renewal. According to Dana Sutton:

> The satyres are grotesque, elemental, not quite human. Comparisons with animals come readily to mind in describing them. . . . They are largely guided by their appetites for food, drink, and sex. They are not fully human because they lack superegos: they are constantly interested in the immediate gratification of their appetites.[6]

On countless vase paintings, satyrs are represented as padded, fat men usually equipped with phalli, long tails, porcine noses, pointed ears, and sometimes miniature horns. They are frequently accompanied by Silenus, their licentious old father who is most often depicted with padded buttocks and belly. According to Jeanmaire, the satyrs and sileni are the equivalent in classic antiquity of "savage men" which are found in the primitive folklore of many peoples:

> The traits that are common to all these creatures, the unkempt and shaggy aspect, the semi-bestiality, the gluttony, the lasciviousness with which they attack, not only their mates — the savage women, the nymphs and the fairies — but the wives and daughters of men, points to an initial affinity between centaurs and satyrs-sileni, which accentuates their common character as men-horses.[7]

Dionysus was not only the bringer of life and abundance, but he was also affiliated with death and dying. Along with the maenads, satyrs, pans, and sileni, his thais incorporated the netherworld demons and spirits that had been a part of primitive fertility cults long before his arrival. In their form as half man–half beast, the satyrs and sileni represent the spirits that animate nature as well as the spirits of the dead. The horse was a funerary symbol in ancient Greece which could represent three things: a messenger from the underworld; the courser who makes the last voyage; and an incarnation of the spirits of the dead. All of these connotations were present in the merger of the individual and god in possession trance. The Dionysian devotee underwent a death of self at the moment of possession. As in African and Afro-American possession rituals, spirit incarnation was described by the Greeks in terms of horse and rider.[8]

Greek mime originated in the mimetic dances and antics associated with possession trance behavior. The dance of the satyrs marks a transition between ancient animal dances involved in ancestral and fertility worship and those that imitated men.[9] Plato in the *Laws* states that the Dionysian dances are a form of "ugliness . . . cultivated by those who indulge in drunken imitations of Pans, Sileni and Satyrs, when performing certain rites of expiation and initiation."[10] The imitation of ugliness by the satyrs, according to Jeanmaire, was not simple diversion, but was originally the result of the bizarre behavior exhibited by the possessed crowd of Dionysian worshipers.[11]

> . . . behind the *sikinis* and all these satyric dances made up of jumps and capers, there is something which is, in reality, the choir of possessed . . . the choir of those who are struck individually by ecstasy (*mania*) and who one cures (or purifies) of mania precisely in letting them dance and cultivate their possession.[12]

MIME AND THE STYLE OF GROTESQUE REALISM

According to Mahadev Apte, as rites are gradually channeled into seasonal festivals that involve the whole community, they provide a context for various types of bizarre behavior and comic entertainment that typify unstructured ritual revels. These include

> spontaneous and often unpredictable behavior of entertainers, who may
> engage in whatever suits their fancy, impulsively switching from one ac-
> tivity to another. They chase spectators, play practical jokes on members
> of the audience and on each other, engage in banter and horseplay,
> simulate sexual behavior, drink and eat all kinds of non-edible objects,
> wear absurd-looking costumes or no clothes at all, jump, dance, exag-
> geratedly imitate others, perform numerous types of antics, and generally
> frolic.[13]

Ritual revels involving phallic processions, lampooning of audience members,
obscene songs and dances, and comic combat is of very ancient origin. They
existed as part of early fertility worship, such as those in honor of Artemis. It
seems that the obscene and satyric elements of these revels were gradually incorporated into the worship of Dionysus and came to play a large role in attic
festivals such as the Anthesteria, Lenaea, and rural Dionysia.

Sixth century Corinthian vase paintings record two types of Dionysian
revels (*komoi*). The first type depicts padded dancers in short tunics engaged
in farcical skits involving Dionysus and his attendants. These representations
are often taken for those of the Dorian mime because of the similarities in
costuming and subject matter. The second type of revel involves a procession
in which the members are disguised as maenads, nymphs, satyrs, old women,
and animals—dolphins, ostriches, birds, roosters, and horse-men carrying
riders. The grotesque types of the satyrs and animalesque spirits, the use of
masked and padded costumes, mimetic dance, obscenity, lampooning, and
comic combat in these revels are all elements that were incorporated into the
Dorian mime.

The first mimes, who were both male and female, were probably mildly
entranced and inebriated devotees, either masked or padded as satyrs, that
mimed scenes that freely mingled sacred, social and folk elements. According
to Sorbom

> there are no reasons to believe that there was a clear cut group of profes-
> sionals making mime performances at this time. . . . There were lots of
> "entertainers" who were professionals. Among other things they had
> mimes in their list of performances as a more or less distinct group. Now
> the word *mimos* denoted both this particular kind of performance and
> the performers of them as we know that this word did later on. . . . Not
> only these professional "entertainers" could perform mimes and thus be
> called *mimoi*. Anyone could, if he wanted, make casual and informal
> mime performances. The essential point seems to be, not the profes-
> sionalism, but the particular sort of performance.[14]

Originally, cult behavior involved a celebration of the world's revival and
renewal in which all took part. There was no distinction between actor and
spectator, male and female. Thus mime in the sixth century B.C. hovered on
the borderline between art and life and was not yet a distinct performance

genre. When cult behavior, however, was reorganized into state run festivals, the transition from the mimetic antics of the possessed worshipers to the comic improvised sketch of the mime was made.

Mime in antiquity, according to Reich in *Der Mimus* was the primary example of the culture of humor. Humor can be extraneous to rituals or an integral part of it; "ritual humor in most cultures seems to fall somewhere in the middle in the sense that some of it is well integrated into the rituals, while some is marginally linked."[15] Apte identifies the following properties as typical of unstructured ritual humor: "an absence of social control; behavior contrary to established cultural norms; extensive sexual and scatological elements; a burlesque of rituals, people in authority, and foreigners; and an appearance of disorder and chaos."[16]

Mime was characterized by comic and lowlife subject matter involving burlesque of the gods and heros. Its purpose, according to Nicoll, was to drag down the characters and subject matter of myth to the level of ordinary life. The Dorian mime also presented scenes from daily life frequently involving obscene or licentious subject matter, such as beatings, drunkenness, sexual talk and play, etc. Diomedes, in a quote from an unknown Greek author, states, "The mime is an imitation and irreverent (i.e. secular) expression of some dialogue, or the lascivious imitation of indelicate deeds and words; it is thus defined by the Greeks: 'The mime is an imitation of life.'"[17]

The essence of carnivalesque humor that was carried forward in the mime lies in the degradation or downward thrust inherent in the fertility rituals themselves, as emblemized by the behavior of maenads, satyrs, pan, sileni, and various underworld spirits that made up the Dionysian thais. According to Bakhtin, "The mighty thrust downward into the bowels of the earth, into the depths of the human body, is the essence of ancient fertility rites. Dying and being reborn. The downward movement is also inherent in all forms of popular-festive merriment. . . ."[18]

The comic quasi-secular mime that developed as pure entertainment side by side with the antics of the possessed devotee and merriment of the crowd at ritual revels is based in what Bakhtin terms "grotesque realism."[19] This style emphasizes the "lower sphere of man" — his basic libidinal attitudes. It reveals a world and individual turned upside down, where the belly, buttocks, anus, and genital organs reign supreme. The emphasis on the lower centers is a celebration of the cosmic themes of fertility, growth, and abundance that form the basis of agricultural rites and unite the individual with the common body of mankind.

There are many theories on the function of humor in ritual. However, its primary function appears to lie in tension reduction and the maintenance of social order.[20] "Much ritual humor . . . appears to be based on incongruity and exaggeration. . . . It stresses either reversal of existing structure or total freedom from it."[21] Dionysus was known as "the liberator." E. R. Dodds, in *The Greeks and the Irrational,* has shown how the Greeks, emerging from a culture of shame and guilt burdened with an overwhelming sense of personal responsibility, had a great need for freedom from self and the constraints of myth.[22] Becoming part of the divine herd of Dionysus offered this freedom. The same releasing mechanism was carried forward in Dorian mime, which essentially highlighted the comic elements that were present in ecstatic behavior of the Dionysian herd of satyrs and sileni.

THE SATYRIC MASK

The carnivalesque grotesque is emblemized by the satyric mask. The mask is a funerary symbol and frequently accompanies possession because it assists in dissociation and creates the strong impression that what is absent—the god, spirit or ancestor—is actually present. Dionysus was known as "the Master of Magical Illusions" and travesty by means of the mask was one of the hallmarks of his thais.[23] A large mask of Dionysus was often present at the ceremony for mixing the wine. And on vase paintings, masks portraying Dionysus appear to stare out at the viewer with startling immediacy, while the other figures in his thais are presented in profile.

In *Dionysus: Myth and Cult,* Walter F. Otto writes, "from earliest times man has experienced in the face with the penetrating eyes the truest manifestation of anthropomorphic or theriomorphic beings. This manifestation is sustained by the mask, which is that much more effective because it is nothing but surface. Because of this, it acts as the strongest symbol of presence."[24]

Especially associated with Dionysus were the grotesque masks of gorgons and other beings of the underworld whose frightening visages were used to ward off evil. According to Jeanmaire, the horse or goat-like demons of the satyrs and sileni and their forest companions were portrayed in possession trance in two ways: through an internal transformation manifested outwardly in the posture and comportment of the spirit, and externally, through masks and disguises.[25] The use of posture, mask, costume and mimetic behavior in ritual possession seems to have carried over directly into the mime.

There has been much conjecture as to whether mimes wore masks. The evidence for mask wearing is primarily derived from two sources. First, the Spartan mimes (*deikelistai*) in ancient Doria are known to have worn masks.[26] Second, many scenes on terra-cotta vases and sculptures frequently show mimes with enlarged and grotesque features that would indicate a mask. However, the argument against masks is that the mimes may have projected the idea of character through facial distortions or grimaces which were then accentuated by ceramic artists and sculptors to suit popular imagination. Another theory suggests that the mimes themselves possessed these enlarged features. It would seem that while some mimes did not wear masks, many did; and those that did not indicated character through facial expressions, posture, and costume.

The strongest evidence that many mimes wore masks derives from references by writers of the time to stock characters that appeared in mime performances throughout Doria. Cornford surmised that mime troupes comprised of stock characters existed which had fixed plots with definite actions which demanded just these characters, each having his proper place and function.[27] Stock characters indicate a standardization of character types based on fixed sets of repeatable traits and behavior that tend to be emblemized in masks. Nicoll, Cornford, and others, primarily on the authority of Pollux, have identified the following stock characters of the mime: two old men with pointed, phallic beards; a witch-like old woman; a foolish doctor; a buffoonish Heracles; and two slaves—one, a ruddy-faced bald headed glutton. Another stock character was the parasite who appeared in the literary mimes of Epicharmus but was probably a well-known Dorian type.[28]

These stock characters appear to be of very ancient Dorian origin—many stemming from types that existed in the dances of primitive fertility cults. Terra-cotta masks found in the sanctuary of Artemis Ortheia at Sparta and the Greek Necropolis of Lipari, which date from the beginning of the sixth century B.C. show striking similarities to character types that are found in the Dorian mime and the New Comedy. These masks are votive copies of the actual masks worn by the performers of some ritual dance in honor of Artemis, probably in the late seventh century.[29] According to Jane Burr Carter, almost all of the masks found at Ortheia at Sparta can be assigned to two types: grotesquely furrowed demons and idealized heroes.[30] The grotesque masks, which include old women, satyrs, gorgon, portraits and caricatures, appear to have a definite link with the character types of the Dorian mime.

The old woman mask found at Ortheia, and adopted by mime performers, was probably a fertility demoness originally. She is depicted in masks as having a heavily lined face and hideous jaws with one or two solitary teeth peering between her lips. She figured predominantly in the *kordax*—the lewd and provocative dance in honor of Artemis in the Peloponnese. The satyr and caricature masks were probably carried forward by the deformed, grotesque characters that made up the bulk of early mime characters. While the former represent the horned figures of mythology, the later included the grosser and more exaggerated masks which fail to come under any of the other types.[31] The masks of two old men which originated in Spartan fertility dances may well be more realistic versions of Silenus, the father of the satyrs. The fat, bald-headed and gluttonous servant/cook, exhibits the grotesque elements that characterize the satyrs as does the buffoonish Heracles with characteristics as a gargantuan eater and drinker.

Along with Dionysus and his satyrs and demons, Heracles and Odysseus were favorite characters of the mime as were mimic fools (*moros*) associated with demonic powers in ritual folklore.

The grotesque masks capture the essential bestial quality of the Dionysian satyrs, pan, sileni, and fertility demons. The combination of animal with human characteristics is one of the most ancient forms of the grotesque. The satyric mask exaggerates and caricatures those body features and deformities that represented man's libidinal attitudes. According to Susan Harris Smith, "The satiric mask is simple and direct. It isolates a negative characteristic from its setting in the total personality and exaggerates it. Thus, a social or spiritual deficiency is manifested as a physiognomical deformity."[32] In the grotesque body:

> The stress is laid on those parts of the body that are open to the outside world, that is, the parts through which the world enters the body or emerges from it or through which the body itself goes out to meet the world. This means that emphasis is on the apertures or the convexities, or on various ramifications and offshoots; the open mouth, the genital organs, the breasts, the phallus, the potbelly, the nose. The body discloses its essence as a principle of growth which exceeds its own limits only in copulation, pregnancy, childbirth, the throes of death, eating, drinking, or defecation. This is the ever unfinished, ever creating body.[33]

ESSENTIALIZATION, EXAGGERATION, AND CARICATURE

Exaggeration and caricature are generally considered fundamental attributes of the grotesque style. While the mimes dealt with comic and realistic subject matter, often drawn from everyday life, evidence suggests that their performances were not realistic in style. From the beginning there was a tendency towards caricature and exaggeration. What the Greeks referred to as miming did not involve an exact duplication or copy of the object of imitation. It appears that the mime performers based their imitations on the portrayal of the characteristic physical or vocal species traits of phenomena—those which distinguished it from other classes of phenomena. "This particular kind of acting [mime] was, as far as we can judge; characterized by a desire to make something clear, to caricature, to choose the characteristic details of something, or strongly emphasize some of the characteristic traits of phenomena in representing them."[34]

The facial masks of the Dorian mime tended to exaggerate features of the lower half of the face—a long hooked nose, large ears, and a crooked mouth with teeth protruding from the corners were common. According to Bakhtin, "Of all the features of the human face, the nose and mouth play the most important part in the grotesque image of the body."[35] They are both orifices that make contact with the external world like the anus and sexual organs. According to Bakhtin, the grotesque meaning of the enlarged nose is that it always symbolizes the phallus. The most important motif of the grotesque is the open mouth, which reduces the face to a gaping abyss.

The exaggerated and bestial characteristics of the mask were essentially a

Statuette of a man (caricature). Inlaid with silver and neillo H. 10 cm. Greek 300-100 B.C. at the Metropolitan Museum of Art, Rogers Fund, 1912 (12.229.6)

microcosm of the global corporeal ensemble. The postures of the Dorian mime types emphasize the belly, buttocks, and phallus. The grotesque style looks "for that which protrudes from the body, all that seeks to go beyond the body's confines." The Dorian mimes are frequently depicted as fat men with padded belly and buttocks, sporting a phallus. A large number of grotesque statuettes in bronze and terracotta have survived, and scholars have identified them as depicting mimes. According to Gisela Richter, the characteristics of these figures are that they usually show bodily deformities, such as a hunchback, a protruding paunch, crooked legs, and exaggerated features, and they all wear a large phallus.[36]

An example of a grotesque mime type may be seen in a bronze figure of a man from the late Greek period which probably represents the hunchback, a stock type frequently portrayed by the mimes. The deformed back, the characteristic trait selected and enlarged by the mime performer, is achieved by means of padding on the shoulders and chest.

Masks represent a microcosm of the essential attitude that underlies a character type. The configuration of the mask demands a particular body posture, walk, and voice which expresses the base attitude. A set of terra-cotta masks found at Lipari complement Pollux's list of masks for the New Comedy. Although the Lipari masks are of a later origin than the stock characters of the Dorian mime, they incorporate the stock characters of the mime as well as more realistic masks of young men and young women. An interesting experiment by Luigi Bernabo Brea involving a reproduction of these masks for stage use underscores that each mask demanded a particular attitude with accompanying gestures and walk. In rehearsals for Menander's *The Woman of Samos*, it was discovered that "the

mask first appeared to possess an extraordinary power of psychological condi-
tioning. No matter how diverse the actors were in age, physical type or social
background, the same voice, the same gestures and the same rhythm came
from each of them when they wore the same mask."[37]

The attitude suggested by the mask called up definite body postures,
gestures, and character voices. "It appears, then, that each mask wants to be
'animated' in its own way. Whomever assumes the role is not supposed to
change it. The actor must conform to the authority of a code."[38] Moreover it
was discovered that each mask was exactly suited to the characters in the play
and that when the wrong mask was assigned to a character, contradictions between the mask and the character immediately became apparent.

VOCAL MIMESIS

While the emphasis of this study is on the corporeal aspects of mime, it
must not be forgotten that vocal mimesis was an essential part of Dorian mime
performances. The early definition of mimos in the sixth century not only en-
compassed a miming or mimicking of the outward appearance and movements
of men and animals, but their sounds as well. On the crudest level, the mimes
indulged in the portrayal of the characteristic sounds of natural phenomena
such as wind and rain, the cries emitted by animals, the noises produced by
the action of objects, and the non-verbal qualities of the voices of characters.
Plato, who deplored the mime's willingness to "imitate anything," gives us an
indication of the mime's propensity for imitating sounds:

> They will seriously try to represent in public all the things we were talk-
> ing about. We shall have the noises of thunder and wind and hail, and
> of axles and wheels, the notes of trumpets, pipes, flutes, and every pos-
> sible instrument, the barking of dogs, the baaing of sheep, and twitter-
> ing of birds. And so this style of expression will depend largely on
> representation by sound and gesture.[39]

Like the speaking actor, the mimes used their voices to represent the non-
verbal qualities of character types — accents, rate, inflection, and vocal qualities.
The performers of literary mime plays, which were largely meant to be read,
were especially adept at conveying character through vocal mime.

POSTURALLY BASED MOVEMENT
AND THE STYLE OF THE MARIONETTE

> Out of these mists step the puppet showmen, the acrobats, and
> the jugglers, and by their side we can just distinguish the comic
> and terrifying forms of the Dionysiac demons who were to enter
> into their bodies, never to be exorcised.[40] — Allardyce Nicoll

The mask, the emblem of the possessing god translates into movement
that is based in the aesthetic of the marionette. The huge masks of Dionysus

were often completed with bodies which were carried or transported through the streets in processions. Some of these effigies had hidden springs or wires by which they were moved in order to create the illusion that they were animated by the god. In a celebration in honor of Bacchus of Nyssa, a huge, seated statue of the god which was mounted on a wagon stood up by itself, poured milk with a ladle, and sat down again.[41]

The marionette, as stated in the previous chapter, is analogous to the possessed body, a body that becomes a mask through which attitudes are conveyed. Attitude articulation in possession trance involves body rigidity achieved by means of the isolation and fixing of segments of the body. This postural style of gesture based in immobility is embodied in the movement aesthetics of the marionette. The Greek scientist Galen in a treatise on anatomy draws an analogy between the "articulation of the body"—by means of attachment of the muscles and tendons to the bones—to the manner in which a marionette is moved by strings attached to its members.[42] According to Petrone, even the vertebrae of the marionettes were so articulated that they were able to assume all sorts of postures and flexions.[43] The technical proficiency of a marionette moved by invisible wires was frequently cited by Aristotle, Plato and others as an analogy for man moved by his passions.

Along with the growth of Dorian mime, the puppet show began to assume a place of importance. Many mimes were expert marionettists (*nevrospastes*) who performed at public festivals and rich men's banquets.[44] Xenophon, in the fifth century B.C., mentions a mime who performed with marionettes. According to eyewitness accounts these marionettes were managed so skillfully that they seemed to be alive.[45] Nicoll tells us that the corporeal technique of the mimes may have emulated the stylized gestures of string puppets. Since the mime and marionette performances were closely intertwined with Dionysian ritual, it seems logical that they would have adopted some of their aesthetics from the ritual performances, especially those which were the most strange and therefore unusual for their audiences: "The puppets naturally took over certain themes which were more largely interpreted by breathing actors, and as a result a kind of double influence ensued, the puppets taking farces from the performers, the performers themselves sometimes viewing in the puppets methods of expression which might be employed on the stage."[46]

MIME TECHNIQUES AND
POSSESSION TRANCE BEHAVIOR

Like Dionysus, who was known as "the master of Illusions," the mimes of antiquity created a world of paradox. Through the aesthetics of transformation they created the illusion that which was absent was indeed present before the spectator. The grotesquely masked and padded mime performers must have seemed to their audiences to be the actual incarnation of netherworld spirits and demons. For this reason, the mimes were sometimes called *paradoxi* (literally "strange beings") and their art one of (*mimus hallucinatur*) "hallucination."[47]

The mime's acrobatic ability contributed to the aesthetics of a demonically possessed puppet. In ritual possession the arrival of the god is signaled by flexions and torsions of the body in which the individual seems to be a mere puppet in the hands of the god. Sometimes individuals appear to be lifted and flung about and engage in other bizarre behavior involving positions and movements of the body that they would ordinarily be unable to accomplish outside of trance. This strange extra-corporeal behavior may have contributed to the development of acrobatic techniques by mimes, such as handsprings and somersaults. In time the mimes elaborated various techniques involving magic and physical daring, which were performed as part of a cabaret-type performance. In Xenophon's *Drinking Party* there is an account of one of these performances in which a female performer does a dance and juggling act involving 12 hoops; another performer executes somersaults through a circular frame full of points sticking towards the center; and a girl does a "wonder act" on a potter's wheel.[48]

MIME, POSTURALLY BASED MOVEMENT, AND DANCE

As indicated above, the mime grew out of dances associated with the ancient fertility cults which were carried over into the worship of Dionysus. The Greeks, according to Pickard-Cambridge "tended to regard all dancing as 'mimetic,' or expressive, especially in its employment of rhythmical gestures and motions."[49] The Greek dance portrayed deeply felt attitudes by means of the repetition of posturally based movement phrases which were modeled upon the selected characteristics of agents and their actions.

The highly postural nature of the art of mime is seen in ancient writers usage of three basic terms, *phora, scheme,* and *deixis,* in their discussions of the dance. These terms have a wide scope and are used with differing connotations by different Greek writers and at different periods. What is important for our study is that there is evidence that one of the key features of the dance was attitude or held poses representing animals, gods, heros, men, and their characteristic gestures or actions. According to Else, mimos and related terms often, but not invariably, referred to miming through the medium of music and dancing in which the essential idea was the "rendering of characteristic look, action, or sound through human means."[50]

In *Poetics,* Aristotle states, "Rhythm alone, without harmony, is the means in the dancer's imitations; for even he, by the rhythms of his attitudes [*schemata*], may represent men's characters, as well as what they do and suffer."[51] In this brief and unique allusion to dance in his works, Aristotle sets forth rhythm, as the essential element of dance, but he also indicates that dance is grounded in the portrayal of characters, actions and passions by means of schemata.

Lillian Lawler, in examining the usage of the term schema among Greek writers of different periods, finds that it had a range of meaning and was used loosely to denote many features of the dance: "it may be translated variously as 'gesture,' 'figure,' 'pose,' 'movement,' 'pattern of motion,' or 'picture,' according to the context."[52]

Some of the schemata are mimetic gestures of the hand, such as "seizing the club" or "sword thrust." Schemata also include such steps or movements as rhythmic walking, running, leaping, twisting or bending the body, writhing, staggering, stooping, hopping, skipping, limping, or a boastful strut. However, the predominant meaning of schema seems to indicate a held bodily attitude, such as "one peering," which was the characteristic pose of Pan, who shaded his eyes with his hand as he peered out over his herd, or looked for enemies or storms. The fact that schema referred variously to movement and pose indicates that it probably consisted of a moment phrase (phora) which was generally highlighted by a briefly held pose of the body.

THE SACRED AND SATYRIC
MOTIFS OF THE MIME

Evidence points to the fact that Dorian mime not only adopted certain of its stock characters and elements of its corporeal style from ancient fertility dances, but important schemata as well. Mimos originally denoted a dramatic or quasi-dramatic representation; in other words, short sketches depicting vocal and physical imitations of men and animals in action. Dorian mime and its descendants relied on a limited range of stock situations depicting general classes of phenomena such as a thief stealing fruit or a slave being beaten. In its earliest form these mime plays were little more than sketches showing general renditions of a simple action. Sometimes these were crudely strung together to tell a story. But the essence of early mime, as distinct from that of the comedy, was in just these short sketches rather than the elaboration of lengthy plots.

ANIMAL MOTIFS

Many of the animal spirits that appeared in the Dionysian thais were the object of dances in primitive Greek cults involving fertility and ancestor worship. Ancient authors have provided us with the names of dances that mime the characteristic gestures of animals. The Crane imitated the flight of these birds in troupes following a leader. The Vultures imitated the characteristic walk of these birds by dancers wearing stilts. The Owl consisted of shading the eyes with the hands or in turning the head to and fro like an owl. Some of the postures and gestures involved in mimetic animal dances were carried over into the mime in the characteristic behavior of the various masks and the portrayal of animals. Evidence indicates that the *fabula Atellana,* which derived from importation of the Dorian mime into Rome, developed a stock type called Cicirrus (the cock) who possessed the features (beaked nose, etc.), walk, and characteristic sound of this bird.

In addition to the miming of characteristic animal behavior, many fertility dances mimed grotesque behavior such as lewd rotations of the hips, beatings, and theft, all of which derive from the downward thrust inherent in fertility worship. The kordax, which was originally a lewd and drunken dance in honor of Artemis, became the comic dance of the Dionysian thais. The sikinnis, the dance of the satyrs, involved capering and leaps, as well as the schema of the owl portrayed by shading the eyes with the hand and turning the head to and fro.[53] Whereas the kordax emphasized the lewd and obscene, the sikinnis involved a parody of all that was noble.

Animal mimesis, which orginates as serious ritual behavior, has a tendency to degenerate into burlesque and parody in ritual revels. As such, these comic dances seem to have had a direct influence on the evolution of Greek mime and comedy.[54] The kordax was a direct expression of the bestial elements in man as symbolized by the satyrs and other horse/man and animal/man incarnations that appeared as a part of the Dionysian thais. The ugliness and obscenity of this dance was not purely diversionary but was ritually sanctioned behavior in Dionysian possession trance in which devotees were possessed by latent libidinal attitudes. While the *emmeleia* was the imitation of the most beautiful and healthy bodies, "the kordax, or comic dance, was the imitation of the ugliest or bodies most deformed by the pursuit of sensuality and base passions."[55] The kordax was based in the imitation of men who by their vices or profession approached most closely an animal type. Characteristic types burlesqued by the kordax were the drunken slave, who stumbles and falls; the gross characteristics of Silenus, the father of the satyrs, with his round face and protruding paunch; and the drunken old hag.

BEATING MOTIFS

Mimetic dances involving ritual beating were common. The purpose of these according to Lawler was "to induce fertility, to stimulate the magic powers of life, and to ward off evil."[56] Bakhtin indicates that ritual beatings embody the downward movement inherent in fertility rituals.

> We also see the downward movement in fights, beatings, and blows; they throw the adversary to the ground, trample him into the earth. They bury their victim. But at the same time they are creative, they sow and harvest. ... The downward movement is also expressed in curses and abuses. They, too, dig a grave, but this is a bodily, creative grave.[57]

Instances of ritual beatings cited by ancient authors include: beating the ground with rods in the cult of Demeter; the ritual beatings of the *pharmakos* (scapegoat) to ward off sin, evil or famine; and the ceremonial beatings of boys in the ritual of Artemis Ortheia at Sparta.[58] With time, the writhing of the dancer or actor pretending to be or actually being flogged became conventionalized and passed over into the mime and from there into comedy. Flogging appears frequently in Old Comedy. In every one of Aristophanes' extant plays a character or member of the chorus either beats or strikes another, or threatens to do so.

FOOD STEALING MOTIFS

Food stealing scenes were a standard among the mimes. Aristophanes indicates that the food stealing motif was used in connection with Heracles in early Dorian mime. In *The Wasps,* the slave Xanthias exhorts his audience, "Expect not from us something mighty grand,/Nor yet some mirth purloined from Megara. We have no brace of servants here, to scatter Nuts from their basket out among the audience,/No Heracles defrauded of his supper."[59]

This motif, which some scholars believe to be a burlesque of an old ritual, was also a favorite of the Spartan mimes (*deikelistai*). Athenaeus mentions that the deikelistai of Lacedaemon portrayed characters who "stole fruit."[60]

Food stealing motifs seem to have been associated with beating dances in the fertility cults. In the cult of Artemis at Ortheia they were called "dance of the theft of food" or "theft dance." Pollux mentions a Laconian dance in which performers portrayed men discovered stealing stale meat and Athenaeus, Pollux, and others refers to "funny" dances involving meat-stealing. In the cult of Artemis in ancient Sparta food stealing mimes were common. In these, young men attempted to snatch the food offered to sacred divinities and were beaten with clubs by shrine attendants. Theft and the subsequent beatings, which seem to have been associated with purification rites, were easily transformed by the mimes into a source of entertainment for the crowd.[61]

SEXUAL THEMES

Release from sexual restraint played a large role in the cathartic value of Dionysian ritual. According to Aylen, the Greek theatre centers on the erotic. The festivals of Dionysus were a "flamboyant celebration of sexuality ... sexual celebration is indistinguishable from religious celebration."[62] Sexuality in all its forms in satyric comedy is evocative of a sense of the fecundity of nature, of a world of life and vitality. Sexuality played a prominent place in the mime performances, just as it did in Dionysian ritual and fertility dances. Before the arrival of Dionysus both Apollo and Artemis were worshiped as divinities of animal fertility.[63] According to Lawler, "The worship of Artemis ... was much influenced by the cults of pre–Greek and Asiatic mother goddesses in which lewd and orgiastic dancers were by no means uncommon." The kordax was a lewd rotation of the abdomen and buttocks. The sword thrusting motif of certain ritual dances appears to have acquired an obscene significance and passed into comedy. There was also another dance motion which was a variation of our modern day bump and grind. It consisted of a stirring motion of the hips with an occasional sharp jerk of the body.

The ritual enactment of myths associated with seduction or marriage and sexual union of the gods was enacted as a part of various fertility rites. These same subjects were also performed by the mimes. In the description of a mime performance at Xenophon's Banquet, Athenaeus describes a girl and boy who do a mimetic dance of Ariadne's seduction of Dionysus to the accompaniment of the aulos.[64] While the performances were discreet and tasteful, the unashamed eroticism appeared designed to arouse the audience sexually — like modern day soft porn.

COMIC CONFLICT

The essence of mime was contained in the small movement fragments of the schemata and it appears that they formed the kernel of small skits involving comic combat or conflict. According to Pickard-Cambridge, the six or so character types of the Dorian mime could be reduced to two essential types, the *alazon* and the bomolochos.[65] The comic conflict between these two types derives from the comic inversion and combat inherent in fertility ritual. Plays treating the combat and the destruction of the Old Man were fairly common in antiquity. They frequently took the form of struggles between masters and servants and burlesque versions of legendary fights. A considerable part of the plays of Aristophanes, as well as those of the New Comedy, involve scenes in which a person of exhalted but pretentious importance (alazon) is made fun of by a buffoon-like character (bomolochos). These types, according to Pickard-Cambridge, originated in Dorian mime and buffoonery.[66] Stock types of the alazon in Dorian mime were a swaggering Heracles, and the pompous doctor of the deikelistai. The fool (bomolochos) was embodied in the stock types of the parasite and the jesting and disrespectful slave.

THE LEGACY OF DORIAN MIME

The focus of this chapter has been on the origins of the mime in Dionysian possession rituals. There were, of course, a variety of performances classed under the rhubrick of mime in ancient Greece. Dorian mime seems to have been coincidental with the appearance of the mimeisthai word group and it is frequently credited by ancient scholars as being the earliest documented occurence of mime as a secular performance genre. However, the diverse forms of mime that appeared almost simultaneously with the Dorian mime reveal enough similarities in style and subject matter to class them as forms of grotesque realism.

Some mime performers were classified according to the type of plays which they performed. Ethologues, Biologues, and Cinedologues dealt respectively with licentious morality, sketches of human life which included portraits of individuals, and comic obscenity.

Other mime performers, the Ithyphalles, Phallophores, and Magodes were classed according to their costumes and were notable for their licentious and obscene performances. Mimes, masked or unmasked, jugglers or tightrope walkers, singers or actors, had one common feature beneath the diversity of their performances — their subject matter was for the most part based in comic and obscene burlesque of myth or everyday life and their style was one of exaggeration and caricature.

The literary mime plays that developed independently of the improvised skits of the Dorian mimes are for the most part short comic playlets written in verse that parody mythological and domestic situations. They were meant to be read by performers, who indicated character with appropriate voice, posture, and gestures.

Epicharmus, the earliest known writer of mime plays, is believed to have begun his career in Dorian Megara. He is credited with raising the Dorian mime in Sicily to literary importance by organizing the crude and very rudimentary sketches of the early mimes into plays with a common plot interest. Like the Dorian mimes, his plays deal with legendary or mythological burlesque in which heroic characters were contrasted with rustic characters from everyday life. His plays reveal how the mythic figures of the Dionysian revels were beginning to be scaled down to the dimensions of everyday life and ultimately to be translated into commonplace authority figures, such as a swaggering Heracles. Other alazon types that figure in Epicharmus are the quack wise-man and the prophet — probably deriving from the quack doctor of the deikelistai.

Sophron of Syracuse (fifth century B.C.) wrote mimes plays in the form of monologues involving naturalistic sketches of everyday life. These plays feature such stock types as the jealous woman and the old bawd and bore titles such as "The Needle-woman," "The Sorceress," and "The Mother-in-Law."

Herodas in the third century B.C. wrote plays consisting of naturalistic conversation pieces from real life which emphasized the seamy side of life. The subject matter of these plays is generally confined to gossip, sex, and scandal. Seven of his plays survive in their entirety. One of them, *The Gossips,* presents the conversation of two women, Koritto and Metro, concerning a leather dildo. Subject matter such as this reveals the connection between the third century plays of Herodas and the primitive farces of sixth century Doria.

The Roman mimes (*mimi*) not only borrowed their name from their Greek counterparts, but incorporated many of their diverse performance genres when they took over Greek territories between 270 and 240 B.C. One of the chief influences on the development and evolution of the Roman mime were the improvised *phlyax* farces that originated among Dorian settlers in Southern Italy in the fifth century B.C. Our knowledge of this type of mime derives from a series of vases known as the phlyax vases found in southern Italy and dating from the fourth century, about a century before any known phlyax plays were written. According to scholars these vases may only depict old and new comedy; however, the scenes of beating, gluttony, food stealing and sexual play reveal striking similarities to the Dorian mime. The phlyax farces probably remained crude, improvised playlets for several hundred years until the third century B.C. when they were incorporated into written mime plays by Rhinthon of Tarentum.

Like the Dorian mime, the subject matter of many of the phlyax farces was mythological burlesques frequently involving Heracles, Odysseus, and Dionysus. The phlyax vases depict scenes of actors, wearing the traditional comic costume and phallus, engaged in Bacchic revels in which can be found motifs of the Dionysian myth.

In addition to subject matter based on mythological burlesque, the phlyax plays also treated subjects drawn from everyday life in which gods and men freely mingled. According to Nicoll, "Of the many scenes depicted on the phylax vases, in everyone of these there is movement, vigor, and rude comic force. Scenes of eating are common; scenes of theft — mostly of wine or food — occur frequently."[67]

The phlyax possessed a set of stock comic masks of pretentious types (alazones) and of buffoons (bomolochoi). Of the stock type of the alazon there was a gluttonous Heracles, cheated of his dinner and a constant figure in Dorian mime and the Satyr plays. Pickard-Cambridge also mentions a type of a swaggering soldier that appears on phlyax vases. Of the bomolochoi there were masks of two types of comic slaves: the stupid slave whose function is to get beaten, and the cunning slave who tricks him into a beating meant for himself and then makes fun of his misery. There was also a foolish, bald-headed character (*stupidus calvus*) who had traits of the parasite; an irascible Old Man who beats any handy bystander with his cane; a cook-slave named Maison who is of Dorian origin; as well as other obscurer masks. It seems that the phlyax farces, like the Dorian mime, started off with a small group of these fixed types, to which others were then created by talented actors, as happened in the Commedia dell'Arte.[68]

The phlyakes in turn seem to have given rise to the Atellan farce (fabula Atellana) which developed in the town of Atella in southern Italy and was transported to Rome in the third century B.C. The Atellan farce consisted of largely improvised, short sketches based on parody of mythology, politics, social customs, and domestic life. As in the Dorian mime, slapstick, beatings, gluttony, trickery, and sexual themes abounded. Four grotesque stock character masks were the centerpiece of the Atellana: Bucco, Dossenus, Maccus and Pappus. Bucco was a loud-mouthed braggart with padded cheeks and accentuated mouth. Dossenus was a sharp-witted and grotesque hunchback. Maccus was a gluttonous fool—probably with a padded belly. Pappus was an absentminded, comic old man. A fifth has been identified as Cicirrus. These stock characters, each with his own mask, costume and behavior, are believed by many scholars to have been the prototypes of the masks of the Commedia dell'Arte. The Atellan farce reached the peak of its popularity in Rome of 100 B.C. At this time it became a literary genre and was gradually replaced by the *fabula riciniata* and the pantomime.

Roman mime originated from a variety of sources. One of these can be traced to Etruria, the northern area of what is now Italy. Etruria existed as a separate territory until it was eventually taken over by the Romans in the third century B.C. Etruscan religious festivals, which included carnivalesque theatrical performances involving acting, dancing, flute playing, juggling, and acrobatics, had a distinct impact on the development of the theatrical offerings at the Roman festivals.

The mime performances (fabula riciniata) were an important part of the Roman festival *ludi Florales* which honored the fertility goddesses. This was a sort of Bacchanalian carnival of the people during which grossly indecent mimes were presented. Unlike the mime performers of phlyax and Atellan farces, these fabula riciniata did not wear masks. Their skits, for the most part, were based on lewd satire of Roman life and customs. In addition to short skits, the mimes also performed a broad spectrum of entertainments, such as tightrope walking, dancing, juggling, and animal acts. Nicoll tells us the Roman mimes were referred to by a variety of terms, among them *saltatores* (literally dancers or acrobats) and *planipedes* ("with barefeet").[69] While there was originally a distinction between the actors of tragedy, comedy and the mime, in Rome the mimes gradually came to be called *histriones*—the generic term for actor.[70]

Mime performances were included in every aspect of Roman life. They were the staple of Roman festivals and were interlaced in most public performances, lectures, and dedications. They also occurred at funerals, weddings, and banquets, as well as on the street corner. Unlike Greece where the mime was considered vulgar, during the Roman Empire mime was the most popular form of entertainment and was regarded highly by all classes of society.

The satyric attitude that underlie possession trance behavior in group fertility worship is the origin and essence of the secular art of mime. The source of mime's grotesque subject matter and style was not the myth of Dionysus but the spectacular and bizarre behavior of the Dionysian choir of the possessed, seeking catharsis from pent-up libidinal attitudes through ritual revel.

Satyric mime humanizes myth; it reconnects the body of the sacred with the body of humanity. In overturning the sacred, it reaffirms its power of release and renewal. The style of grotesque realism grew out of the sacred unity

Terra-cotta statuette of an actor in the Atellan Farce. Roman, first century B.C. Louvre, Paris, France. Photo La Réunion des Musées Nationaux.

of man, god, and beast which brings together the three levels of existence: the underworld, the human plane, and that of the gods. The grotesque mask is the vehicle of this union. It incorporates the mystery of otherness. It manifests the presence of a divinity in all its terrifying otherness — not as an idealized hero but as an antihero — more powerful because it incorporates the realm of the ugly and deformed with its appetites and gargantuan desires. These too are sacred, as well as beautiful, because they capture in a physical and direct form the terrifying forces that lie buried in the individual and the sacred mythology of which he is a part.

The key to the origin of mime lies in the power of the mask. It enabled the worshipers of Dionysus to externalize their impulses and act them out in a sacred context. It disguised the wearers and allowed them to step out of their everyday selves and reconnect with the fundamental impulses that generate life. The grotesque disguises and padding created a mask of the body to which the posture of the individual conformed. The attitudes contained in the body mask were expressed in corollary behavior, antics, and mimetic dance. From these were born small skits that encapsuled the primary attitudes of each mask as they related to one another. The essential gestures of each mask were posturally based because they articulated the conflict between the self and the other latent self, the alazon and bomolochos They dramatized the battle between the forces that limit the individual to a social plane and those that seek to rupture the plane to experience the sacred participation in the cosmic energies of life.

Posturally based gesture is the essence of attitudes held from going into action. The stronger the emotion behind the gesture the greater the immobility. The greater the immobility the greater the force is to overcome it. Possession behavior explodes and exaggerates. It siezes upon the gesture that characterizes an internal state and pares it to what is essential. It then repeats it over and over again until the attitude exhausts itself. There is no need to create a play complete with plot. The gesture encapsules everything that needs to be said; hence the short ribald skits and lampooning that accompany the ritual revels.

Mime developed from the unstructured play of the tipsy and mildly entranced devotees at ritual revels. When rituals are incorporated into public festivals in which all participate, they begin to degenerate into parody and humor. While these elements are present in the rituals themselves, they take on an aspect of performance to amuse the crowd. The same attitudes of release and renewal remain operative but their end is different. As in type two possession the performances begin to center around a fixed set of masks and themes inspired by the mask. The sacred world of the gods and the profane conflicts of everyday life intersect and in this meeting the genre of the mime is born. Characters and subjects from daily life begin to mingle with the figures of the gods and their stories. Themes that were originally enacted as a part of a sacred rite take the form of sociodramas, incorporating on a human scale the original attitudes that were enacted under the guise of possessing deities.

Mime took its particular form from the style of grotesque realism because it is basically an unstructured ritual form. Its power lies in overthrowing the spiritual and social hierarchy in order to allow life-giving energy to flow into society. Like the ancient comedy which grew out of it, its function was to release the psychophysical tensions latent in the population. However, its basic form was anarchic. The state channeled this potentially destructive impulse into its conception of the democratic city-state. It charged the playwrights to appease the people by providing representations founded in terms of the laws of the city-state and to create through art a controlled outlet of the constellation of mental attitudes that lay at the core of the ancient Dionysian ritual. The genres of comedy and tragedy were born, but the mime remained free.

Mime lies precisely in the psychophysical laws of this possession behavior. Its techniques are those of identification, metamorphosis, and role playing by means of posturally based gesture. Grotesque realism is the essence of its style. It has no need to feel ashamed that its subject matter is licentious and that its pieces are only sketches. It does not lie; it does not create to please the institutionalized powers that be. Its source and its audience are the common people, who it delights by tearing down all that enslaves and diminishes them. The truth of its uniqueness as a performance genre distinct from the drama and dance can be found in its virility and ability to survive on the fringes of society from century to century.

Chapter Three

The Satyric Masks
of the Commedia dell'Arte

The embryonic satyric comedy that was present in the stock characters and sketches of the Dorian mime reached fruition in the Renaissance in the Commedia dell'Arte. Commedia dell'Arte was a comedy of skill in which troupes of professional players employed techniques of improvisation, mime, mask, music, song, and dance to create comic plays centering on a set of stock character types. The commedia had three categories of characters: lovers, old men, and servants. The essence of the commedia's longevity and broad popular appeal lay in the antics of its masked characters. The basic commedia masks from which many related types branched off are the two old men (*Vecchi*), Pantalone and the Doctor; and two or more comic servants (*Zanni*)— Harlequin, Pulcinella, and or Brighella. While there is no clear line of descent tracing the commedia from the Dorian mime through the Atellan farce and medieval mime, the similarity in stock character types, subject matter, and style point to a derivation and development of the satyric revelry associated with fertility festivals.[1]

The unique style and aesthetics of commedia is based in carnivalesque "grotesque realism" as emblemized by the commedia masks. According to Bakhtin, "Such manifestations as parodies, caricatures, grimaces, eccentric postures, and comic gestures are per se derived from the mask. It reveals the essence of the grotesque."[2] The commedia masks embody a vision of a world turned upside down in which humor is generated by parody of the existing order—young triumph over old, the fool over his master—and in which blows, beatings, births, deaths, gross jokes, and swearing (all typical of the fecund ritual humor) abound.

The continuity of stock types of the Doctor, old man, and comic slaves, from ancient times up through the peak of the commedia in the eighteenth century, as well as their continued popularity today, suggests that they embody archetypes representing fundamental human attitudes.[3] The conflict between the alazon and bomolochos; the confrontation between the old and the new which parodies the existing social hierarchy serves the important function of release and renewal.

The central players in this drama of renewal and regeneration are the masks of the commedia Zanni (the bomolochoi or fool masks). They are what Jung terms the Trickster figure, which is an essential archetype in the development of the psyche; the "Trickster is a figure whose physical appetites dominate his behavior; he has the mentality of an infant."[4] According to Joseph Campbell the Trickster represents "the chaos principle, the principle of disorder, the force careless of taboos and shattering bounds. But from the point of view of the deeper realms of being from which the energies of life ultimately spring, this principle is not to be despised."[5]

The Trickster is a positive force. In its bold and uninhibited energy lies the ability to overturn the status quo and to erase all boundaries. It represents the irrepressible life force manifested in the exuberance and abundance of spring's regeneration. Harlequin has survived to today, especially in popular forms of art like the mime, precisely because they are seen as representations of our culture's antiheroes—its original rebels.

In the Dorian mime and Greek comedy the bomolochos, who frequently appeared as a jesting slave, makes fun of a person of elaborate pretensions, the alazon. The alazon is generally an established member of society who takes himself too seriously. Pantalone and the Doctor in the commedia are both alazon masks. Pantalone, in particular, functions dramatically to block the wooing and marriage of the young lovers. The Zanni play tricks are upon the old men and they assist in aborting their schemes. In this tripartite cast of old men, comic servants, and young lovers is to be found vestiges of the ritual structure of the old year in conflict with the new in which ritual clowns and buffoons serve to overturn the existing order and hasten in the new year.

The contrast between the alazon and bomolochos, the former which generally come from the upper classes, and the latter, in the form of servants which come from the lower classes, has been seen by some as a satire of class structure. According to Lorelle, the commedia masks represent "sociotypes" based in a satire of the social structure of Italian society of the sixteenth and seventeenth centuries.[6] Pantalone is a satire of the mercantile class, the Doctor a satire of culture considered an end in itself, and the Zanni a satire of the Bergamask porters, etc. Scholars have tended to base their evidence for this theory on the importance of dialects as a basis for distinction between characters. For example, Pantalone's dialect signals he is from the Venetian merchant class. However, Nicoll states that "it is entirely false, on the basis of such employment of dialectal forms to suggest that the Commedia dell'Arte was a 'class conscious' form of theatre."[7]

The purpose of the commedia was the same release from constraints through merriment that typified the Dorian mime. It was a satire of types who represent a human tendency to deny life through the pursuit of knowledge, money, or reputation and was a celebration of the forces that turn it topsy turvy. Henri Bergson in *Laughter* states that comedy springs from "rigidity . . . clashing with the inner suppleness of life."[8] The commedia did not seek to caricature particular classes per se, but rather that which goes beyond the limit, that which is carried to an excess. Since the class structure and social decorum represent fixed systems of behavior that constrict the natural flow of life, they become part of the subject matter of satire that aims in its broader strokes to shatter rigidity in all its forms. Zanni and Vecchi alike are ridiculed for a single-minded pursuit of their objectives which reduces them to mechanized puppets of desire. The masks are at once a combination of the rigidity of fixed character types and an expression of the satyric excesses of the ribald and joyous upheaval of life originally contained in the carnival festival.

The masks distill the original satyric behavior of the possession demons and the spirits of carnival festivals into characters whose essence lies in a fixed set of repeatable gestures. The comic in character, according to Bergson, does not spring so much from action as it fuels a plot as it does from the unconscious gestures, postures, and language that signify an underlying comic attitude.

> *. . . instead of concentrating our attention on actions, comedy directs it rather to gestures.* By *gestures* we here mean the attitudes, the movements and even the language by which a mental state expresses itself outwardly without any aim or profit, from no other cause than a kind of inner itching. Gesture, thus defined is profoundly different from action. Action is intention or, at any rate, conscious; gesture slips out unawares, it is automatic.[9]

The masks represent a constellation of emotions and tendencies that have more or less remained constant throughout the Renaissance, despite the changes wrought by the genius of individual performers. The masks isolate and exaggerate facial features which accentuate fecund and netherworld body aspects — phallic and bulbous noses, padded cheeks, jutting beards, baldness, piercing eyes and blackness. Each mask in turn demands a characteristic posture or set of postures which signify a particular constellation of psychic tendencies. The postures that support the commedia masks are macrocosms of the attitude contained in the configuration of the mask. With the assistance of costume and bodily padding, they emphasize and exaggerate those anatomical features (belly, buttocks, genitalia) which protrude beyond the body.

The bodily postures typifying each mask have remained relatively fixed from the early commedia in the sixteenth century through the eighteenth century. The principle documentation for mask postures comes from art works of the Renaissance. While often mask postures may have been altered by artistic convention and or the artist's limitations in portraying the human body, there nevertheless appears to be enough collaborative evidence to arrive at some suppositions about the nature of these postures.

Jacques Callot (1593–1635). "Le Pantalon du Cassandre." Print Collection, Miriam and Ira D. Wallach Division of Art, Prints and Photographs, the New York Public Library, Astor, Lenox and Tilden Foundations.

First, they are built upon the courtly posture of the Renaissance period. This posture is essentially the neutral posture for the age, and any deviation from it through exaggeration creates the excessive attitude that characterizes the mask. Second, the postures of the commedia masks are based on a variation of an undulation of the spine starting at the feet and moving through the head. Using the language of body centers, we may speak of each character in terms of the body element which is most predominant, i.e. belly centered, buttocks centered, genitalia centered, etc. The satyric attitudes of the commedia are clearly visible in the following discussion of four basic masks: Pantalone, the Doctor, and the two most popular servant masks, Harlequin and Pulcinella.

THE VECCHI

PANTALONE

Pantalone is a Venetian merchant whose mask has historically revealed many variations. In the sixteenth century he first appears with the dominant characteristics of a miser and a lecher. To bring out these traits and the inflation that makes this character an alazon, the actor who performs this role, according to Riccoboni,

> should try to provoke laughter at appropriate junctures by his self-importance and stupidity, and in this manner represent a man ripe in years who pretends to be a tower of strength and good counsel for others, whereas in truth he is blinded by amorous passion and continually doing peurile things which might lead an observer to call him a child, for all that he is almost a centenarian. The actor should also demonstrate how Pantaloon's avarice, common enough in men of his advanced age, is dominated by a more virulent vice, love, which makes of him a callow graybeard ... lost to all sense of decency.[10]

The conflict between the pretensions and self-importance of this mask, manifested in a kind of serious dignity, and the more bestial impulses stemming from the lower center's greed for sex and money is what creates the grotesque comedy of the mask.

Pantalone's lecherous nature is conveyed by a genital-centered posture which consists of a thrust forward pelvis (often accompanied by hands on the hips) and a pushed back chest, which is counterbalanced by a thrust forward chin and long hooked nose, creating an S-like undulation. The genital-centered posture of this mask is further accentuated by a pouch (which in the sixteenth century barely concealed a phallus) and a sword which were made to stand out when the character stood in his characteristic profile position. The byplay between the old body sprouting the phallic nose and genitalia indicates its ancient lineage with the sileni of the Greek mime. A second characteristic posture accentuates his prying, inquisitive, suspicious and miserly nature. The chin and nose are thrust forward and the entire torso inclines forward at a 45 degree angle over bent legs.

The phallic attitude that animates Pantalone's postures is expressed outwardly in a characteristic walk. According to Lea, "Pantalone comes on to the stage masked as a lean inquisitive old man; in his loose slippers he walks like a hen, one hand is thrust behind to hold back his 'zimarra.'"[11] In Latin cultures the cock symbolizes both the virile male and the cuckold, two roles most often played by Pantalone. The cock-like aspect of this mask was further accentuated by its pointed yellow turkish slippers, skinny legs enclosed in black tights, and long black cloak which was frequently thrust out behind his body. In addition, the jabbing movements made by the thrust forward beard and beaked nose recalls the pecking of chickens.

MARC ANTOINE ROMAGNEZI.

dans le personnage du Docteur Balouard.

(Comedᵉ Italienne)   (Année 1850.)

Marc Antoine Romagnezi as the Doctor, seventeenth century. Billy Rose Theatre Collection. The New York Public Library for the Performing Arts, Astor, Lenox and Tilden Foundations.

THE DOCTOR

The Doctor is the second old man of the commedia. His mask, like the very similar "quack" doctor's of the Dorian mimes, represents the rigidity and pretensions of the alazon type. This mask derives from the town of Bologna which was famous for its universities. The Doctor is a pedant who satirizes humanist learning carried to an excess. He continually lets off verbal hot air in the form of clichés, malapropisms, and misquoted and mispronounced passages of Latin and Greek. In addition to verbosity, he is also a glutton whose penchant for good food has resulted in obesity. Like Pantalone, who is both friend and rival, the Doctor has large sexual appetites; he "is madly eager for amorous adventure, but ends up a cuckold and an object of derision to the Zanni, the butt of their Lazzi, and the Lover's mockery."[12]

The verbal inflation and gluttony of the Doctor are fittingly indicated by a belly-centered posture. The Doctor's rotundity is portrayed by a thrust forward belly accentuated by ample padding. This is counterbalanced by a protruding buttocks and a forward thrust head. The obesity of the global corporeal posture is distilled in the facial mask, which consists only of the forehead, bulbous nose with a huge red wart, and a huge black mustache which accentuates the actor's cheeks.

The inflation of this mask is carried forward in its stance and walk. The Doctor's tiny feet and narrow legs are often depicted in a ballet first position. This stance narrows the character's base and imparts a balloon-like lightness to his considerable bulk. The contrast between the girth and weight of the belly and the prissy lightness of the support is further emphasized by the tiny mincing steps and a swaying motion of his walk. One of his characteristic gestures, according to Oreglia, was that he often "holds a small but very thick book in one hand and gesticulates professorially with his index finger."[13]

THE ZANNI

The commedia Zanni have an ancient lineage. Although their origin is obscure, they reveal strong affinities with the satyrs and netherworld demons of the Dionysian thais, whose characteristics were continued in the travesty and mimetic behavior of Greek and Roman revels and in the carnivals of the Middle Ages. Scholars have traced one possible derivation of the term Zanni to *Gianni*, a familiar name for the devil in Italy,[14] and to the Latin *sannio* (buffoon).[15] The Medieval carnival characters often wore black or white face colorings to simulate the dead or the creatures from the underworld who, when they entered a city, turned it upside down with their bizarre antics. "According to the magico-religious interpretation of the ritual, they were, as spirits from the earth, assisting in the process of rebirth, helping the old year, with all its sins on its head, toward death and a new beginning ... and demonstrating the capacity for renewal through energy and animal spirit."[16] Harlequin and Pulcinella, the two predominant Zanni of the commedia, can be traced to the development of distinct character types within the carnival. Indications are that Harlequin originated in France as a specter devil who led a troupe of demons who played tricks and created confusion. Pulcinella developed as a supreme carnival demon in southern Italy.

The commedia Zanni have all of the characteristics of the plotting slaves of ancient Greek comedy. Their type is based on the Bergamask porters who plied their trade in Venice and other cities in northern Italy in the sixteenth century. They represent the bomolochoi whose comic essence lies in making dupes out of themselves as well as their masters. As in the Dorian mime, they appear in pairs. According to Lea, the pair of Zanni in commedia troupe "soon realized that the sparks of comedy were struck from the flint and steel of opposite natures."[17]

HARLEQUIN

The mask of Harlequin, more than any other character, captures the satyric essence of the Commedia dell'Arte. There is strong evidence that Harlequin was influenced by spectre-devils of the medieval carnivals. Long before the arrival of the Italian actors in France, the word *herlequin*, pronounced harlequin, existed in France and denoted "a reveller associated with the charivari and the comic devils of the miracle and mystery plays whose antics and license of speech recalled his devilishly ancestry and whose mask and hairy garments his beast developments."[18] His continuing popularity beyond the demise of the commedia in the eighteenth century attests to the fact that he is a potent archetype of the infantile period in the development of the human psyche. The comedy created by this character is that of the logic of libidinal impulses given free rein, "wherein concepts of morality have no being, and yet, despite such absence of morality, he displays no viciousness. . . ."[19] Riccoboni writes, "The acting of Harlequins before the seventeenth century was nothing but a continual play of extravagant tricks, violent movements, and outrageous rogueries. He was at once insolent, mocking, inept, clownish, and emphatically ribald."[20]

Harlequin exhibits several remarkable corporeal techniques that affirm his connection with the netherworld demons of fertility festivals including his acrobatic prowess and the ability to metamorphose into variety of personages and animals. Like one possessed, he is capable of the most amazing physical feats. Somersaults, hand springs, tightrope walking, tumbling, and diving are all associated with Harlequin's normal means of locomotion. Like the Trickster figure, he frequently engages in transformations or appears in disguise. For this reason, he has been described as a "chameleon which takes on every color."[21]

Harlequin's amazing ability to rapidly transform himself is apparent in a scenario entitled "Arlequin Lingère au Palais." Dressed half as a man and half as a woman, Harlequin appears alternately in a scene involving a lemonade-stall (where Harlequin appears as a woman) and a linen draper's shop (where Harlequin presents himself as a man). "Harlequin passes rapidly from one shop to the other, pivoting about so fast that Pascariel cannot tell whether he is dealing with the linen-woman or the lemonade-man. In the end Harlequin appears as a nurse with a child in her arms. . . ."[22]

Harlequin has two centers. First, he is buttock centered with thrust-backwards buttocks produced by a convex arching of the lower back, compensated by a forward thrust chest and head. This posture signifies his curtailed development at the anal stage. This S curve is also apparent in a frontal posture in which one hip is thrust to the side and compensated by the chest and head.

LE MERCURE TERRESTRE DES AMOUREUX DE CHAQUE
SEXE CHERCHANT LA PIERRE DES PHILOSOPHES.
De Groote Gardenier der Liefde kruidhoven, meest achtende de
Gulde kroon Imperiaal.

35

Wilh. Koning excud. Amst.   *Ignatio Folkema fecit.*

NICOLO CACCATRIPPA, FAMOSA CANAIA BERGAMASCA,
AMBASCIADOR D'AMORI DEL SIG? GRATIAN DI BLOUNIA.

*Non manca mi Spirit, per far el Ruffian
Adess la Zinzola Sarà per Grazian
La Smeraldin per me, Ceruell si vuol auer
Per procurar formai, macaron e bel mager .*

*Messager de l'amour je fais le fol partout
Car c'est propre a cet art. He! tel valet tel maitre
Un insensé voudroit tout le monde renaitre
L'Amour est trop grand dieu, pour le dompter au bout.*

*'K Ben Minnepostiljon, dat past tog best de gekken
Ik volg myn meesters net op 't spoor ook blind verliefd
Maar meest op splint zo mag ik voor Sinjoor verstrekken
Het zot gevley al licht een doetjes hert doorgrieft.*

Harlequin. Dutch engraving, eighteenth century. Billy Rose Theatre Collection.
The New York Public Library for the Performing Arts, Astor, Lenox and Tilden
Foundations.

Secondly, he is eye centered. His mask is generally dark and has round, slanted
eye holes that give him a characteristic devilish expression. Typical of the carnivalesque grotesque, his eyes appear to protrude beyond the mask. The tension
between these two opposing centers creates a comic counterpoint in the
character between the front and the back. It also allows him to engage in the
most amazing acrobatics because he is weighted both in the rear and in the
front.

Harlequin has a set of automatic and mechanical gestures which evoke the
movements of a machine. The union of the human with the object is an element of the style of grotesque realism. Many of Harlequin's gestures involve
the rigidity of one or more parts of the body as a basis to create characteristic
postures, walks, or gestures. Harlequin's walk when he enters the stage consists
of a straight-legged and flat-footed strut with the feet turned out (an exaggeration of the Chaplinesque walk). He has a unusual jack-in-the-box head movement in which he pulls his head down onto fixed shoulders by scrunching his
neck and then suddenly pops his head up without moving his body. He also
can hump his back to make himself look like a hunchback, while he has a set
of comic manipulations of his cap and his wooden bat, similar to the keystone
cops.

PULCINELLA

Pulcinella is a composite of the physical and psychological traits that typified the satyric excesses of the ancient Greek mimes and their Latin counterparts, the Atellenae.

With his humped back, padded belly, large phallic hooked nose, and
huge coarse mouth, he is the physical heir to the Dionysian satyrs and netherworld demons whose spirit can be seen in the early grotesque statuary which
depict mimes. Pulcinella's physical deformities are expressed behaviorally by
a set of contradictory qualities in which the negative aspects of the libido
predominate: "He is faithful, revengeful, sly, gullible, nervy, audacious,
jealous, cowardly, bullying, sentimental, lazy, a scandalmonger, and full of
malice in turn...."[23]

He is the embodiment of the darker elements of the Jungian trickster,
who "Lacking any purpose beyond the gratification of his primary needs, ...
is cruel, cynical, and unfeeling."[24] Ducharte describes Pulcinella in similar
terms: "Being self-centered and bestial, Pulcinella had no scruples whatever,
and because the moral suffering from his physical deformity reacted upon his
brain at the expense of his heart, he was exceedingly cruel."[25]

While he is capable of unexpected and capricious kindness, his cruelty
and readiness to use his wooden bat to flog his victims, distinguishes him from
the essentially good-natured and childlike Harlequin.

The mask is probably the most frightening and comic of all the commedia
masks because of its unpredictable and changeable nature. Pulcinella is not

Jacques Callot. Signa Lucretia and Pulliciniello (detail). Print Collection, Miriam and Ira D. Wallach Division of Art, Prints and Photographs, the New York Public Library, Astor, Lenox and Tilden Foundations.

one individual but a collection of traits that have allowed him to appear in dozens of roles, from a dull-witted fool to a cruel and vulgar rogue. Nicoll states that "Pulcinella was a characterless dummy which could be dressed up in any way a particular actor—or particular public—desired."[26] Not only is the audience unable to predict how Pulcinella will behave, but they often do not know in what disguise he will appear next. Since this mask has no clear set of fixed traits, Pulcinella is characterized most by his constant transformations.

Pulcinella's complex and contradictory behavior and his striking blend of physical characteristics have led many scholars to make connections between this mask and the buffoons of the Atellan farces, Maccus, Bucco, Doxenus, and Pappus. Pulcinella seems to be a montage of all of the grotesque elements that typified the early mime. Like Maccus, whose humped back, padded stomach, and long spindly legs he shares, he is slow-witted and cruel. Like Bucco, with whom he holds in common a large sensual mouth and padded cheeks, he is a flatterer, braggart, thief, and a coward. Affinities can also be found with the hunched-back Doxenus and the gluttonous of Pappus.

Pulcinella's base posture accentuates the duality inherent in this character, as in the case of Harlequin, between the front and back. The mask is both belly and back centered, created through padding in both these areas. The deformity of the back signifies the cruelty and bestiality of the mask; the large, protruding belly signifies the sensual and gluttonous nature. The contrast between these two centers creates a feeling of opposition and tension that, in contrast to the ingenuous and optimistic nature of Harlequin, can be at once sinister and obscene. Pulcinella's sinister and satyric aspect is further heightened by a black mask with a huge, hooked nose and the large wooden bat that he frequently carries. In contrast to these frightening physical attributes, the costume is strikingly neutral, consisting of a pointed hat or cap, loose white trousers, and a large shirt. Its origins can be variously traced to the costumes worn by the peasants in the region of Acera where Pulcinella first arose, or to the loose white costume signifying spirits which is worn at carnivals in northern Italy.

PLAYING THE MASK

The Commedia dell'Arte masks demand a postural style of performance. To play the mask, as the saying goes among commedia artists, the actor must manipulate it in such a way that the various facets of the character are indicated to the audience. Because the masks do not depict any emotion, they require a performance style in which postures or body-attitudes freeze the mask in various angles and positions in order that the audience may clearly read exaggerated and stereotyped expressions of emotion.

In order to play the mask, the commedia performers needed to be expert mimes. The mimetic ability of the commedia performers was one of the main reasons for the broad popular appeal of this genre in countries throughout Europe, even where the audience could not understand Italian. In the many drawings and paintings of the commedia that have survived, the element that stands out most is the energy of the masked characters. So often they are depicted in precariously balanced, exaggerated postures. This is a stylistic device, accentuating the inner drama of attitudes held from going into action that forms the basis of corporeal mimesis. Frozen postures, animated by opposing forces within the performer's body, result from energy going in two directions. The impulse to burst forward in movement is checked in moments of precarious balance by another force within the performer's body which holds him back. This alternation between moments of dynamically balanced stasis and bursts of violent action typified the performing style of the commedia.

LAZZI: THE SHORT COMIC
SKETCHES OF THE COMMEDIA

The constellation of attitudes that are represented in each mask are expressed outwardly in characteristic gestures or behavior; for example, Harlequin's lowers his head and extends it suddenly like an accordion, or the Doctor holds a small book and wags his index finger. When the attitudes that underlie the mask are elaborated dramatically the gesture is expanded to a comic sketch or gag (*lazzo*; plural form is *lazzi*).

Indications of how the commedia performers expressed satyric attitudes can be found in the descriptions of lazzi that have survived to present day. Mel Gordon, in the most complete study of lazzi done to date, defines lazzi as "comic routines that were planned or unplanned and that could be performed in any one of dozens of plays. Put another way, lazzi allude to any discrete, or independent, comic and repeatable activity that guaranteed laughs for its participants."[27]

Scholarship, according to Gordon, has tended to concentrate on the scenarios of the commedia and to almost ignore the equal if not greater importance of lazzi in the performance. The Commedia dell'Arte was primarily an improvised form of comedy in contrast to the aristocratic literary comedy (*commedia erudita*). The performers worked from scenarios tacked on the stage wall which indicated the outlines of the plot and many of the lazzi. The loose structure and schematization of the plot suggests that the scenarios may have primarily functioned as frameworks for the short comic sketches or lazzi. The lazzi probably existed prior to the commedia in carnivalesque skits similar to those of the Dorian mimes. Lea indicates that many lazzi were "episodes in miniature, each involving some dramatic knot which must be solved before the play can proceed."[28] Nicoll cites this same function, referring to them as separate "intermezzi."[29] We need only look at such comic bits such as Chaplin in *The Gold Rush* using two dinner rolls to mime a dance (lazzo of transformation) or eating his shoe (lazzo of food) to see that comic business is often the most amusing and memorable part of burlesque, comic performances.

A quick glance at the 12 categories identified by Mel Gordon of almost 400 lazzi performed between 1550–1750 reveals many common themes between commedia and its ancient ancestor, the Dorian mime: acrobatic and mimic lazzi, comic violence/sadistic behavior, food lazzi, illogical lazzi, stage properties as lazzi, sexual/scatological lazzi, social/class rebellion lazzi, stage/life duality lazzi, stupidity/inappropriate behavior, transformation lazzi, trickery lazzi, and word play lazzi.[30]

Many of the lazzi were purely mimed scenes involving both real and imaginary props and mimic sounds as in the lazzo of the axe grinder in which Mezzettino sharpens a knife by mimicking the movements of a knife-grinder while making the noises created by the blade and stone. Mimic lazzi involving the characteristic behavior of animals were associated with Harlequin. In lazzi of the cat, Zanni (or Harlequin) imitates the actions of a cat, demonstrating how it hunts for wild birds or how it cleans itself, scratching his ear with his foot, and washing his body with his tongue.

Transformation lazzi are a specialty of the Zanni. In these, the character appears to change form by mimicking traits of an animal, human being, or object. For example, Harlequin is turned into a crane whose neck grows longer or a dwarf whose body shrinks, or Pantalone is turned into a ass who is ridden by Harlequin.

Playing the mask demanded that the commedia performer assume postures and poses indicating emotion. In some of the lazzi, these postures were exaggerated and held for comic effect. For example, in the lazzo of silence, Pedrolino (Pulcinella) freezes in an attitude of amazement when his master shouts at him for doing what he thought he was supposed to do.

Commedia's carnivalesque connection to the scatological subject matter of the Dorian mimes is most apparent in the lazzi of comic violence and or sadistic behavior. These seem to be a vestige of the ritual beatings in which blows were symbolic of the downward thrust inherent in fertility rituals. The lazzo of the innocent by-stander, lazzo of the cuff, lazzo of beating his father, and lazzo of the flogging are only a few of the many lazzi which derive humor from beatings.

The Zanni's gluttony and obsession with eating is revealed in the food lazzi, several of which create humor through the "eating of the self," which has definite ritualistic and carnivalesque overtones. In lazzo of eating oneself, the starving Harlequin, unable to find anything to eat, begins to eat himself starting with his feet and working up to his knees, thighs, and upper torso. As in fertility ritual, food and beating motifs often appear together. In lazzo of being brained, Scaramouche hits Harlequin so hard on the head that Harlequin's brains begin to spurt out. Afraid that he will lose his intelligence, Harlequin sits and proceeds to eat his brains. Numerous lazzi involve scatological behavior associated with bodily products, representing the fecund nature of the body's taking in and giving forth. For example there are the lazzo of the enema, the lazzo of vomit, lazzo of urinating on her and lazzo of spitting. Many sexual lazzi involve simulated sexual acts.

The acrobatic and mimic lazzi as well as transformation lazzi are vestigial behavior of possessed individuals who engage in bizarre behavior and gymnastics while entranced and who frequently metamorphose into animals. Handsprings, cartwheels, flips, dives, falls, tightrope walking, and stilt walking were associated with Harlequin's normal means of locomotion and are also engaged in by the other masks. Acrobatic lazzi were not just used in the commedia to amaze the audience with daring technical feats and displays of virtuosity. They translated strongly felt inner attitudes — anger, joy, surprise, etc. — into dynamic and bizarre motion. For example, joy might be expressed through a flip and a series of somersaults. Acrobatics also served to express the spontaneous and automatic nature of comic character types. These machine-like movements, which engage the body in unnatural and repeatable motions, equate the human being to an object. For example, in the lazzo of somersaults, Harlequin's comic confusion reduces him to a human missile and he executes a series of handsprings or somersaults that catapult him from one character to another.

While the commedia is known for its acrobatic and frenetic activity, it also demanded moments of immobility as a contrast. This was especially apparent in the mime of the Zanni and often occurs in lazzi involving transformation. The most frequent use of this device was in statuary lazzi. In one such example, Harlequin is brought in as a statue and plays tricks on the other characters when their backs are turned, always returning to the statue position when they face him. Immobility often involved only a part or parts of the body. In lazzo of the chase, the Captain and Coviello mime running while fixed in place, slightly out of reach of each other. A stationary leg supported the body while the other created the illusion of running. This lazzo involves the technique of fixed point in space (*point d'appui*) which was to be elaborated centuries later in the work of Etienne Decroux and Marcel Marceau. In a scenario entitled "Pulcinella the Brigand Chief," Pulcinella, who is being pursued by a policeman, transforms himself into a weather vane, fixing his body and moving his arms like windmills, then into a milestone in a garden, and detected once more he hides under a basket and pretends to be a tortoise. Ducharte, who compares this series of transformations to those made by Charlie Chaplin in *Shoulder Arms* states, "All the comicality of Pulcinella's and Chaplin's acting in these cases lies in the contrast between absolute immobility and sudden agility. . . ."[31]

The Commedia dell'Arte is an elaboration of the satyric mime into a formalized theatrical genre which derives its style of performance and subject matter from the laws of the grotesque mask. The genius of the commedia is in the melding of the archetypal masks of the ancient and medieval carnival with the stereotypical traits of types from the Italian society. This union produced sociotypes which were employed to enact dramas centering on the social differentiation of personality structures and on the conflicts and tensions engendered by the socio-cultural system.

The style of playing the grotesque mask is based in the intensification and exaggeration of the element of posture. Each mask possesses a characteristic bodily posture that exaggerates the lower centers of the character. The bodily posture, which is a macrocosm of the configuration of the mask, encapsules a latent attitude which is rooted in those elements of the psyche which unite man with the elemental forces of birth and death. In addition, each mask has a set of corollary postures and gestures which articulate the conflicting energies that make up the attitude by means of posturally based movement. This style of corporeal expression is analogous to that of the marionette. The commedia masks seem to be manipulated by their inner attitudes like puppets on strings. Movement oscillates between frozen and dynamically charged, held positions of the body and frenetic explosions of the attitude into gesture and action.

The play between the masks dramatizes the conflict of attitudes on its most basic level in the opposition of the alazon and bomolochos. This struggle between the old and the new translates the tensional forces operating in the mask into a dramatic representation of conflicting attitudes posited as a dialogue between self and other. The essence of the commedia spirit derives from the energy articulated both in the dynamically charged mask postures and gestures and in the by-play between mask attitudes. The rapid fluctuation between tension and release directly engages the audiences in the play of attitudes on a corporeal and kinaesthetic level. As in possession ritual, the audience is engaged, not so much by the unfolding story, but by the moment to moment participation within the muscles and bones of their own bodies in the drama of unfolding attitudes.

The commedia retained many of the essential plot elements from ritual revels such as the conflict between the old and new year, the reversal of the social order, carnivalesque uncrownings, and the scapegoat. It channeled these themes into comic socio-dramas, crafted on classical canons of comedy, which served to release pent-up libidinal attitudes while demonstrating to the people socially unacceptable behavior. The satyric mime which informed the commedia scenarios continued largely unchanged in the short comic skits or lazzi which involved gluttony, beatings, trickery, and metamorphosis and which were interspersed throughout the performances. The lazzi were a direct manifestation through gesture of the constellation of psychic impulses that constituted the inner attitude typifying the masks.

The impulse behind satyric mime is the overthrow of the established order and a reveling in libidinal energies. Its essence is to release and purify through comic catharsis rather than to instruct through plots that are contrived according to social and artistic convention. The commedia gradually reverted to its primitive source in the lazzi and the more grotesque masks as it began to wane in the seventeenth century. The reassertion of the pure satyric impulse that is present in spontaneous and grotesque antics of the ritual revels can be seen in the rising popularity of Pulcinella.

Pulcinella's ascendance may be traced to the fact that he is a direct and uncensored expression of the satyric spirit that infused the original mimes. The behavior of this mask encompasses many of the major elements of the style of grotesque realism, and it reestablished the lazzi rather than the scenarios as the fundamental impulse underlying the commedia. Lea laments:

> Why labor with the complications of a neo-classical intrigue when the appearance of Pulcinella in one disguise after another, turning off practical

jokes or quarrelling with Rosetta, is what the audience enjoys? . . . As ivy the tree, so he first kills the Commedia dell'Arte and then supports it when the sap, the vis comica, is dried up.[32]

It could be argued that Pulcinella and his ilk are "sap" from which the tree of commedia grew and from which it sustained its life. The forms that satyric mime fills are transitory and depend upon the continuance of a set of social and artistic conditions. However, the deeply felt need in humanity to express taboo attitudes through comic play remains the kernel of satyric mime. Essentially the demise of the commedia meant its return to the type of short, ribald, and obscene skits that characterized the essence and origin of mime in Dorian Megara.

Chapter Four

The Masks of Jacques Lecoq

France has been the nexus for a regeneration of the art of mime during this century. Renewed interest in mime developed as a by-product of attempts by theatre artists in Europe and Russia to renovate the art of theatre. Disillusioned with the style of realism and naturalism which had come to dominate the stage, reformers such as Evreinov and Meyerhold in Russia, Fuchs in Germany, and Copeau in France turned towards the great ages of the theatre of the past in order to discern in the performance techniques of the Greek tragedy and the Commedia dell'Arte what made these genres so compelling and vital. In the process, emphasis was shifted away from literature and psychological realism in the direction of the actor's performance, pure spectacle, uninhibited stylization and above all theatricality to reinstate a lost fusion of actor and spectator.

In France in the 1920s, Jacques Copeau and his school, the Vieux-Colombier, were at the vanguard of experimentation with new forms of acting and theatre performance. Working primarily with the idioms of Greek tragedy and the Commedia dell'Arte, Copeau sought to hone a new type of actor who would be "an instrument capable of serving a Tragedy of Modern Times and a New Comedy."[1] In the course of his experimentation he established mask work and mime as the basis for a new acting style that would situate the actor-creator as the central element in the theatrical performance. His school has had a profound influence not only on influential theatre artists, but on all of the great French mime teachers, performers, and practitioners in France from 1921 to the present. Etienne Decroux, Jean-Louis Barrault, Jacques Lecoq, and Marcel Marceau have each been shaped directly or indirectly by what was taught there.[2]

Jacques Lecoq is a director, actor and teacher whose École Internationale de Théâtre, established in Paris in 1956, has served to deepen and extend the discoveries made at the Vieux-Colombier in mask and mime. He was introduced to the work of Copeau in 1945 when he joined the company of Jean Daste and Mari-Hélène Copeau in Grenoble. Daste, a student and the son-in-law of Copeau, had acquired Copeau's passion for the Commedia dell'Arte and a love of the mask work which was taught at the Vieux-Colombier by Suzanne Bing.

More importantly, the Dastes had been members of les Copiaus (Little Copeaus), a troupe of students from the Vieux-Colombier school that worked to develop the New Comedy through masked character-types and a strongly physical style of performance inspired by the Commedia dell'Arte. The Dastes continued to work in this direction with their company in Grenoble and transmitted to Lecoq the echo of Jacques Copeau, "but above all the spirit of the Copiaus."[3] The corporeal training he received while working with the company inspired Lecoq's further exploration of how mime and mask techniques could be used to train and produce a new generation of theatre artists.

Lecoq spent eight years in Italy which permitted him "to expand the possibilities of mime."[4] In 1948 he accepted an invitation to teach movement at the University of Padua Theatre School and subsequently opened his own theatre school at the Piccolo Teatro in Milan. The two greatest influences on his work during the Italian period were his "encounter with the spirit of the Commedia dell'Arte" and then his friendship with the great mask-maker Amleto Sartori. "It is at Padua, in contact with the peasants of the region and my friend, the sculptor Amleto Sartori, that I was able to sense the force of a forgotten Commedia dell'Arte, which exists among the people."[5] In observing the small dramas of the village and marketplace, where life is a matter of passion and survival, Lecoq came face to face with the direct and uncensored spirit of the mime. In the masks of Amleto Sartori, he found the tools which could be used as a basis for releasing the natural inborn gift for mime in his students.

Lecoq is important to our study because his training program presents a systematic analysis of the psychophysical basis of corporeal and vocal mimesis. He has said, "Mime is pre-eminently a research art; all forms of art originate in its silent depths, for everything moves, stirs, shifts, evolves, is transformed. It is in that common mimetic source that the artist prepares for his choice of thrusts toward the different forms of expression."[6]

Lecoq has sought to rediscover the essence of mime as it existed in classical Greece and Rome, when the art of mime was total theatre and the mime performer was simultaneously an acrobat, singer, actor, dancer, and playwright. His search, which has taken him to the sources of dramatic corporeal expression, places him directly in line with the primitivist trend in twentieth century art. Like Artaud before him, he believes that the renovation of the art of the theatre lies in the performer's rediscovery of the original mimetic impulse (*mime de fond*) that exists before it is formulated into a secondary language of speech and codified gesture (*mime de forme*). "I bring a mime unburdened by its codes, and its aesthetic formalisms."[7] In this process, he has rediscovered and applied in his teaching methods, perhaps without being aware of it, the same techniques of dissociation, identification, and masked role playing that are found in possession trance initiation.

Lecoq describes the student's progression through his two-year training program in shamanic terms as a "voyage" of discovery structured around stages of development marked by a particular mask. He recognizes that the mask is the key to unlocking the student's mimetic instinct. It serves as both a guide and model around which attitude expression is structured into a coherent language.

Attitude-models are provided to the student through seven basic types of masks: neutral, expressive, contra mask, larval, Commedia dell'Arte, buffoon, and red-nose.

Of these masks, three form the core of his training program: the neutral mask, the commedia mask, and the clown nose. These masks mark a progression from the cultural model of the ideal human being through the socio-types of the Commedia dell'Arte masks to the personal expression of hidden latent attitudes revealed by the clown nose. This progression, which is accompanied by a gradual softening and disappearance of the mask to reveal the naked face, parallels the three types of possession trance that exist in African and Afro-American societies: type one, predominantly cultural; type two, cultural and psychological; and type three, psychological.[8]

THE NEUTRAL OR "HEROIC" MASK
(LE MASQUE NEUTRE)

Lecoq's training program begins with the neutral mask, which he describes as "a mask without a particular expression or character traits, which neither laughs nor cries, which is neither sad nor gay and which is supported by silence and a state of calm. The form should be simple, regular and not present conflicts."[9]

The neutral or noble mask, as it was termed by Copeau, was one of the most original discoveries of the Vieux-Colombier. To be neutral is to be without the habitual attitudes that constitutes the self. Copeau was disturbed by the fact that "the actor always starts from an artificial attitude, a bodily, mental, or vocal grimace."[10] This attitude is what constitutes the personality. The socially acquired attitude not only inhibits the free and spontaneous expression of the primitive self, it deforms everything the performer does.

The attitude to posture and movement contributes a particular constellation of Effort qualities that are not in balance. A truly neutral attitude is one in which the elements of time, weight, space, and flow are perfectly manifested in the middle range — not too light or heavy, not too fast or slow. This means that one exerts just the right amount of Effort to accomplish a task and not any more. Since the posture is integral to a neutral attitude, one must sense that the posture is perfectly balanced and aligned.

DISSOCIATION

Work with the neutral mask strips students of their habitual mental and corporeal attitudes through a process analogous to possession trance dissociation:

A neutral mask. Photo by Patrick Lecoq.

"The students do not arrive new at the school, many have already had theatrical experiences, and have preconceived and ready made ideas. It is necessary from the beginning to demystify what we know in order to put ourselves in a state of non-knowing and to make ourselves available to the discovery of the elementary."[11]

The students do not achieve the inarticulate loss of consciousness that is associated with complete dissociation. Rather, through exercises in relaxation and work with the neutral mask, they become mildly entranced—open to stimuli both from within and without.

The mask is a tool which aids in dissociation. Jean Dorcy, who participated in mask work at the Vieux-Colombier, asks, "What happens to the actor who puts on a mask? He is cut off from the outer world. The night he deliberately enters allows him first to reject everything that hampered him. Then, by an effort of concentration, to reach a void, a state of unbeing. From this moment forward, he will be able to come back to life and to behave in a new and truly dramatic way."[12]

The mask, neutral or otherwise, shuts the wearer off from external stimuli and forces him to focus within. The sense of claustrophobia and closure, often accompanied by constriction of breath, are hallmarks of dissociation and typify many student's first experiences with masks. Shut off from the external world, the wearer enters into the often frightening darkness of the world within. As the student gropes for direction, he or she inevitably turns to the attitude-model in the mask, its neutrality.

Like Copeau before him, Lecoq is most interested in assisting the development of a truly creative actor. For him this means an erasure of past experience and a rediscovery of the essential roots of human expression. The student must be guided back to the preliterate world of childhood which is akin to a neutral state of unknowing; impulses arising in the individual are not filtered through the consciousness, which usually buffers and channels them. Rather the response to the images is in a purely sensory way and is manifested directly in gesture and action.

Work with the neutral mask is similar to techniques acquired through meditation. Zen Buddhism, for example, seeks to impose a neutrality and calm through contemplation of the mind and body from a state of emptiness. During meditation, one watches impulses arise and die within in the mind and sees how the mind and body are taken by these impulses away from the central point that constitutes the essential self—as in the Zen Koan, "the face before you were born." Dissociation does not lead to loss of self or depersonalization; rather Lecoq sees it as process of essentialization which eliminates the superfluous to arrive at the core of the personality.[13]

As in the practice of Zen Buddhism in daily life, where attention is focused on doing activities with just the right amount of Effort, work with the neutral mask teaches the student economy of movement. Dorcy continues: "To re-establish dramatic harmony, it will be necessary to act according to the law of the mask; to create and comply with the rhythm imposed by the theme, to emphasize contrasts and to eliminate superfluous movements and amplify or exaggerate the remaining motions. All this constitutes the first step towards the mime."[14]

The first exercises with the neutral mask begin from sleep, a metaphor for dissociation. The students are then asked to enact a neutral image, such as "The figure wakes in the desert and walks into a city. The figure wakes in the desert; goes to a river and walks in it." In the process they must discover how their movements deviate from neutrality by the addition of extraneous Effort and action.

The neutral mask demands elimination of the inessential to get at the universal qualities of an action. Masks, according to Lecoq, "allow one to search for the pivotal point within an action, within a conflict; allow one to find the essential, the gesture that will epitomize the many gestures of daily life, the word of all words."[15]

With the neutral mask, the students also explore economy of movement from an external perspective while doing simple tasks such as lifting an object. The exercise involves the breakdown of the movements involved in an action into its various components. These components are in the nature of phrases, which are highlighted by a briefly held body attitude. Once the student has isolated all of the component attitudes that make up an action they reduce the movement to only those attitude-phrases that contain the essence of the movement.

Work with neutral masks is analogous to type one possession trance, predominantly cultural, which according to Walker, involves "highly motivated, theatrical role playing," based upon deity-models that "are very far from man and embody very universal and general human attiributes."[16] Highly motivated role playing would seem to be the opposite of the intended function of the neutral mask, which is to strip the student of acquired cultural habits. It also seems to be antithetical to the school's emphasis on searching out the mime de fond.

The neutral mask is not a blank canvas, it is the representation of the ideal attitude which must be *learned* by the student. The learning of how to be neutral already implies going beyond mime de fond, which is a primitive and direct gesture that is not shaped by cultural models. The mask is an instrument to move the student towards the ideal creative state of neutrality. It is a way to teach the ideally sought attitude that allows for the free surfacing of impulses and attitudes, which are then analyzed against the template of neutrality.

The neutral mask is both a tool for dissociation and the attitude-model of the perfectly balanced individual. It calls up in the wearer the universal qualities that inform all men and women: "It attempts to erase the individuality; to get at the essence; to get at Man rather than *this* man."[17] For this reason, it was first termed the noble mask by Copeau and the universal mask by some who use it. It is the great teacher or principle model upon which all subsequent mask work is built. In a sense, the actor wears the neutral mask beneath every other mask and every other character. Lecoq likens the neutral mask to "the bottom of the sea," whereas "the expressive mask is like waves."[18]

The deities in cultural possession (type one) are generally very far from the personalities of the devotees and thus do not allow them to express latent aspects of themselves. Spontaneous possession by the deity is rare, and ritual dissociation must be learned through a long initiation process. By comparison, the neutral mask is the most difficult mask for students to conquer because it is furthest from their habitual attitudes. Students spend three months with this mask, more time than working with any other mask during the first year, because they must learn how to adopt the model-attitude of neutrality through the techniques of dissociation and identification.

IDENTIFICATION

In cultural possession (type one) the repertoire of roles are based on powerful nature deities which are concerned with the working of nature and the universe. Similarly, exercises in the neutral mask involve identification with natural phenomenon; i.e., elements, materials, flowers, and trees, which engage students in the original impulse towards movement (mime de fond). Mime de fond is a product of complete identification with phenomenon where there is no separation of "I and thou." It is the most direct and basic expression of mimesis and is found in the natural tendency of children to mime the gestures of phenomenon from the surrounding world. Some scholars believe that it was man's first language, existing prior to the formulation of spoken language. In type one possession, trance deities are the figurative embodiments of natural forces, and mimesis demands a highly codified language of comportment and gesture. Exercises in mime de fond while wearing the neutral mask give students a taste of the impulses from which culturally shaped and highly theatrical genres such as the Commedia dell'Arte originated.

The first principle of Lecoq's teaching method is that mimesis is based in identification with the gestures of phenomenon.

> Man understands that which moves by his ability to 'mimic' it; that is, to identify himself with the world by re-enacting it with his entire being. Beginning in the silent body of man the impulses towards expression take shape — dramatic impulse and then dramatic creation.[19]

Like Marcel Jousse, Lecoq recognizes the source of all learning is to be found in the imprinting of the gestures of phenomena upon the body of the individual; "the bodily impression is more important than the bodily expression."[20] It is this mimetic source of recorded *mimemes* that the student must contact before he or she proceeds to elaborate an image corporeally through analysis and acquired technique. "The passage from the impression to the expression must be formulated by a 'touch within' the body of the mime."[21]

The neutral mask is used in exercises involving identification with matter (identification aux matières): trees, wood, sea, fire, etc. Impulses towards movement originate in immobility: "All that is great tends toward immobility (immobility is also a gesture)."[22] Movement originates in the neutral body of the mime which, freed from gratuitous activity, maintains itself in an immobile state of calm for image to touch impulse. One of the first exercises Lecoq gives his student is to observe a tree and to "become it." This exercise is based upon the essential immobility of the rooted tree, which demands that the students search within their body-memory to discover how a tree might move, walk, and sound.

> It consists in gathering together in the depths of oneself, that which the product of observation has deposited (impression). Take, for example, the observation of a tree: in going beyond the ideas which surrounds it and the personal feelings which it arouses, one encounters a physical sensation which reveals the dynamism of the life of this tree. It is to this [impression] that the expression must refer in order for the tree to live. As if the body had a skin for touching the space within and another for touching the space without.[23]

Identification with elements and matter assist the student in rediscovering the recorded gestures of phenomena that lie buried in their sensory apparatus. "The fire that I look at blazes within me. I can know that fire by identifying with it in action; I give my fire to that fire."[24] The essence of this exploration lies in identification with the essential Efforts that are unique to each phenomena and which impart to them a particular internal energy or rhythm that is conveyed externally by the student through breath and rhythmic gestures.

Once the student has identified with a particular element or material object, they are asked to discover its characteristic sound or cry. Thus the corporeal expression is expanded to the relationship between physical gestures of phenomenon and their sound gestures. Just as the mimesis of the gestures of phenomenon forms the basis of mime de fond that precedes the structured and socialized language of acquired gesture systems, the sounds and cries emitted by phenomenon forms the basis of spoken language.

Discovery of the characteristic gestures typifying elemental and animal agents is the first step towards character expression. "The neutral mask is identified with the elements; trees, wood, sea, fire. This identification with the elements then becomes the basis for the character work: man as tree; man moving as the sea."[25]

The Efforts that characterize elemental and material agents are similar to those that animate human agents. Everything in the universe exists as though it were "taking an attitude." The gestures that animate fire, water, or a lion provide constellations of Effort (time, weight, space, and flow) that are analogous to those that make up character attitudes. The students proceed to exercises in which they construct characters based on elements and or animals. Here the focus is on the gestures of phenomenon as they evoke a corresponding emotional state. Once the students have grasped the physical and auditory gestures of agents they move on to the action of these agents upon other agents (la rencontre des matières), such as fire melting ice. This tripartite expression involving improvisation between two materials contains the seed of conflict.

Identification involves exploration of the impulse towards movement by allowing the image to work internally to summon up impressions that are conveyed externally through movement. However, the students also explore how impressions are created externally through the isolation and rhythmically repeated motions of parts of the body. For example, they experiment with the arm swinging motions involved in throwing a ball.[26] In the process they discover that a rhythmically repeated gesture evokes both images of actions based on the gesture as well as a particular emotional state. Mimetic expression is filled with homonyms. The arm-swinging motion of throwing a ball can with slight variations become a bird in flight or a gesture of disgust.

The primitive impulses prompted by the release of an attitude through gesture are the essence of mime de fond. They summon up impressions recorded in the body and trigger the creation of images that are tied to one another by analogy. From this wealth of sensory material the student can express a variety of images that are prompted by the release of an encapsulated attitude through movement.

An expressive mask. Photo by Patrick Lecoq.

EXPRESSIVE MASKS
(LES MASQUES EXPRESSIFS)

With the expressive mask, the students shift from the exploration of the gestural traits of matter to the study of masks which represent human-types dominated by certain elemental or animal characteristics. This stage of exploration is centered around masks which provide attitude-models of psychological character types, such as the sly, the arrogant, the bully, and the miser, etc. The expressive mask serves one of the main historical functions of the mask, which is "to isolate a human characteristic from its setting in a total personality."[27]

While the neutral mask served to distance the wearer from his habitual attitudes, the expressive mask begins to tap into these attitudes. It marks a movement away from the cultural mask of neutrality to an exploration of the psychological dimensions of its wearer.

In type two, "predominantly cultural and psychological possession trance," there is a deliberate rapport between the (deity) mask and that of the wearer: "The individual may exhibit facets of his personality normally hidden from himself and others, in the guise of the deity, thus in culturally approved form."[28] This work builds on the discoveries of the neutral mask involving identification with non-human phenomena. The students find that the basic attitudes which animate nature are also those that animate human characters, emotions, and actions.

POSTURE AND ATTITUDE

As training proceeds with the expressive mask, the students explore the importance of posture or held positions of the body in the creation of stereotypical attitudes. Exercises with the expressive mask are based in the psychophysiology of attitude expression. The mask is an emblem of the attitude which the students must seek to reproduce in corporeal postures.

Discovery of the emotional basis for characterization is approached both internally and externally. In early work with the expressive mask, the students spend several days studying the mask before placing it on their face. They allow the lines and volumes to speak directly to the muscles and bones of their body. When they finally place it on their face they proceed slowly, discovering the characteristic posture, walk, and gestures prompted by the attitude-model contained in the mask. As in their work on the elements, they must sense the Effort qualities that animate the postures and gestures of the mask.

External exercises involve the discovery that a physical disposition of the body or one of its members produces an internal state or attitude. The students are asked to isolate one part of their body and position it differently thus creating a postural adjustment. These newly acquired postures, which are based on the fixing of parts of the body, create corresponding inner feelings or attitudes. "We try to feel that when an arm is raised, it creates in us a corresponding dramatic state, and that an attitude of the body is related to an internal attitude of mind."[29]

Likewise the students discover that reactions to an external sensory stimuli or environments (hot, cold, etc.) cause a corresponding inner postural adjustment that leads to a feeling. Walking against the wind or on a mountain slope require a realignment of the body, creating a corresponding internal attitude.

These exercises apply the psychophysical principles of attitude expression to the creation of emotion. The postural inner adjustments of the skeleton when held up from going into action are manifested in a feeling, which in turn can lead to an action. The postural study of attitude expression builds upon the earlier exercises that involve the release of emotion through rhythmically repeated gesture. These two aspects are combined in the work in the expressive mask, which demands a deviation from the balanced posture of the neutral mask and the outward expression of latent attitudes through posture and rhythmical gesture.

LARVAL MASKS
(LES MASQUES LARVAIRES)

The larval masks are simplified and embryonic forms of the human face which are "devoid of human features so that no specific characterization is suggested by it."[30] These masks function to release the student from the tyranny of a specific emotion demanded by the expressive mask. Thus, they allow more creative latitude in arriving at a characterization. Unlike the expressive masks, which call for smaller and more precise gestures in evoking the specifics of character, the larval masks, because of their large and abstract forms, demand a broader and more simplified gesture. As in all the other mask work, the students improvise to invent relationships among masks and construct an imaginary world.

Each larval mask serves to evoke an emotional state in the wearer. As in the expressive mask work, the students seek to discover a specific bodily posture and the basic Efforts that animate the rhythms of the mask's gestures and walk. They also explore how these masks might sound, but they do not use language at this point.

THE CONTRA MASK
(LE CONTRE-MASQUE)

Conflict, or the play of opposition, is the essence of dramatic mimesis. The study of the contra mask follows mastery of the expressive mask. It introduces students to the complexity of character. Characters are rarely one dimensional; they are most often a combination of contradictory attitudes and tendencies. The contra mask teaches the student how to simultaneously express both the obvious external attitude of the mask as well as its latent, contradictory side.

Lecoq says:

> Each larval or expressive mask can be acted twice; by the mask and in contra mask. If I act a mask which represents an idiot, I attempt to identify with the role that it suggests and organize my body and acting in this sense. But I can act the opposite and express an intelligent being under the mask of an idiot. In so doing I create another character more rich than the first, who carries within himself this conflict of having the air of an idiot and not being one. This is the contra mask.[31]

In type two possession trance, individuals may become possessed by deities that are very similar to their everyday personalities or by dieties who are their complementary opposite. Possession by opposing deities allows individuals to act out aspects of themselves that are generally hidden. However, all forms of possession involve an internal struggle in which the individual attempts to stop himself from being possessed—that is, to keep his self intact. Work with the contra mask in which the students play the opposite character type from the mask they are wearing serves to expose the internal conflicts which make up a particular character and which maintain it in a state of precarious balance. In these exercises, the student must struggle against the attitude imposed by the mask in order to carry two contradictory attitudes simultaneously.

After the expressive mask, students move to the exploration of archetypal masks of the Commedia dell'Arte, which represent fixed psychological and cultural types. Here, as in type two possession trance, students must learn how to take impulses released by the mask and express them in terms of clearly defined character-types and a formalized set of performance codes.

The work up to this point has focused on components that build upon one another: neutrality, identification with phenomenon as a basis for characters, fixed psychological types, contra masks, abstract masks, gesture and posture as they create an internal state, conflict, sound proceeding from mask and movement, and improvisation. These stages of training have centered on freeing the student physically, emotionally, and vocally as well as providing a foundation in the basic elements of mimesis. In the Commedia dell'Arte, the students must combine everything they have learned so far and channel it though a formalized language of expression.

With the Commedia dell'Arte, the students focus on one of the great historical forms of masked theatre, which like Greek tragedy and comedy, traces its roots to the satyric excesses of Dionysian revelry. As in type two possession where the gods are the figurative embodiment of personality structures, social conflicts and tensions engendered by the socio-cultural system, the masks are stereotyped expressions of fixed cultural and psychological character types of the Italian renaissance. They demand a particular style of playing the mask which, like possession roles, has been encoded into them by generations of performers.

In type two possession, it is essential that the devotee's personality coincide with that of the deity: "there is deliberate rapport between the deity personality and that of the individual who is chosen to serve him. Care is taken to insure the proper matching of deity and devotee, since trouble will result if the choice is incorrect."[32]

Lecoq students are encouraged to work with the mask with which they feel the most affinity. The rationale here is that if the mask directly expresses latent aspects of the wearer's personality, identification (possession) will be deeper and more fruitful.

Improvisation proceeds from the behavior associated with each mask and is structured around simple plots involving a theme or conflict. As in type two possession, the students enact, under the guise of masks, their ordinary profane social interactions and tensions.

As before, students proceed from impulses offered by the configuration of the masks; "Each movement should be made with dramatic motivation so that it is not exterior or mechanical."[33] The student must learn how to impart their own individuality to these masks while working within the strict boundaries of the performance style. Lecoq says:

> The masks of the commedia dell'arte bring about bounded corporeal acting, which manifests itself in remarkable attitudes. One cannot act under the mask "like in life." It is necessary to carry it beyond naturalism, it is necessary to act it, to invent that which prolongs the dimensions of life and what life has never shown us.[34]

Each mask imposes a distinct body attitude upon the wearer and demands to be animated in its own way. Copeau discovered in his work with the masks that

> The actor who performs under a mask receives from this papier-mâché object the reality of his part. He is controlled by it and has to obey it unreservedly. Hardly has he put it on when he feels a new being flowing into himself, a being the existence of which he had before never even suspected. It is not only his face that has changed, it is all his personality, it is the very nature of his reactions, so that he experiences emotions he could neither have felt nor feigned without its aid. If he is a dancer, the whole style of his dance, if he is an actor, the very tones of his voice, will be dictated by this mask — the Latin "persona" — a being, without life till he adopts it, which comes from without to seize upon him and proceeds to substitute itself for him.[35]

The masks are not just simple manifestations of fixed constellations of attitudes; they represent a complex of contradictory tendencies which makes them at once human and stereotypical. The essence of the playing the mask lies in finding the contradictions in the character. Lecoq continues, "Thus Pantalone the old man, rich merchant of Venice, greedy and amorous, sick and in full health, is the condensation of several characters, old and young at the same time. Amorous, he dances; if one asks money from him, he is going to die."[36]

The contradictions manifested by the mask are based in earlier work with the contra masks, which create the internal conflict that represents complex character types. The humor and tragedy of Commedia dell'Arte is created by the struggle in the mask between conflicting psychological impulsions and by a struggle between it and other masks which attempt to block its path to the attainment of desire.

Work with these masks demands a study of the bodily attitudes and gestures for each mask. The style of playing the mask is highly postural and demands not only precariously held positions of the body, but also demands highly postural gesture: "Corporeal training is necessary, based in movements which depict the body in its grand attitudes, in which each part performs separately."[37] This work builds upon earlier exercises in which the body or its parts are held in positions or isolated in movements to produce emotion and action.

The attitude-models presented by the commedia mask have their source in the fixed psychological-types of the expressive masks, but they represent human passions taken to the extreme in the struggle for survival. According to Lecoq:

> The commedia dell'arte is based in the passions of men pushed to the maximum of their consequences. It manifests the absurdity of our behavior. It has nothing to do with elegant entertainment; it expresses the urgency of living, closer to survival than life, which is already a luxury. Planted in the misery of the people, in its naïveté as well as in its intelligence, it stratifies the society in a stable manner, without the revolt of a valet towards his master. But each one arranges, with all the compromises possible, to exist and satisfy his hunger, his greed, his passion: and all this world lives together. Each one tries to trick the other and falls into ridiculous traps. The smile does not exist. One cries or one laughs.[38]

The Commedia dell'Arte that Lecoq teaches in his school is close to the pulse of human life and its scope is essentially tragic. Its themes encompass "that of fear; fear of death; fear of living; fear of everything. It is cruel, present, and without regret."[39]

The style of playing the mask in the Commedia dell'Arte is based in exaggeration. It demands that impulses be carried to their extreme in bodily attitudes and gestures that are larger than life and full of frenetic energy. This work explores one of the central premises of Lecoq's pedagogy that "all corporeal movement pushed to its maximum limit, in retaining its fixed fulcrum points, tends towards equilibrium; and conversely, all corporeal movement reduced to its limit tends towards the immobility of its respiration."[40]

The neutral mask engaged students in an exploration of the zero state of movement in which mimetic impulses arise from a fulcrum point of calm. Movement is characterized by quasi-immobility in which gestures are pared to their minimum. It is from this neutral state that all movement arises and to which it returns. The expression dictated by each commedia mask originates in the same zero point, but impulses are exaggerated and extended to their furthest limit. Work with the commedia mask is undertaken "so that the student can become familiar with a maximum level of theatrical play employing the human being in his entirety."[41]

Buffoons. Photo by Alain Chambaretaud.

BUFFOONS
(LES BOUFFONS)

Just as the expressive masks were followed by the larval masks in the earlier stage of training, the intensive study of the Commedia dell'Arte masks is followed by a study of buffoons. The purpose of this sequence is to give free reign to the students creative imagination while building upon the discoveries made with the earlier masks. In a sense, the students work backwards from the codified form of the Commedia dell'Arte to discover the source from which it sprang in the free and untrammeled expression of the satyric mimes in carnivalesque revelry.

Buffoons are similar to the netherworld demons of half-men/women–half-beast that have appeared as part of carnivalesque fertility festivals since antiquity; they "are deformed creatures that make fun of life."[42] When Lecoq demands that each student find the magic of his creation and then make fun of it, he is essentially asking them to revel in the joy of the earthiness, the release of libidinal energy in a socially sanctioned group setting.

Type three possession (predominantly psychological) is found where religious institutions are in a state of disorganization and decline. "One of its major defining characteristics is the individual invention of private possessing agents corresponding to impulses striving for expression."[43] In this stage of their training, the students create grotesque body masks which represent a personal and concrete expression of latent attitudes by means of body padding, protuberances, and appendages. The buffoon body mask is based on an externalization of postural imbalances and internal forces that cause the body — those aspects of the body which the students sense as deforming their body-image — to deviate from neutrality. Students tend to emphasize bodily elements that represent the freeing up of the energies of the lower centers; i.e., breasts, buttocks, genitals, noses, breasts, etc. The buffoons tend towards the shape of gigantic spheres with appendages. They have "enormous stomachs, huge chests compensated by gigantic bottoms."[44] The gestures of the buffoon "are transposed and find their organization in the costume which obliges one to only make certain movements that verge on catastrophic acrobatics and which would be impossible to effect with a normal body."[45]

The study of the buffoons frees up students' imaginations and teaches them not to censor impulses but to carry them to their extremes of vocal and physical expression. Improvisations ground them in the importance of relating their actions to a group theme that arises spontaneously out of the behavior of the various masks. These improvisations, which involve sounds and music as well as exaggerated behavior and acrobatics, often have the appearance of a Dionysian revel. One observer writes, "I watched this pair of deformed societies forming, competing, regrouping, bumping bellies, touching humps, dancing horn-to-horn, and sometimes merging briefly in what looked like a midnight bacchanal in a cemetery...."[46]

Buffoons exist on the borderline between type two and type three possession, because while the behavior of these creatures is still culturally determined, it has not yet disintegrated into the purely personal expression of an isolated individual which will be undertaken with the clown nose. Students engage in masked improvisations in which they create inverted societal structures which parallel and burlesque our own.

As in carnivalesque revels, the antics of the buffoons celebrate a world turned upside down and the breaking of social taboos. This Dionysian connection is evident in Lecoq's statement that "Buffoons come from beyond, they are linked to the verticality of mystery, they form part of the relation of the sky with the earth, whose values they invert. They spit at the sky and invoke the earth: in this sense they are in the same space as tragedy; they cross on the same verticality."[47]

Buffoonesque role-playing is a form of protest or revolt against societal rules, norms and values. However, buffoons do not usher in chaos. They install an ideal world which is the mirror image of our own. According to Lecoq, they "are organized hierarchically and live in a perfect society without conflicts, where each one finds his exact place."[48] Their sole reason for existing is to parody and make fun of "our society, the themes of power, of science, of

religion in 'follies' organized following precise rules where by the most debili-
tated directs the others and declares war because he is bored."[49]

Buffoons are beings from the pataphysical universe of Pere Ubu, which
Alfred Jarry describes as a world parallel to our own with its own laws based
in the libido. A blend of the reveries of childhood and the devil, buffoons provide insight into the truth about our world. By inverting the world order, they
bring a vision of the demonic beauty and mystery of life's hidden forces. The
recreation of the Dionysian chorus of netherworld demons leads the students
on to tragedy, the chorus, and to the final mask, the red nose.

THE RED NOSE OF THE CLOWN

In *Mime, Movement, Theatre,* Lecoq writes "For several years the study
of clowns has taken on larger importance in the school, not in the sense of the
traditional circus, which is dead, but in searching out the ridiculous in man.
The clown in the spirit of today has replaced the hero, who no longer exists
in the theatre."[50]

The mask work has proceeded at this point from the rigid, neutral and
expressive masks, which covered the student's entire face, to the half masks of
the Commedia dell'Arte, to the body masks of the buffoons, and finally to the
smallest mask of all — the red nose of the clown. The gradual uncovering of the
face coincided with the full emergence of language in the Commedia dell'Arte,
but more importantly it signifies the increasingly personal and complex expression of character mimesis.

Graves says:

> Starting as a device for isolating the performer from the world of everyday
> reality, the mask eventually becomes more or less committed to this ideal
> and tries to get closer to the appearances of the individual men. The pro-
> gression, then, is from the unnatural freezing of a single human charac-
> teristic (e.g. avarice, lust, sloth) to the revealing of an entire spectrum
> of human characteristics — an even greater naturalism of representation.[51]

The diminution of the facial mask to a red nose marks the unmasking of
the student. Lecoq does not consider the red nose a mask. A mask serves the
function of hiding the wearer; the red nose reveals. What it reveals is the student's central flaw (*bide*). According to Laurence Wylie, the students must
realize that "One plays a role in order to hide his 'flaw' and that is exactly the
opposite of what must be done."[52]

The clown nose serves as a releasing mechanism for the individual's
repressed self; repressed because if expressed it would entail socially unacceptable behavior. The discovery of the personal clown within is a natural extension
of the expressive mask. While the expressive mask isolated a predominant trait
from the complex of attitudes that comprise the self, the red nose requires the
student to express his personal and deeply repressed contradictory latent attitudes.

Here the student can no longer hide behind the rigid face mask; his own face must become the pliable mask connoting character.

The red nose presents difficulties for many students because they are in a sense stripped bare, as they were with the work on the neutral mask. With the neutral mask, the exploration of the self focuses on a deviation from an ideal state of balance. With the red nose they must become fully identified with the tics they sought to eliminate with the neutral mask. Lecoq describes the clown in terms of freedom and solitude. The clown is "the one who has grown up within us and which society does not permit us to express. It is total freedom, where the individual can be himself, only himself; it also offers the experience of solitude...."53

The clown is basically studied as a solo mask in Lecoq's school. "The difference between the clown and the buffoon is that the clown is alone, whereas the buffoon forms part of a band."54 The solo nature of the clown places this type on the borderline between the pantomime and mime. Lecoq states that his research into clown work, begun in 1962, was inspired by a desire to know what happened after the Commedia dell'Arte and the pantomimes of the nineteenth century pantomime blanche. The clown is the ultimate antihero of our age. He is the direct expression of a world turned upside down, as seen in the behavior of trickster shamans and the antics of mimes at carnivalesque fertility festivals. According to Lecoq, the clown's actions are "often the inverse of logic; he puts a certain order in disorder and thus brings about the overthrow of the established order."55

Whereas buffoons make fun of us, it is we who make fun of the clown: "clowns are people who try to do everything well and fail."56 The humor in clown work is directed at the self rather than the structures of society. The essence of the training here is not only to touch base with that part of oneself which is outlawed but to come to love it and accept it as well. The expression of attitudes that are not socially sanctioned is deeply cathartic, allowing for their acceptance and integration into the total self. Humor serves to deflate the terror that this process holds for the student. The latent aspects of the personality, when fully integrated into the psyche, provide the student with a greater reservoir of creative potential and power.

If the ultimate goal of the school is liberation from self in order to achieve a truly creative state, then the ultimate end of the study must be the uncovering of the repressed self that is vented in ritual under the guise of a personal, possessing deity. The search began with the neutral mask — which with small extension is the mask of the hero — and ends in the expression of personal idiosyncrasies.

The neutral mask opened the way for the blossoming forth of the truly creative center of the individual, which is lodged precisely in the powerfully repressed impulses that fuel his latent attitudes. The expression of the clown within is essentially a revolt against society and its constraints. This can lead to

solitude and a profound sense of alienation in which the individual is so focused
on the self that he represents his own phobias and paranoias: "In such situations, where cultural determinism and control are lacking, possessions tend to
be expressions of the individual's own private impulses, with no cultural mold,
hence their content is idiosyncratic, rather than culturally determined, and
may tend towards pathology."[57]

According to Roger Bastide, the expression of neurosis outside ritual
structure leads to profound alienation:

> There is no true creation but by the constraint of rules; instead of
> creating a new language, there is no more than the "me" which speaks;
> that is, the revolt against society only ends in a profound alienation, in
> its own complexes. Even though one does not wish to repeat the gestures
> of the gods anymore one does not cease to repeat something; but one
> repeats only the traumas of one's childhood, which have no interest (ex-
> cept for the psychoanalyst...).[58]

However, Lecoq does not ask his students to immerse themselves in personal hysteria. In his classes, mimesis always occurs within a carefully structured
pedagogical matrix. The clown nose has been prepared for by the previous year
and a half of study. This has provided students with a technical foundation
which assists them in channeling potentially anarchic behavior into artistic expression.

Lecoq is basically a teacher of the satyric mime. He employs work on the
chorus and the hero, but these are not as fully fleshed as his work in the areas
of the expressive mask, commedia masks, buffoons, and clowns. Outside of the
neutral mask, which serves primarily in teaching the techniques of dissociation, identification, and economy, Lecoq does not have an heroic mask. Instead he concentrates on the discovery of the heroic in the flaws of the various
masks. Elements of the tragic hero are to be found: in the point where the cry
meets the scream in the desperate struggle for survival in the commedia mask;
in the Dionysian beauty of the buffoons; in the solitude and suffering of the
clown confronted by his flaw; in the tension created between the chorus and
the lone individual; and in the contra mask. Perhaps the absence of an heroic
mask is due to the fact that Lecoq does not believe that there are any heros today. The real truth is that the mime de fond is grounded in the satyric spirit
and that its natural elaboration leads to comedy rather than tragedy.

Tragedy, as it existed among the Greeks, is an artificial form. It does not
spring naturally from mimesis. While it was present in the suffering, death,
and resurrection of the gods in ancient ritual, the behavior of the crowd of worshipers tended towards joyous renewal through the release of the body in
throes of ecstasy. The Dionysian thais reveled in the exposure of human flaws.
The tragic form of the classical Greek theatre arose as a function of state-run

festivals which sought to channel the satyric impulse of the populace into the ideals of the city-state. The crowd of worshipers became the chorus of tragedy who suffered as a result of the deeds of the hero. Catharsis was achieved through pity and fear. The elements of suffering and death were artificially separated from the joyous aspects of renewal that were the essence of primitive fertility worship.

Tragedy does not evolve naturally from the free play of the mimetic instinct. The body of man delights in the freedom of being other than the self. Tragedy is born when this play of the mimetic impulse is trammeled and subverted. It demands a quality that Lecoq explores only superficially in the work on the various masks. These are the elements of corporeal risk, denial and struggle which are antithetical to the spirit of satyric mime. This is the heroic attitude which originates out of the solitude of the clown, but a clown who does not accept. This non-acceptance is a physical attitude, won through a technique composed of opposition that is deliberately created in the mime's body so that the performer feels the suffering at the same time he or she is expressing it. It is based in an acquired anti-natural technique that is diametrically opposed to the natural impulse that Lecoq seeks to unleash in his students. The hero is one who risks with his body; he or she cures the ills of mankind by making the body the battlefield of this confrontation. This is the element that separates the satyric mime from heroic mimes and pantomimes. Lecoq engages his students in the element of conflict most fully in the contra mask, which like the neutral mask is worn under the more complex masks of the commedia dell'arte, buffoons, and clown. However, he does not carry this forward to its full tragic dimensions in the creation of an heroic mask.

Lecoq's preference for the satyric mime over the tragic form parallels his preference for the mime de fond over the mime de forme. The only full fledged exploration of a secondary language of acquired gesture is undertaken with the masks of the Commedia dell'Arte. (He also touches on a study of the codified language of the pantomime blanche in which gestures are substituted for words.) It is interesting to note that in the study of the masks of the Commedia dell'Arte, he approaches most closely the spirit of tragedy. This is, in part, due to the intensification of the techniques of the contra mask, but it is more importantly the result of the formalized body attitudes and gestures which provide a platform for the channeling of attitudes into potentially tragic expressions.

Tragedy is a highly cultural form of expression. It probably exists in its purest form in type one possession rituals which exhibit highly codified languages of expression. In these rituals, the gods and legendary heros are enacted by performers who possess a rigorous corporeal training, precisely because the model-attitudes are so distant from their everyday personalities. Heros are made, not born. Type one possession masks are contra masks for their wearers. They exhibit universal attributes of the gods while masking the conflicting habitual attitudes of the wearer. However, rather than enacting this struggle, the devotees distance themselves from the mask and only become mildly entranced. Formalized gesture takes over and becomes a secondary language (mime de forme) which carries the performance.

This is the pitfall that Lecoq seeks to avoid by concentrating on mime de fond. He is rigorously against locking students into what he sees as an artificial style which limits the students' creativity. His training seeks to leave the students' expression as direct and uncontaminated by social and artistically conditioned clichés as possible. It acquaints them with the fundamentals of mimesis and encourages them to apply what they have learned to their own personal modes of artistic expression. His teaching does not consist, as in ritual practice, in the transmission of a sacred body of knowledge and set of techniques:

> The pedagogue can only cultivate, orient, and fortify the inborn talent, bring out that which is larval or discover that which is hidden. . . . Therefore, it consists for Jacques Lecoq, and this is fundamental, not only to never forget that the student comes to him with a desire, a vocation, a gift, a talent (or sometimes also an illusion . . .) but, more importantly, to give him the means to go to the end of his desire, to propose to him the references, to awake his curiosity for life, both within and without, to educate his actor's body, gesture and word, and to provoke his imagination as actor-author. To propose and sustain a creation inspired by a true theatre of gesture which "moves truthfully" and which "speaks truthfully, this is the pedagogical aim of Jacques Lecoq."[59]

That Lecoq has succeeded in his efforts is evidenced in the original and diverse directions that his students have taken in their professional activities.

PART II
Heroic Mimes

Chapter Five

The Shaman

Shamanism is probably the oldest form of religious experience. It dates as far back as the stone age and has persisted into the nineteenth and twentieth centuries in many non-agricultural, hunting societies, especially in Siberian, Central Asian, Northern European, and Native American cultures. Elements of shamanic practice and world view are to be found in most surviving religions, including possession trance. Although there is no clear dating to determine which is the older phenomenon, many believe that shamanism predates the group possessions that appear in many parts of the world.[1]

Shamans are psychopomps, spiritual healers, and wisepersons who voluntarily enter into trance to make contact with the spirit world to acquire knowledge and power which is used to help others. They are generally rugged individualists who possess prodigious powers and artistic abilities. According to E. T. Kirby, "shamanistic ritual was the 'great unitarian artwork' that fragmented into a number of performance arts, much as Wagner believed had been the case with ancient Greek tragedy."[2] Shamanic techniques and practices may include painting, clowning, juggling, tightrope walking, puppetry, magic, dance, story telling, acrobatics, chanting and mime, to name a few. However, the primary source of shamans' knowledge and power lies in their unique ability to call upon one or more spirit helpers for guidance and assistance.[3] Their most characteristic and striking corporeal techniques are the ability to become possessed by these spirits and the spiritual voyage:

> A shaman is a person who at his will can enter into a non-ordinary psychic state (in which he either has his soul undertake a journey to the spirit world or he becomes possessed by a spirit) in order to make contact with the spirit world on behalf of members of his community. The neutral term "person" is used to indicate that a shaman may be of either sex.[4]

SHAMANIC ECSTASY

At first glance shamanism appears to hold much in common with possession trance. However, they are essentially opposed phenomenon. The opposition between shamanism and possession lies in the nature of the trance as it pertains to each. Shamans, according to Eliade, are to be differentiated from

Koryak woman shaman performing. Neg/Trans. no. 4164. Courtesy Department of Library Services, American Museum of Natural History.

other types of medicine men and spiritual healers by their particular employment of the techniques of "ecstasy."⁵ His usage of the term ecstasy for shamanic trance follows Western mystical tradition where it denotes the state of divine rapture achieved by saints and religious mystics, who in solitude, silence, and the immobility of prayer receive mystical visions.

The term ecstasy is usually applied interchangeably with trance to the altered states of consciousness as they appear in shamanic performance. The confusion of terms derives partly from the great variety of shamanic and possession trance behaviors which frequently interpenetrate one another. If we situate shamanism at one pole of a continuum and possession at the other, however, we could speak of ecstacy as the *a priori* root of the shamanic experience and trance as the *a priori* root of possession, with many variations in between as the two forms overlap.

Rouget sums up the differences between shamanic ecstasy and possession trance as follows:

Ecstasy	*Trance*
immobility	movement
silence	noise
solitude	society
without crisis	with crisis
sensory privation	sensory stimulation
memory	amnesia
hallucinations	absence of hallucinations⁶

THE SHAMAN AS ARCHETYPAL HERO

Possession and shamanism are products of very different societies and by the same token different personality structures engendered by these societies. Studies have shown that personality structures differ according to whether the society is agrarian, with a stable food supply, or a hunting and gathering society, where the food supply is uncertain. Possession trance exists primarily in agrarian societies where the qualities of conformity, obedience to authority, and placing the good of the group over individual welfare are highly valued. For this reason, possession frequently takes the form of submission to the gods and amnesia. Shamanism, on the other hand, exists in hunting societies where a high value is placed on such qualities as independence, self-reliance, creativity, and experimentation. Hence shamans tend to be rugged individualists who remain aware and in control during ecstasy to ensure their survival and success.[7]

The shaman is the central agent of a drama involving life and death matters relating to her community. She is not a passive subject who is involuntarily possessed by spirits in order to effect her own cure, nor is she a mystic who is visited by the spirits. Rather, she is the heroine of her entourage who actively goes out in search of a cure or lost soul. Rouget sums up the essential difference between shamanic ecstasy and possession trance in the opposition: *"agir/subir"* (to act/to submit).[8] Shamans act upon the spirit world in order to wrest some positive benefit for their community, while the possessed individual is acted upon by these same spirits.

The shaman's ability to act is closely allied to the spiritual voyage. According to Eliade, the voyage is a uniquely shamanic technique and specific to ecstasy, "hence any ecstatic cannot be considered a shaman; the shaman specializes in a trance during which his soul is believed to leave his body and ascend to the sky or descend to the underworld."[9] Shaman's prodigious powers lie in the fact that they alone are able to effect the hero's paradigmatic voyage into the upper and lower worlds. Jacques Bourgaux states:

> Over the course of the séance the shaman becomes the locus of the drama, the unique actor of a drama with innumerable characters among which, he, the shaman, plays the principle role, the role of hero. The hero is the original non-alienated, non-dissociated person of the shaman....[10]

According to Andreas Lommel:

> The shaman's soul-journey is a mimed repetition of a myth; that is to say it repeats the memory of the travels and adventures of a shamanistic tribal hero of ancient times — a memory that is preserved in tribal tradition, ever-renewed, changing and in this sense "living" — in whose figure many historical personages are fused into one.[11]

While possession trance involves a visit of the spirits to the secular world, shamanistic ecstasy involves going to the spirit world. The shaman is his society's emissary to the spirit world and his primary task lies in creating access to the sacred through the medium of ecstasy. Central to the shaman's craft is the ability to effect a dangerous voyage there and back during which he must wrest power, knowledge or cures from the spirits through skillful battle and physical daring.

SHAMANIC IMAGES AND MIMESIS

"The shaman's histrionic achievement lies in his almost complete identification with the 'images' in and through the trance."[12]

The shamanic voyage is based in what Harner and others term the Vision Quest—experiencing externally projected psychic imagery as present reality. The term ecstasy as applied to shamanic trance denotes the state of rapturous delight that the shaman feels as he or she moves into an altered state of consciousness. It is characterized by the shaman sensing himself as being part of nature: "Through mystic trances, bodies participate in the rending of the sky by lightning, in the lapping of the ocean waves on the beach, in the germination of plants and in the copulation of the animals of the forest."[13]

The shaman's experiences during ecstasy, states Michael Harner, "are like dreams, but waking ones that feel real and in which he can control his actions and direct his adventures."[14]

Shamans do not experience their visions as fantasy, but as real and tangible realities which they can see and with which they can interact. The reenactment of imagery can take place in two distinct modes according to Eveline Lot-Falck: either as a "soul journey" as in the "cataleptic trance" or in the form of pantomimic enactment as in the "dramatic trance."[15] Shamanism comes closest to ecstatic experience of the mystic in what Lot-Falck terms the cataleptic trance. In this trance the body of the shaman is "rigid, it is nothing but an empty envelope, deserted by the soul, which has left to accomplish some mission."[16]

In the case of the aboriginal shaman in a cataleptic trance, the vision "is no mere hallucination. It is a mental formation visualized and externalized, which may even exist for a time independent of its creator. . . . While the person is experiencing the vision, he cannot move, but he is conscious of what is going on around him."[17]

The cataleptic trance in turn is diametrically opposed to the dramatic trance, which manifests itself as role playing and mimesis: "the shaman simultaneously lives and describes the stages and incidents of his voyage. The scene is extremely animated, the shaman mimes the voice and the comportment of the beings which he meets or those which accompany him."[18]

In the dramatic trance, shamans serve to make their visions of the sacred world, with its magical spirits and properties, present before an audience.

This strong appeal to the imagination is undoubtedly the principal motive which induces the prophet, priest and seer to make extensive use of ritual. His own communion with the spirit world takes place in his own soul. But the shaman is a *psychopompos,* and the spiritual representative of his tribe. He must stimulate the imagination of his audience, however crudely, to see his own vision, to realize the truths which he himself apprehends spiritually. . . . He may demonstrate by mimesis, or teach orally.[19]

During ecstasy, the shaman interacts with spirits that are absent for the audience. This type of mimesis is fundamentally different from that of possession trance, where images are given concrete presence through group role playing and the use of real props. The shaman creates the semblance of actual events and agents by means of vocal and gestural mimicry, dialogue, illusion, and magical feats. He functions simultaneously as an actor, who becomes different characters, and storyteller, who indicates and narrates events as they unfold. Rouget states that "During the dramatic trance . . . the shaman describes what he sees during his voyage in the upper and lower world and recounts his adventures in chanting and hitting a drum, which gives place to a veritable theatrical representation, or more exactly a *one man show*. . . ."[20] According to Bourgaux, those who have witnessed a shamanic séance "all agree that it is a spectacle without equal: everything is represented, everything is made concrete by gesture, voice and accessories — 'Total' theatre animated by one man."[21]

There are numerous references in scholarly works to rites in which the shaman physically mimes her sacred voyage. Andreas Lommel states, "Many processes during the soul journey, in particular obstacles in the way, are represented dramatically."[22] Stephen Larsen refers to one such sacred voyage by a shaman in an Eskimo rite involving a visit to the "Mother of the Sea Creatures," a rite which symbolizes the society's social situation and infraction of taboo: "The shaman, as emissary of the community, re-enacts it [the rite] personally and it is believed, actually. This enactment then belongs in and through the experience of the shaman. The shaman flies personally to the numinous, mythogenic realm, *there* to enact the symbolic drama."[23]

Lucile Charles writes of shamanic exorcisms:

Actual performance includes dramatic invocation of evil or benevolent spirits, or both, for diagnosis and advice as to treatment; possession of or battle with the shaman by the spirits through ecstasy or frenzy which may be considered a supreme example of dramatic impersonation, often with elaborate use of voice, dialogue, and body pantomime.[24]

Shamans experience the phenomenal world as kinetic, animated motion in which agents and objects are perceived in terms of their gestic qualities. Through the use of verbal and corporeal mimesis, shamans make the hidden realities of the spirit world visible to their entourage. The performance space becomes a vast cosmic canvas upon which their visions are painted with feats of magic and physical daring.

The externally projected dream world of the shaman during dramatic trance involves an alteration of the laws of time and space. Bogoras states that the spirits which the shaman sees and interacts with are relative in size and shape and that they change in connection with the various alterations of the surrounding objects and with the actions of other spirits, men, or shamans.[25] The supposed reason for this mutability is that human beings and spirits belong to different worlds, separate and distinct from each other. According to Bogoras the prevailing or victorious spirits, are represented as big and even gigantic, while the losers are depicted as small in size. The size of spirits seems to be bound up with the shaman's attitude towards them—that which is potentially threatening is perceived psychologically as being bigger and more powerful than it might be in actuality, and that which is nonthreatening, is seen as smaller and less powerful. The shaman is also able to condense space. During her voyage she moves easily through the vast dimensions of space which symbolize the cosmos. This movement is often indicated by a spiraling or circular walk or turning motion.

Ecstasy also alters the shaman's attitude towards time. Bogoras states that the inner time of the shaman's dream world is projected outward upon reality and manifests itself in two distinct modes. The first of these is compression of time in which a series of events or long duration of time is condensed into a single action or short period. The second of these is a slowing down of time, which creates a type of slow motion. These two may be combined when, for example, the shaman covers vast amounts of time and space with a slow motion walk comprised of several spiraling circles which portray his movement through the various layers of the cosmos.

Audience participation in shamanic rite is also fundamentally different from that of possession trance rituals where the audience interacts with the possessing deity. In rites of possession, the sacred and secular realms interpenetrate as the gods are made present among men and women. The fact that gods have been brought to the human plane makes them approachable. The audience talks to them, offers them food and drink, and caters to their every whim, and in this sense plays a small role in the unfolding improvisation.

The particular magic and aesthetic of the shaman's performance is his verbal and corporeal reenactment of his voyage to the Illud Tempus. The audience ascends, as it were, with the shaman and identifies with the unfolding drama in and through his visions. During the voyage, the audience serves as a kind of the tragic chorus both by witnessing and participating in the suffering and triumphs of the shaman-hero. Shirokogoroff tells of a séance of a tungus shaman:

The rhythmic music and singing, and later the dancing of the shaman, gradually involve every participant more and more in a collective action. When the audience begins to repeat the refrains together with the assistants, only those who are defective fail to join the chorus. The tempo of the action increases, the shaman with a spirit is no more an ordinary man or relative, but is a "placing" (i.e. incarnation) of the spirit; the spirit acts together with the audience and this is felt by everyone. The state of many participants is now near to that of the shaman himself, and only a strong belief that when the shaman is there the spirits may only enter him, restrains the participants from being possessed in mass by the spirit.[26]

The audience's participation in the shaman's ecstasy serves not only to initiate them in the secrets of the spiritual world but to cleanse and strengthen them as well. As in tragic drama, with which it holds much in common, the shamanic voyage is a dramatic embodiment of harmful psychophysical attitudes of an individual and or community which seek recognition and purgation. Shirokogoroff continues:

> After shamanizing, the audience recollects various moments of the performance, their great psychophysiological emotion and the hallucinations of sight and hearing which they have experienced. They then have a deep satisfaction — much greater than that from emotions produced by theatrical and musical performances, literature and general artistic phenomena of the European complex, because in shamanizing the audience at the same time acts and participates.[27]

SHAMANIC INITIATION AND CORPOREAL TRAINING

Solitude, silence, and immobility are hallmarks of both the rigors of monastic life lead by monks and nuns and the shamanic experience. When a future shaman receives a calling, usually in the form of visions and involuntary possession, she generally undergoes a long period of initiation away from the social group in a cave, special enclosure, or the wilderness. During the initiation she is instructed by a master shaman in the techniques of her craft and its underlying theory, including the techniques of possessing and controlling the spirits as well as a repertoire of magical gestures for exorcism and curing. While she learns from the great traditional models, her initiation is undertaken in solitude and her knowledge is won by personal ordeal.

Initiation essentially involves a rigorous corporeal training in which the shaman is divested of the acquired attitudes that make up her everyday personality and discovers her hidden personal powers. During initiation, the future shaman undergoes the archetypal voyage of the hero or heroine, an adventure of death and resurrection — the structuring theme that serves in all

future voyages. "The voyage for the shaman and for the community by identification is a means of restructuring the personality, a search for the ego in the
face of a multiplicity of 'alter egos,' of doubles which are the concretization of
impulses."[28]

In addition, Campbell states, "the painful crisis of the deeply forced voca-
tional call carries the young adept to the root not only of his cultural structure,
but also of the psychological structures of every member of his tribe."[29]

During the voyage of initiation future shamans witness the painful
destruction of their bodies, which are stripped of skin and flesh and often
boiled until nothing remains. In this process they come to see themselves on
the inside; that is, they come face to face with their "bone essence."

> Though no shaman can explain to himself how and why, he can, by the
> power his brain derives from the supernatural, as it were by thought
> alone, divest his body of its flesh and blood, so that nothing remains but
> his bones. And he must then name all the parts of his body, mention
> every single bone by name. . . . By thus seeing himself naked, altogether
> freed from the perishable and transient flesh and blood he consecrates
> himself in the sacred tongue of the shamans, to his great task through
> the part of his body which will longest withstand the action of sun, wind
> and weather, after he is dead.[30]

The crisis of initiation involves a radical opening up of latent powers or
attitudes locked in the spinal column of the neophyte shaman. The spinal
column in the image of a world tree or *Axis Mundi* is of central importance
to shamanism. In Siberia, it is believed that the shaman is hatched in a tree
and in order to obtain his special knowledge and power he

> must climb the tree, branch by branch, heaven by heaven, bone by bone.
> It is a journey during which he meets various personages and adventures,
> and which he recounts to his audience in great detail. He impersonates
> all the characters of this other world, and acts out his own laborious
> efforts.[31]

The backbone represents a hierarchy of powers locked within the deepest
recesses of the self, which the shaman releases in the figurative embodiment
of spirits and their actions. The shaman is able to use his latent attitudes as
agents of the drama.

> His dissociation appears as a crisis of dismemberment, which can be
> understood as a radical unseating of cathexes throughout the body; a
> crisis into which he is sometimes drawn as though down a tube, whose
> bodily referent remains to be diagnosed. He is in touch with spirits,
> which must be those cathexes transformed from parasites of the body-
> mind into its instruments. They travel through the various levels and do-
> mains of a well-ordered cosmos, or personified image of nature; and they

stage their adventures in front of an audience for the benefit of a client, a patient, or an entire congregation.[32]

The keystone of the shaman's corporeal technique is the acquisition of one or more spirit helpers during initiation which provide him with his magic powers. The shaman's helping spirits are his alone and have never been seen by anyone else. In possession cults, on the other hand, the gods are well-known members of a spiritual pantheon that have been visible to the entire village since time immemorial. The shaman's spirits represent in Jungian mythology the powers that are latent in every individual, which only the shaman has direct access to. In carrying out his task it may be said that he derives "in-spiration" from them. According to Jung in many myths of the hero,

> the early weakness of the hero is balanced by the appearance of strong "tutelary" figures — or guardians — who enable him to perform the super-human tasks that he cannot accomplish unaided. ... These god-like figures are in fact symbolic representatives of the whole psyche, the larger and more comprehensive identity that supplies the strength that the personal ego lacks. Their special role suggests that the essential function of the heroic myth is the development of the individual's ego-consciousness — his awareness of his own strengths and weaknesses — in a manner that will equip him for the arduous tasks with which life confronts him.[33]

The helping spirits symbolize a real connection between the natural and sacred realms of existence. Archaic peoples believe that in primordial times heaven and earth were connected and that humans lived on equal footing with the plants and animals. The shaman has been termed a microcosm of all flora and fauna, because he understands their language and is able to converse with them. In hunting societies, which depend upon animals for their health and well-being, the deities are primarily animal-gods. By incarnating the power of an animal (i.e., its strength, swiftness, sinuousness, etc.) the shaman taps into her own strengths or latent efforts that mirror those of the deity. "Animals," according to Laban, "are perfect in the efficient use of the restricted effort habits they possess; man is less efficient in the use of the more numerous effort shadings potentially possible to him."[34] The shaman is able to employ the clear and simplified expression of animal Effort to effect important changes or bring about desired results for the benefit of an individual or the group as a whole.

Unlike the possessed devotee, the shaman uses latent attitudes in the form of helping spirits to strengthen his everyday personality. He retains his consciousness during possession because the helping spirit does not displace his everyday personality. The opposite is true for possession in which the individual seeks release from habitual personality in order to enhance his power or status. The shaman is therefore always responsible for his actions where as the possessed devotee generally is not. Erika Bourguignon sums up the differences between possession in trance as opposed to ecstasy. In the former:

> The individual enhances his power and his status by total abdication and self-effacement before the spirits. He abandons his body to them as their mount; his spirit vacates its place before them. He can achieve dominance and assertion only indirectly, through the unconscious pretense of obedience and submission. On the other hand, the shaman who acquires power, and the witch as well, do not impersonate spirits, do not abdicate their own identity. ... Those who through some form of possession acquire powers for good or for evil have these powers supplement their own; their selves are strengthened rather than displaced.[35]

SHAMANIC ROLE PLAYING

According to Siikala, the enactment of counter-roles or spirit helpers by the shaman manifests itself in several alternative techniques. The first is role identification, in which the shaman is changed directly into a spirit. The second is dual role, in which the shaman plays her own role and that of the spirit with whom she creates a vocal and gestural dialogue. The third is description of a counter-role, in which the shaman sees or hears a spirit which is external to herself and remarks on it.[36]

The shaman frequently becomes totally identified with a main helping spirit which takes up abode inside him. This spirit is often identical with the shaman's ancestor or dead predecessor. Frequently, the helping spirit is in the form of an animal. When the shaman becomes possessed by the spirit, he may don a mask and a costume with animal trappings, i.e., feathers fur, etc. He may also assume its characteristic posture and gesture. N. K. Chadwick cites the Baganda shamans who "make their appeal through the eye, by assuming the role of the animal in question, roaring like a lion; turning the head and snapping like a crocodile; growling like a leopard; crawling and wriggling like a python.[37] Shamans also make the characteristic sounds of the animals that they incarnate. Lommel states, "When the animal spirit has entered into the shaman he has to behave outwardly in conformity with the animal in question: he howls like a wolf, barks like a fox, whistles like a jakesnipe, snorts like a walrus...."[38]

The most common helping spirit is a bird which carries the shaman on a magical flight through the layers of the cosmos and assists him in his adventures. "Among the Buriat, the animal or the bird that protects the shaman is called *khubilgan*, meaning 'metamorphosis,' from the verb *khubilku*, 'to change oneself, to take another form.'"[39] In the Lascaux cave paintings in southern France, there is a picture of a shaman dressed in a bird costume, lying prostrate in a trance with the figure of a bird perched on his staff beside him, signifying shamanic flight.

Among the Tungus shaman of Siberia the primary helping spirit is a

Tlingit shaman's mask. Neg/Trans. no. 330968. (Photo by Rota.) Courtesy Department Library Services, American Museum of Natural History.

horse. However, unlike possession trance in which the devotee is mounted by the god and becomes its horse, the shaman mounts his horse and directs its behavior. This points to the fundamental difference between the shaman who acts in order to bring about some benefit for the community and the possessed individual who submits to the god in order to benefit himself. "In other words, in possession the subject enters into trance because he changes his identity, in shamanism he enters into trance because he changes the world."[40]

SHAMAN AS ANTIHERO OR "TRICKSTER"

The shaman may not only become possessed by helping spirits but by evil spirits representing disease and deformation. It appears that in some shamanic-based rituals the representation of evil spirits has become the basis for clown-like behavior on the part of the shaman. According to Gananath Obeyesekere, in Ceylonese curing rituals, known as demon plays, demons, acted out by masked performers, were originally representations of physical illness but then came to portray the psychological meanings of symptoms and psychosomatic and psychological illness in particular.[41]

Because of his special magical ability to assume an animal form and to metamorphosize into good and evil spirits, the shaman has often been depicted as a trickster figure in folklore. The trickster, according to Joseph Campbell, appears to have been the chief mythological character of the paleolithic world of story where "he was the archetype of the hero, and the giver of all great boons—the fire bringer and the teacher of mankind."[42] Often seen as a clown, liar, fool, and cheat, he represents the principle of disorder, the creative chaos of which can come a new order. As such, he is also a Promethean figure—the bringer of culture. Among his many guises, according to Campbell, are the coyote of the American Plains Indians, the great rabbit who became the basis for Br'er Rabbit, Prometheus, Hermes, and Dionysus of the Greeks. The trickster survives "in the numerous clowns, buffoons, devils, Pulcinellas, and imps who play the roles, precisely, of the clowns in rites of the Indian Pueblos and give the character of topsy-turvy day to the feast."[43]

The shaman/clown results from a blend of elements derived from shamanic ecstasy and possession trance—a mix that evolved as hunting societies were gradually transformed into agricultural societies. Campbell gives an account of this process among the Hactin in the origin of the Tsanati dance society of the Jicarilla Apache in which 12 shaman were painted and turned into clowns:

> It would be difficult to find a clearer statement of the process by which the individualistic shamans, in their paleolithic style of magical practice, were discredited by the guardians of the group-oriented, comparatively complex organization of a seed-planting, food-growing community. Lined up, fitted into uniform, they were given a place in the liturgical structure of a larger whole. The episode thus represents the victory of a socially anointed priesthood over the highly dangerous and unpredictable force of individual endowment.[44]

IMMOBILITY

Immobility is a primary corporeal technique of shamans who engage in cataleptic trance. During ecstasy, the body of the shaman appears completely dead to the world. Her soul is believed to have left her body to make a journey to the upper and lower spirit worlds. In actuality, the shaman is reliving psychic imagery in the depths of her dreaming imagination. During the voyage the shaman's internal world is projected outward as superimposed on reality. The immobility of the shaman has the appearance of deep sleep, but in actuality the shaman is actively engaged in a waking dream or reverie in which she internally mimes the gestic content of imagery within the muscles and organs of her body.

This same visualization and kinaesthetic participation in the gestic content of imagery forms the basis of shamanic mimesis in the dramatic trance. Immobility is the essence of shamanic mime. The shaman engages in a conflict of attitudes within her body. She must maintain her own attitudes while summoning up latent and opposing attitudes. The dramatic struggle within the shaman between conflicting attitudes produces strong oppositional tensions in the body which manifests itself in spectacular posturally based movement.

Shamanic corporeal mimesis is similar to that of possession trance mimesis, with a fundamental difference being that shamans preside as master controllers of the drama being enacted within their bodies. Throughout the séance,

> they must respond to the demanding expectations of their entourage. They must show proof of a solid nervous constitution, an acute power of concentration, extraordinary muscular strength, a perfect control of the smallest and most violent movements of the body, and finally, a prodigious memory.[45]

They are able to employ images, which are the figurative embodiments of latent attitudes, as instruments of their will. Like master puppeteers, their conscious will presides over the strings of imaginary characters from the spirit world in order to relay back important messages necessary for the mental health of the community.

SILENCE AND MUSIC

While possession trance is characterized by group dance to orchestral accompaniment and often noisy audience interaction, shamanic ecstasy is marked by silence and absorption in imagery. According to Rouget, "Between the practice of ecstasy and that of music, there is incompatibility. . . . Unless the experience is deliberately sought, immobility, silence and the sensory privation are incompatible with music."[46]

In the dramatic trance the shaman does employ music, but in a manner that is fundamentally different from that of possession trance. The shaman, according to Rouget, is the musician of his own entrance into trance as opposed to the possessed devotee who is passively moved by the music. "It is not in hearing others sing or drum for him, but on the contrary, in chanting and in drumming himself that he (the shaman) enters into trance."[47] The shaman uses both song and rhythmic drumming or other percussive media to induce ecstasy and to sustain him throughout his journey. While music is employed in possession trance to call forth various spirits by playing their melodies or beats, as well as to maintain and quicken the pace of the unfolding drama, the shaman uses music, along with costumes, lighting, and dramatic setting, to assist in evoking the mood or atmosphere of the world of the spirits. Thus, music becomes another dimension of the performance whose purpose is to make the sacred realms visible for the audience.

Music, in the form of song and drumming, helps to heighten the mystery and magic of the sacred realms and the events that unfold therein. To this end, the shaman employs a variety of vocal techniques in conjunction with drumming to clarify and dramatize events as they unfold in the chanted or sung narrative.

> Every effort is made by the seer or shaman to convey to his audience his experiences on these journeys in order to make them familiar with spiritual regions. Tatar shamen, Dyak manang, Tibetan lama—all take their audience with them in a kind of charade with running commentary, and the indelible impression which these journeys make on the lay mind can be gauged from the paramount place which they hold in the literature of entertainment.[48]

SHAMANIC MIME AND POETRY

Many scholars have termed the vocal utterances of the shaman as the beginnings of poetic art. Lommel states that the shaman is not merely a "sorcerer," but also "the poet and artist of his group. It is he who molds the spiritual world of his group into impressive images, and who gives ever-renewed shape and fresh life to the images that live in the group's imagination."[49] He functions as a mediator between the profane world of everyday life and the spiritual world that constitutes the core of the subconscious.

The shaman's recitation constitutes an oral tradition which serves to transmit the myths of her society. Whereas in possession cults the myths are acted out in group performances, the essential technique of the shaman is to narrate the myths to her group. According to Rouget, the most important aspect of the shaman's song is in its reference to the world, to things said.[50] Not only does she mimetically enact mythical dramas of which she is the heroine, but she also recites, chants or sings the verbal dialogue that accompanies her actions.

Radlov's classic account of the voyage of the Altaic shaman offers an example of a mimed and chanted shamanic voyage. In a state of ecstasy, the shaman performs his own role and dialogues and interacts with various spirits and personages along his journey. The séance begins with the invocation of helping spirits through drumming and the sacrifice of a horse whose soul is to accompany the shaman throughout his celestial journey. The mimed and chanted representation of the mythic events goes as follows. He straddles a scarecrow in the shape of a goose (helping spirit) and "rapidly waving his hands as if to fly, sings: 'Under the white sky,/Over the white cloud;/Under the blue sky/Over the blue cloud:/Rise up to the sky, bird!'" The shaman then imitates the cackling of the goose's reply. Sitting astride the goose, the shaman pursues the soul of the horse (which is supposed to have fled) and neighs like a charger.

> With the help of those present, he drives the animal's soul into the palisade and laboriously mimes its capture; he whinnies, rears, and pretends that the noose that has been thrown to catch the animal is tightening

around his own throat. Sometimes he lets the drum fall to show that the animal's soul has escaped.[51]

The actions performed by the Altaic shaman portray the characteristic and transitory gestures of agents acting upon one another (Agent-Agissant-Agi) that forms the basis of the language of dramatic mimesis. Moreover, these postural and gestural signs are denoted verbally in the shaman's accompanying recitation. However, the sung and enacted shamanic imagery is charged with an emotional significance which goes beyond the denotational aspect of spoken language to reveal hidden truths through lingual and gestural metaphor.

Many sholars adhere to the theory that spoken language is a secondary development out of the gestures of phenomena that lie recorded in the body of the individual. According to Wilhelm Wundt, "vocal language is nothing but a sector of the entire system of expressive movements. The sounds emitted by the vocal organs being nothing but a vocal gesture, fragment of the mimic of the ensemble."[52] Marcel Jousse states that archaic peoples intussuscept the aural mimemes (sound gestures) of phenomenon as well as their gestural mimemes. An agent not only possesses a characteristic gesture, it also has a characteristic sound. For example, an owl's characteristic sound might be a hoot, a cat's might be a meow, and so forth. Furthermore, each agent performs a fixed number of transitory sounds such as the flapping of wings sound of flight for the owl.

The shaman portrays the sound qualities of the objects of imitation by articulating the efforts that underlie spoken imagery. Like the poet, he makes his recited imagery come alive vocally by selecting words which through their particular tonal or sound quality convey the attitude on a deeper level than denotation. According to Rouget, the shaman's recitation consists of "a succession of musical episodes and the most diverse styles: melodies, recitatives, invocations, spoken passages, dialogues, imitation of the cries of animals or the noises of nature, onomatopoeia, vocal imitations."[53] This same poetic quality is mirrored in the accompanying pantomime which translates the chanted or recited words in equivalent gestural images.

Shamanic corporeal and vocal narration is metaphoric. It links the attitude to concrete phenomenal realities in a way that is emotionally evocative. "Metaphor is the supreme agent by which disparate and hitherto unconnected things are brought together in poetry."[54] On their most basic level lingual and gestural metaphors abstract the characteristic gestic traits of phenomena which serve to link them to other classes of phenomena with similar gestic traits. For example lightning, which is perceived by archaic peoples in terms of its gestural trait of serpentine, is figuratively embodied by archaic peoples as a snake or a snake-like god. The sun, which is perceived in terms of its gestic qualities of flight because it moves across the sky, frequently appears in gestic, lingual and pictorial expressions as the heavenly flier, an arrow, or a bird. These lingual and gestural sings also serve as metaphors for the attitudes of the ritual performer and the community as a whole. It is this aspect more than any other that charges the image with emotional significance. The serpentine gesture of the snake, for example, depending on the cultural attitudes towards this phenomenon, might be associated with such qualities as deviousness or sinisterness. The person performing this gesture would find his inner attitudes mirrored in the slowly twisting and serpentine movements of the snake.

Metaphor is created through relationship. The vocal or gestural mimesis of an agent by itself has no real ideational and emotional significance. It is only when the image is combined with other images that their true meaning and impact can be achieved. Each image consists of a tripartite action which articulates an attitude through the enactment of agent acting upon agent. This is the smallest unit of dramatic meaning which in revealing relationship takes on metaphorical overtones but still remains primarily at the level of denotation. The true evocative power of shamanic narrative lies in the coupling of individual images, for example as in "under the white sky," "over the white sky," "rise up bird into the sky." At the end of the performance, the metaphorical meanings and gestic resonances of the individual images combine to create a unified and emotionally significant vision which transcends its purely denotational meaning to illuminate the mysteries of the spirit world.

CODIFICATION OF GESTURES

With time and repetition, the original spontaneous gestural expression in ritual becomes codified into a language which still retains its original metaphorical overtones, but the signs, which have become increasingly abstract, take on the denotational quality of words in language:

> as soon as an expressive act is performed without inner momentary compulsion it is no longer self expressive; it is expressive in the logical sense. It is not a sign of the emotion it conveys, but a symbol of it; instead of completing the natural history of a feeling, it denotes the feeling, and may merely bring it to mind, even for the actor. When an action acquires such a meaning it becomes a gesture.
>
> Genuine acts are completed in every detail unless they are forcibly interrupted, but gestures may be quite abortive imitations of acts, showing only their significant features. They are expressive forms, true symbols. Their aspect becomes fixed, they can be deliberately used to communicate an idea of the feeling that begot their prototypes. Because they are deliberate gestures, not emotional acts, they are no longer subject to spontaneous variation, but bound to an often meticulously exact repetition.[55]

For the most part, the performance of the shaman, although following patterns laid down by the First Shaman, reveals his unique individuality.

Unlike the possessed devotee in type one rituals, he is not merely going through a learned pattern of ritual behavior, he is both the author and actor of his own personal voyage. And while his postures and gestures may become codified through repetition, they reflect a degree of spontaneity and variation that is not found in reified ritual languages in which participants merely go through the motions of performing ritual acts. As belief in shamanism declines, however, ritual performance is replaced by theatrical performance. The evocative and metaphorical language of the original performance tends to pass over into a secular form of pantomime, in which gestures replace words.

Shamanism and possession represent two poles of a continuum that includes a variety of hybrid forms. This opposition may be summed up as follows:

Shamanism	Possession
solo performer	group performance
heroic	satyric
possession of spirits	possession by spirits
voyage to the spirits	visit of the spirits
voluntary trance	involuntary trance
mastery of spirits	submission
memory	amnesia
visions	absence of visions
immobility/lack of movement	a great deal of movement
silence	noise
narration	dialogue

The key to the opposing techniques exhibited in shamanic ecstasy and possession trance lies in a radical difference in the personality structures of the performers. Shaman's have great willpower, independence, personal daring and self-reliance. They are the embodiment of the mythical heros and heroines of their entourage who are able to stand alone against the crowd. Unlike the possessed devotee, they do not submit to being mounted by the gods; rather they act upon the spirit world for the benefit of the community for whose wellbeing they are responsible.

The many tasks that are placed before them demand perilous voyages into the upper and lower worlds which are fraught with danger and possible death. As psychopompos, they must journey to the lower world to accompany the dead or receive lost souls. As diviners, they visit the future to foresee events and perhaps alter the course of history. Their primary role, however, is as healers of psychological and somatic illnesses. In this capacity, like the tragic hero, they take upon themselves the flaws of an individual or society. The struggle with these flaws (which are nothing other than latent attitudes that when repressed cause sickness and disaster) is the tragic theme which is played out on the battleground of their bodies. The voyage into the body constitutes a voyage into the spirit world where they meet with the figurative embodiments of latent attitudes which become agents in the unfolding drama.

The heroic stance of the shaman is diametrically opposed to the group possession rituals in which individuals enact latent aspects of their personality by becoming the god. In this process there is no separation of the performer and their role. While possession enactment is shaped according to the models acquired during initiation, impulses are expressed without conscious awareness on the part of those possessed. Devotees are the puppets of the gods who inhabit their bodies.

The most typical form of possession trance is that involving equal portions of cultural and psychological material (type two). In these, devotees enact ethnodramas based on tensions latent in themselves and the group. Performances take the form of improvised plays structured around the ritual occasion and the attributes of the possessing deities. While these performances generally give rise to themes involving potentially tragic conflict, the tendency is more often towards burlesque and comic behavior.

Possession trance performers are not tragic heros who are superior to other men and their environment. They are the common men and women of the original tragic chorus who, lacking models of heroic stature, have reduced the great tragic themes of mythology to the profane level of latent individual and group tensions. Through possession by deity they take on power and authority which they are denied in everyday life. On coming out of the trance they can remember nothing of what has happened and are absolved of all responsibilities for their behavior while possessed.

Shamans are the mythical heros and heroines of their entourage precisely because they have access to knowledge unavailable to other men and women. They do not become spirits in order to take on power. They already possess power in the form of prodigious techniques acquired over a long and demanding initiation period. These ensure their survival and success during the voyage and by extension that of the community for which they are responsible.

Their foremost technique lies in the ability to master and control the spirits, requiring both aggressiveness and strong will to prevent becoming possessed. Unlike the possessed devotee, they are able to stand at a distance from their body and events in order to manipulate them for their ends. This distance and control is the essential technique that situates the performance of the shaman diametrically opposite that of the possessed devotee.

Shamanic mimesis is a form of instruction as well as edification for a society. Because shamans are the sole individuals in their communities that are able to effect the voyage to the spirit world, they must remain aware and in control in order to relay back important messages. The unfolding elements of the voyage and the encounter with the spirits are only visible to the shaman. Therefore, they must narrate the sequence of events to make them present for their entourage. Vocal narration is often accompanied by gestural narration in which the body acts as a cipher for the events occurring in the spirit world. Mimesis unfolds linearly as images are juxtaposed one after another and parallel the spoken or sung recitation. The solo and narrative style of the shamanic performance is similar to epic narration. Shamans are tellers and mimers of great tales whose mythical subject matter is still alive. The audience's participation in and through the recreated events of shamanic narration is the primary method by which sacred history is relived, and in the process, healing is achieved.

Chapter Six

The No Actor

The No is a form of musical dance-drama which originated in fourteenth century Japan under the patronage of the shogun, Ashikaga Yoshimitsu. Vocal and corporeal mimesis form the core of the No performance, whose purpose is the transmission of the deeply felt attitudes of the central character (shite).[1] The subtle refinement of the highly symbolic and codified gestures of the mime dance by the elegantly costumed and masked shite and the beauty of the chanted and sung poetic text and musical accompaniment serve to create a hallucinatory vision of the dimension of the sacred.

The No has close connections with shamanic ritual and may be seen as a ritual bridge between the mime of the shaman and the mime of the dancer. The narrative structure of the No mime dance, which serves to translate the pathos of the central character by means of highly postural and conventional signs, and the special shamanic techniques of the No actor situate the No mime-dance in the tradition of the heroic pantomime. Many No plays are structured in a manner similar to the telling of a story by the possessed shaman; they are "very much like an illustrated, acted-out narration of a past event — more like a narrated reenactment than like the apparent presentation of the actual event itself."[2] There is a dream-like quality to the unfolding drama which is heightened by a series of transformations by the shite that have all the hallmarks of possession. The controlling will of the No actor presides over a highly trained corporeal instrument which communicates the inner emotional landscape of the central character in an evocative language of symbolic signs. As such, the central actor (also termed shite) in the No is an embodiment of the shamanic hero who takes his audience on a visionary journey to the world of the spirits as contained in Japanese legend, which comprises the substance of the No plays.

SHAMANIC ORIGINS OF THE NO

The Japanese No is an amalgam of a variety of influences: popular folk dances, mimes, and entertainments at agrarian festivals and temples (*sarugaku* and *dengaku*); Buddhist dance-drama forms imported from Korea and China which were incorporated into courtly entertainments; Buddhist ritual and

moralistic mimes; indigenous popular mime (*waza-ogi*); and shamanic practices and entertainments associated with Shintoism (*kagura*—God Entertainment). During the Heian period (A.D. 794-1192), sarugaku, which included comic
skits, mimes, dances, popular songs, acrobatics, and magic acts, shifted to a
concern with realistic imitation. It was performed both as a popular entertainment at small shrines and temples and also at the court where it came under
the influence of the refined music and dance of courtly ceremonies. While
sarugaku disappeared from the court with the collapse of the Heian dynasty,
it continued to strengthen its appeal with audiences and patrons in the provinces by adding theatrical enactments of myths to its entertainments at shrine
rituals honoring the gods. Under the patronage of the Ashikaga court during
the fourteenth century, the religious and popular elements of the sarugaku
were refined and perfected by Zeami Motokiyo, a great actor, writer and theo-
rizer of the No drama. The aristocratic genre of *Nogaku* (No) was born.

While the No is a complex sum of a variety of interrelated entertainments
deriving from folk festivals, ritual performances, and courtly entertainments,
its spiritual qualities, unique style, and aesthetics point to a deeper source. Recent studies have shown that the origin of No can ultimately be traced to
shamanic rituals involving spirit possession, which were refined and shaped by
Buddhist spirituality: "their function should be compared to that of a powerful
generator of energy; all pervasive, influencing throughout, and capable of ex-
plaining most phases of the prodigious development of No."[3]

Zeami, in his treatise on the No, attributes the origin of sarugaku No to
the Age of the Gods in which the goddess Ama-No-Uzume performed a legendary kagura ("The Myth of the Heavenly Cave"). Divinely inspired, the goddess danced and performed mimetic antics in order to entice the Sun Goddess
out of the cave where she had hidden herself plunging the world in darkness.[4]
Primitive kagura was a form of ancient Shinto ritual drama involving shamanic
ecstasy, spirit possession and entertainments by means of mime, music and
song.

Scholars generally acknowledge that the trance dance of Uzume in "The
Myth of the Heavenly Cave" is a "projection into the mythical past of ancient
shamanic practices, typified by *miko* trance performances in ancient kagura."[5]
The primitive miko was essentially a shaman or spirit medium attached to a
Shinto shrine who in a state of trance invites a god or spirit to use her voice
and body to name itself and make its utterance.[6] Miko serve as mouthpieces
for three types of spirits; a god (*kami*); a spirit which leaves the body of a living
human being in a faraway place; or the ghost of a dead person. Some miko
merely act as mediums for monks who serve to conjure the trance and control
the actions of the spirits. However, others are often able to self-induce possession and, once possessed, retain a partial consciousness and control of the
spirits.

Another form of ancient kagura involving the shamanic voyage can be

No performance at the Meiji Shrine in Tokyo. Courtesy Japan Information Center, Consulate General of Japan, New York.

traced to *yamabushi* ascetics. These were itinerant monks who formed part of a mountain cult that practiced a religion combining Buddhism, Shintoism and Taoism. The early yamabushi were essentially shamans, who in a state of trance, made magical flights to the upper world during which they became possessed by a succession of spirits. They used a medium as a receiver and one or several priests as conjurers of the trance. Their journey was accomplished either by means of a cataleptic trance, in which the soul makes the voyage leaving the body in suspended animation, or by means of a dramatic trance involving "symbolic mimesis; the other world projected by means of powerful symbolism onto the geography of our own. . . ."[77]

The shamanic kagura consisted of two elements: a ritual portion involving purification, invocation of the god or spirit, possession, and hymns (*kami-kakari*) and a section of entertainment for the possessing deity (waza-ogi).[8] The kami-kakari designated a state of possession in which the devotee produced the comportment of the god. The waza-ogi, which consisted of an invitation to the gods by means of imitative gestures or buffooneries, was a type of comic mime performed to entertain the gods. It continued to be associated with Shinto and Buddhist ritual and had a large influence on the evolution of the arts in Japan, especially the No. It is to these entertainments that Zeami refers in attributing the origin of sarugaku No to primitive kagura.

Many aspects of primitive kagura exerted an important influence on the development of the No. The principal roles of the No, the *waki* and the shite owe their origin to shamanic practice. The waki or second actor in the No finds its counterpart in shamanic ritual in the priest who conjures the trance. In the No plays, the waki appears either as a shrine official or retainer; a Buddhist priest or monk; or as a warrior, townsman or country person. He is essentially the reason for the shite (protagonist) to appear. He does not enter into the action of the play, but rather sits to one side and evokes appropriate responses to the thoughts, feelings and pleas of the main character. The shite is the counterpart of the medium or ascetic who becomes possessed by a ghost, or spirit of a living being — human or sub-human. The No play centers on the spirit's enactment of the story of its pre- and after-life by means of mimetic dance, narrative recitation, chart and song.

The No plays are based primarily in the expression of the deeply felt emotions of the shite. Characterization in the No emphasizes emotion, inner spirit, mood, and suggestion rather than realistic action. According to Komparu, "The image of the human character, which is of greatest relative importance, is not evoked through interaction with other human beings; rather, the character is given life and breath by depiction of the complexities of life and death involved in that figure's personal battle with fate — that is what is deeply impressed upon the consciousness of the viewer."[9]

No plays are structured around the vocal and gestural narration of a single event in the life of the shite. In nearly all the classical repertoire of the No plays, the shite role is based on well-known figures in Japanese history or legend. Each play is divided into two sections. In the first part, the shite is generally a god, spirit (human or non-human) who appears in the guise of a human; in the second part, the shite metamorphoses into his real form and performs a mime-dance, accompanied by chant, in which he acts out or dances an attitude relating to present or past events.

There are five categories of No plays based on the types of shite which appear in them. A brief glance at these categories reveals the important role spirit possession and the expression of attitude plays in the No.[10] The first category comprises god plays, *kami–No,* which are dedicated to gods and shrines. The kami, which are numinous presences or powers believed to exist in natural phenomena, have been the principal object of worship of Shinto cults since pre–Buddhist times. For the most part they are natural phenomena which are perceived as supra-ordinary, awesome, powerful or terrifying. "Thus the emperor, dragons, the echo, foxes, peaches, mountains and the sea" are all seen as kami because they are mysterious and full of strange potency.[11] In spirit incarnation, the kami are figuratively embodied in the images of a "snake, an old man dressed in white with long white hair and a beard, and as an animal, bird, or plant."[12] The figure of the old man, who appears in *Okina* plays, is thought to be the representation of the divine ancestor, commonly associated with many of the kami.[13]

As a rule, kami–No are divided into two parts. In the first, a god appears in the form of a mortal and tells his story to the waki, who is visiting the place. In the second part, he appears in his own form and performs a *mai* (mime-dance) giving a blessing to the land. Since the kami are generally associated with beneficial powers, the attitudes associated with their enactment tend to express joy and thanksgiving.

The second category are the warrior plays, *shura-mono.* In a typical warrior play, a ghost of a warrior who has fallen in battle appears in the guise of an old or young villager and recounts something that has happened in the past. In the second part he appears as the ghost in full battle attire and acts out that tale in a dramatically concentrated form in the present. The emotions expressed through mime-dance are those which characterize the warrior's struggle with destiny. The mood which they evoke is one of poignancy and regret.

The third performance category are the woman's plays or *kazura-mono* ("wig-pieces"). Here the shite usually appears in the guise of a young and elegant woman. In most cases she is a ghost, or spirit, sometimes a living woman. When she is a ghost or spirit she appears to a monk in the first part in the form of a local woman and tells a story relating to the place. In the second part, she appears in her real form as a princess, a dancer, an old woman, spirit or ghost and performs a mime-dance. Many of the women's plays deal with the pathos of longing, sorrow and regret over lost love or beauty.

The fourth is a miscellaneous category which gives prominence to madness plays, *kyoran-mono,* which derive from the apparent madness of exorcism and spirit possession. Madness in the No is the result of such extreme emotions as intense suffering over the loss of a loved one, rage, jealousy, hatred, or violent love, which are so great that they cause a temporary loss of normal consciousness on the part of the shite. The state of "unknowing," which is similar to trance, has been compared by scholars to the Zen Buddhist state of "nothingness."[14] Often madness in the No is the result of the temporary possession of the shite by a spirit or ghost. In many of the madness plays the shite appears in a disguised form in the first part and in the second undergoes a transformation. The emotions of sadness and lament predominate, often arising from the loss of a child or lover.

The fifth category are demon plays. The shite in this group of No is a lesser deity, dragon god, ghost of a mighty general or highway man, monstrous animal, etc. In the first part the shite appears in various human forms, such as a monk, old man, young woman or a boy, then is transformed in the second part into its true form as a monster or demon in order to demonstrate its power and to help or attack humans. The dancing in these plays is energetic and the mood triumphant.

IMITATION AND THE ART
OF THE NO ACTOR

The No actor's art originates in *monomane*, variously translated as imitation, mimicry or role-playing. In the "Fushikaden," Zeami states that monomane "forms the fundamental basis" of the art of No.[15] The No actor undergoes a long period of training where he learns the techniques of his craft which are grounded in the imitation of the various shite roles in the No plays. In training for these roles, Zeami urges the actor to study the comportment of ministers, generals and courtiers, as well as that of natural things such as flowers, birds, the wind and the moon. However, when an actor proceeds to a higher stage of training, he should not be satisfied with the mere imitation of the outward appearance of a character, such as posture, walk, dress and voice. He must penetrate the *hon-i* (variously translated as true intent, interior essence, or inmost nature) of the object.[16]

The No actor's art is predicated upon the loss of habitual personality which interferes with his ability to achieve complete oneness with the hon-i of his role: "'First truly become the thing you are performing' represents a principle that applies to every variety of Role Playing (monomane) in sarugaku."[17] According to Buddhist philosophy, unless one becomes empty of all of the attitudes associated with the temporal self, one cannot be filled with the Buddha nature or true self. The essence of this experience is to become like a little child again. In the "Fushikaden" Zeami states that the appearance of the child is the basis for beauty (*yugen*) in the No. In the child-like state (which is similar to trance) the limits of the body are loosed and the dualism of man and nature is breached.

IDENTIFICATION

The theory of monomane, as set forth by Zeami, contains the principle of identification. In the East, the concept of identification is partly derived from Buddhism and involves the observer's merging into or becoming one with the object of perception. Identification means becoming one with the unconscious, both inner and outer. Unlike ritual trance, which is primarily grounded in motor archetypes, the Buddhist unconscious is a larger metaphysical concept, which encompasses the idea of a spiritual soul or Buddha nature which permeates all matter. The unconscious within the actor is a mirror of the larger unconscious of the universe. The No actor strives for the cessation of the temporal personality and the assumption of the larger true self. When the actor reaches the state of *mushin*, the unconscious is realized. Mushin is "something identified with a state of ecstasy in which there is no sense of 'I am doing it.'"[18] The ultimate stage of imitation in the No actor's art is the attainment of the state of non-imitation. In the art of Zen archery, this state is achieved when "the hitter and the hit are no longer two opposing objects, but are one reality."[19] At this stage the actor has entirely entered the thing he is imitating. Zeami states in the "Fushikaden":

> In the art of Role Playing [monomane], there is a level at which imitation is no longer sought. When every technique of Role Playing is mastered and the actor has truly become the subject of his impersonation, then the reason for the desire to imitate can no longer exist.[20]

When the No actor has reached this level of artistic development, he performs as if truly possessed. In other words, he lacks the conscious will to imitate and has become completely identified with the thing imitated.

IDENTIFICATION AND
METAMORPHOSIS IN THE NO

The No actor performing the role of the shite usually undergoes several transformations within the course of a play. Before he enters the performance space he performs a ritual in the Mirror Room, *kagami-no-ma*, which is analogous to shamanic spirit possession. According to Komparu, the performer "uses the mirror as a medium"; it invokes "an important psychic element related to spiritual possession."[21] The mirror kagami originally meant god (kami), but later came to mean one's true self or essential way of being. In Zen Buddhist philosophy the mirror is a metaphor for the pure and undefiled Buddha nature of the individual, which reflects the myriad forms of the universe but whose essential nature is nothingness because it does not keep or hold anything. As the No actor looks at himself in the mirror through the tiny eye holes of the mask, he gradually becomes loosed from his ordinary consciousness and the attitudes that make up his personality. In this process, he comes to identify the image in the mirror with one of the many forms of his latent subconscious. The transformation is complete when he comes to sense the externalized image (the character) as himself. In the second part of a No play, the actor must again transform himself into another image (character) by undergoing the same process. In and through these transformations the actor becomes the medium through which the audience experiences the emotions or attitudes of the shite. This does not entail a form of identification on the part of the audience; rather the shite is himself a mirror in which the audience is able to experience a reflection of its own latent attitudes.

ATTITUDE AND POSTURE
AS A BASIS FOR ROLE PLAYING

Monomane in the No is based in the expression of the various character roles by means of posture, gesture and rhythm. The *santai* (three roles) form the basis for the representation of character in the No. Zeami regarded the woman, old man, and warrior as basic personality types and all others as "applied styles which developed out of these according to the personality of the performer."[22] According to Masakazu Yamazaki, the santai represent "the basic attitudes of man towards his world": "The old man represents the attitude of retiring from life, and the calm contemplation of it. The warrior shows an aggressive and vigorous attitude. The woman stands between the two, symbolizing an attitude of harmony with the world."[23]

According to Carl Woltz, the santai were shaped by three influences operating in the Ashikaga court during the time of Zeami: *bushido* (chivalry), a code of ethics and conduct of the samurai which are embodied in the warrior (whose straight forward, practical, healthy and forceful qualities were representative of the rural plebeian); *miyako*, the elegant world of the Imperial court nobles in Kyoto, whose polished manners and refined grace are embodied in the role of the woman; and Zen Buddhism, the spiritual training in the form of meditation adopted by the samurai in the twelfth century, whose qualities are best exemplified in the role of the older person.[24]

The No artist "did not see attitudes of man on the spiritual plane alone but also regarded them as very concrete attitudes of the body."[25] While acquiring the external details of costuming and gesture is an important aspect of monomane, the actor's primary task is to adapt himself completely to the norms of posturing for each role. The character postures for the three roles are based on subtle variations in the basic standing position (*tsune-no-kamae*). The No actor's trunk, which is held as one unit and slightly inclined forward, acts as a platform and energy source for movements of the arms and legs. The back is elongated to achieve a straight line by tucking in the chin, the knees are slightly flexed, the pelvis tilted forward, and the arms are rounded and held a little forward of the body in order to display the long sleeves of the kimono. Whether the actor is standing or sitting, the kamae must never reveal any relaxation in any part of the body. "In other words, the actor must concentrate every part of his body and all his senses on the kamae in order to fully express the character he is playing."[26] To portray the santai the No actor makes subtle modifications in the basic standing posture. According to Zeami:

> When performing the part of an old man, for example, as such a character will naturally have an aged posture. The actor must bend at the hips, walk in a frail fashion, and use small gestures when moving his hands. After having truly assumed this kind of posture the actor's dancing, stage deportment, and chant will seem to emanate from within the character itself. When performing a woman's role, the actor should slightly bend the hips, hold his hands high, sustain the whole body in a graceful manner, feel a softness in his whole manner of being, and use his physique in a pliant manner.[27]

As in all aspects of corporeal expression in the No, the postures and gestures comprising a role should be subtly understated.

EFFORT AS A BASIS
FOR ROLE PLAYING IN THE NO

The actor, according to Zeami, should not be concerned solely with the depiction of the external traits of a character role, but must penetrate its surface to discover its essential spirit (hon-i). The hon-i or primary meaning of the object of imitation, as mentioned above, is the central element in the actor's monomane of character in the No. O'Neill writes, "Zeami was not advocating a thoroughly realistic and detailed form of imitation. It is clear from his notes on the representation of particular roles that the important thing was to grasp and convey the essential character or spirit of a role."[28]

The hon-i of a role essentially refers to the powers it possesses in the form of Effort attitudes. Because many of the characters of the No are the figurative embodiment of natural phenomena (kami) they possess the Efforts or powers associated with these, which serve as metaphors for latent attitudes. Thus, the ultimate stage of identification should bring the actor into contact with the characteristic Efforts or energies which constitute the hon-i of a role.

"Asiatic art," according to Coomaraswamy, "is ideal in the mathematical sense; like Nature, not in appearance but in operation."[29] Asian artists tend to perceive nature in terms of its gestic aspects, while Western artists tend to be concerned with the formal qualities of phenomena; i.e., its shape or structure. For example, a Westerner views a knife as a handle and a blade, placing generic emphasis on it. The Chinese, on the other hand, see the essential nature of a knife in terms of its cutting quality and that of a willow tree in terms of its swaying suppleness.[30] When Zeami exhorts his actors to capture the hon-i of a character, he appears to be referring to the Effort qualities that animate its characteristic postures and gestures. Effort is an important element in character enactment in Mime. Rudolf Laban writes:

> The value of characterization through dance-like mime movements lies in the avoidance of the simple imitation of external movement peculiarities. Such imitation does not penetrate to the hidden recesses of man's inner effort. We need an authentic symbol of the inner vision to effect contact with the audience.[31]

Rather than being concerned solely with the superficial external details of a character, the No performer seeks to capture the characteristic inner attitudes of the object of imitation as expressed through a unique configuration of the four Effort factors of time, weight, space, and flow.

The essential quality for the representation of the woman is suppleness; for the older person, the important element is calm serenity; and for the warrior, the basic quality is forcefulness.[32] Zeami states:

The style of acting appropriate to a quiet solemn god is adapted from the style of the old man; roles requiring great taste and elegance come naturally from the style of women's roles, and roles requiring powerful body movements and foot stamping grow from warrior roles.[33]

While Effort is a key element in the basic body attitudes of the santai and the various applied styles, it is also the essential vehicle by which the character's emotions or mental attitudes are transmitted to the audience. Thus, when Zeami tells the actor to capture the hon-i of a role he means its body posture and Efforts as well as the emotions which color and temper this attitude. His comments in the "Fushikaden" on how to act a frenzied or mad person's role provide an insight into the importance of attitude expression by means of Effort:

> The really difficult parts involve those characters whose thoughts have become confused because their minds have become crazed — a parent searching for a lost child, for example, a wife thrown over by her husband, or a husband who lives on after his wife. Even a relatively skillful shite may fail to make the distinction between them, and he will create his mad gestures in the same manner, so that no emotional response is engendered in those who watch him. In the case of characters of this sort, the actor must have as his intention the manifestation of the precise feelings that can indicate the character's emotional disturbance, and make them the core of his Flower; then, if he feigns madness with all the skill he has at his command, there will certainly be many arresting elements in his performance. If an actor possesses this kind of skill, and if he can make his spectators weep, his art will represent the highest attainment possible.[34]

The "emotional disturbance" is the primary psychic attitude (hon-i) of the character which constitutes the core of its personality. If the performer can capture the essential "mental tensions" of the mad person's disturbance, the muscular configuration of his postural tonus and his gestures will be subtly altered by the Efforts associated with this mental attitude. When the actor becomes "one" with the dynamic mental attitude of the character of the mad person the "primary cause" of the insanity is revealed to the hearts and minds of the spectators.

THE MASK AND ATTITUDE
EXPRESSION IN THE NO

The No mask is a microcosmic condensation of the essential energies of a universal character type, such as the old man, young woman, or demon. Almost all the shite characters in the No wear masks, while the waki are maskless. In those few plays in which the shite performs without a mask his face is (according to tradition) mask-like. The waki too must maintain this mask-like aspect. The paradox here is that the mask-like face is made to live while the unadorned face is kept in a mask-like rigidity. This creates the psychological juxtaposition of the real and the not real — the living and the dead, which derives from the phenomenon of spirit possession, the subject matter of many of the No plays.

The actor's transformation into a role is effected by the assumption of a mask. It makes that which was present (the actor) appear absent and the imitated phenomenon appear present. While character transformation is an important aesthetic function of the mask, it serves a more important psychological function of transforming the consciousness of the actor. The No mask is the embodiment of the essential spirit (hon-i) of a character and when the "whole heart and soul of the actor" is "concentrated on the mask" he feels his entire body imbued with its emotional and spiritual qualities.[35] Thus, the facial mask assists the actor himself in becoming the mask of character.

While the No masks emblemize the particular age, sex, and social status of the different characters, they are more importantly "the impersonal expression of a personal emotion."[36] For example, the mask used for the madwoman play *Hyakuman* depicts the grief-stricken face of a mother who has become slightly deranged in the search for her lost child, while the old man's mask depicts calm serenity. Moreover, the masks are carved in such a way that the expression appears to change based upon the movements of the actor. They can be made to express sadness, grief, joy, contemplation, as well as a variety of other emotions.

Just as the various shite in the No represent the figurative embodiment of the powers of natural phenomenon, the terminology for mask choreography are metaphors which link an emotion with a natural phenomenon. *Omote o kumorasu*, which means "to shade the face" by tilting the mask down and putting it in shadow, expresses sadness.[37] *Omote o terasu*, which means "to make shine" by tilting the mask up and catching the light, expresses joy.[38] *Omote o shioru*, which means "to wilt or fade," indicates the attitude of crying.[39]

THE ACTOR'S WILL IN THE NO AND THE MARIONETTE

According to Komparu, when the actor undergoes the process of transformation by looking at his image in the mirror through the tiny eye holes of the mask, "before entering the stage, a kind of will power is born."[40] This will, which is most directly expressed through the No mime-dance, is analogous to the shamanic ability of controlling the spirits (the figurative embodiments of latent attitudes which have surfaced from the unconscious and taken possession of the body). The No performer, while totally identified with his role, must be able to stand at a distance from himself in order to judge the effects of his performance on the audience. Zeami writes:

> To see the figure (of an actor) from the audience is a view detached from the self. This being so, then to see it with one's own eyes is a "self view."

This is not a detached view. To see with a detached view is to see as if of one mind with the audience. When this happens, the self is enabled to perceive its own figure.[41]

The No actor appears to be able to double his consciousness. While he is fully identified with his role, he is able to simultaneously maintain the necessary objectivity to observe his performance from the vantage point of the audience (detached view). This complex creative process is embodied in the concept of *kokoro,* which briefly defined, encompasses "such things as feeling and emotion, soul and spirit, mind and the objective knowing process, consciousness and self, intent and will, a pure and non-conscious mind, and a spiritual state representing the deepest levels of the total self."[42]

The basic elements comprising kokoro appear to be the unconscious mind of the performer, with its feelings and emotions, expressed through a spontaneous state of ecstasy (mushin) in which the actor is unaware that he his acting; and a rational or conscious mind, "which is aware of what and how the styles and effects are produced, but which keeps such secrets to itself and does not let this consciousness be reflected externally on the stage."[43]

The quality of control which enables the actor to project his inner attitudes through the subtly animated forms of his body (seemingly moved by a superior force) reveals the influence of the Zen Buddhist Big Mind concept. The Big Mind possesses concentration, will and the ability to control all of the spiritual, mental and physical powers of artistic expression. Kokoro, which is essentially the one mind linking all powers, has been compared by Zeami to the strings of a marionette:

> "Indeed, when we come to face death, our life might be likened to a puppet on a cart (decorated for a great festival). As soon as one string is cut, the creature crumbles and fades." Such is the image given of the existence of man, caught in the perpetual flow of life and death. This constructed puppet, on a cart, shows various aspects of himself but cannot come to life of itself. It represents a deed performed by moving strings. At the moment when the strings are cut, the figure falls and crumbles. Sarugaku too is an art that makes use of just such artifice. What supports these illusions and gives them life is the intensity of mind of the actor. Yet the existence of this intensity must not be shown directly to the audience. Should they see it, it would be as though they could see the strings of a puppet. Let me repeat again: the actor must make his spirit the strings, and without letting his audience become aware of them, he will draw together the forces of his art. In that way, true life will reside in his No.[44]

The gestural enactment of the No actor is based upon a precise and stylized technique bound up with the expression of attitudes (powers). What holds the elements of the performance together is the mind, which must not be disclosed to the audience. If the audience senses that the performer is doing it, it is just as if the marionette's strings are visible. It is this perception which destroys the magic and beauty of the performance.

The No actor performs at a distance from the self. While he feels the emotion of the character he is portraying, he must never allow himself to be so overcome that he is unable to judge the emotion that his performance is engendering in his audience.

Emotion must be cooled down and translated through technique in order to create an impersonal expression of a universal emotion. Only in this way will the actor be able to lift his audience to a perception of profound truths about the nature of reality.

The secret of unifying the body and spirit lies in controlling the *seika-no-itten,* the single spot in the lower abdomen. The importance of seika-no-itten in the No appears to have been influenced by the Zen Buddhist concept of *hara,* the point below the navel which is considered to be the focal point of meditation. It is the source of breath and energy and is, moreover, the locus of both the Big Mind and the emptiness or mindlessness associated with the larger unconscious. The actor's performance in the No, Woltz states, originates in the energy (*ki*) that is gathered in the seika-no-itten, which he imagines as lines of force emanating from this spot into all directions in space. The projection of spiritual power from the center of the performer's body creates the impression that he is an animated marionette or statue which is moved by an unseen force.

The visual style of No performance is highly sculptural and is partly the result of the external transformation of the actor's body into a mask of character through the assumption of the No mask and costume. However, it is even more so the product of the limited use of posturally based gesture. Ueda relates that a certain sculptor once said, "The No has the elements of sculpture more than any other histrionic art. I even feel as if the No were an extension of sculpture. ... The No studies how one can move with a minimum of movement...."[45]

The control of the energy which is situated in the seika-no-itten is closely bound up with posture. As in Zen meditation posture, in which the spinal column is kept erect and immovable above the hara, the No actor's spine in the basic *kamae* (standing position) is held in one unit and appears to be transported by the slightly bent legs. The lack of free play and divisions in the spine creates the impression that the torso is a wooden sculpture which is carried through space, while movements of the limbs and head, which are effected from the fixed base of the torso, seem to be controlled by invisible strings.

IMMOBILITY

The No, which is primarily based in the portrayal of the attitudes (emotions) of a single character (shite), presents in the corporeal technique of the performer the essence of "movement held up from going into action," which forms the psychophysical basis of mimesis. Gesture evolving from and ending in immobility contributes to the strong presence that the No actor has on stage. This presence is a product of a play of oppositions within the actor's body. In ritual mimetic enactment, the opposition of the balancing forces within the possessed individual's body expresses the conflict between habitual attitudes and those of the possessing deity. This struggle manifests itself in tense or bound bodily postures and gestures. In the No, this same conflict forms the basis for mimetic expression. The No actor Hideo Kanze reveals that the energy (*ko-shi*) radiated to the audience through the performers' art is created by a tension between two opposing forces within the body of the performer. He relates how the actor achieves this energy in the No walk (*hakobi*): "My father never said 'Use more ko-shi,' but he taught me what it was all about by making me try to walk while he grasped me by the hips and held me back."[46]

The immobility achieved in all movements and postures in the No is predicated on a precarious balance between forces of resistance and momentum. This resistance is effected not only on the horizontal plane, but on the vertical as well. The Kyogen actor Mannojo Nomura relates that the No actors of the Kita school said, "The actor must imagine above him is suspended a ring of iron which is pulling him upwards and against which it is necessary to resist in order to keep one's feet on the ground."[47]

The emotional high point of the No play is often conveyed by the shite during the *kuse*, a narrative song-poem that the shite usually dances. Sometimes this dance is performed, however, as an *i-guse* with the shite sitting immobile in the center of the stage. While to the uninitiated there appears to be nothing happening during these moments of nonaction, the actor is in actuality dancing the oppositions that form the basis of his monomane within the depths of his body. Benito Ortolani relates that a No actor once conveyed to him that dancing the i-guse was like a seagull flying through the water with open wings. The spiritual energy which the actor projects through his crystallized posture is conveyed outwardly to the audience by means of the actor's single-minded will (kokoro). He must preside over the play of oppositions within his body in order to project the deeply felt attitudes of the character to the audience.

The i-guse is perhaps the most exhausting and challenging part of the No, because the actor must use greater energy to project the emotion than he would if dancing. Zeami has a saying, "What is felt in the heart is ten; what appears in movement seven."[48] The struggle of movement held up from going into action limits the No actor's movements in space and charges these movements with an accumulated energy that would ordinarily carry out a much larger action. To restrict the actor's movements to apparent immobility would demand a maximum of energy employed in time and a minimum of movement employed in space: "No matter how slight a bodily action, if the motion is more restrained than the emotion behind it, the emotion will become the Substance and the movements of the body its Function, thus moving the audience."[49] The actor must possess a strong controlling will in order to channel this energy within his body and to radiate it outward in space to the audience. According to Zeami, "It is the moments of 'no-action'" in which "the artist never relaxes his inner tension," that the audience finds the "most enjoyable."[50]

While the i-guse represents a prolonged moment of immobility, it provides insight into the essential nature of gesture in the No. According to Komparu, "the times of action in No exist for the sake of the times of stillness."[51] Movement in No evolves out of the immobility of a frozen postural form and ends in the stillness of another form or sculptural pose. However, the action that culminates in a pose, while it stops in space, continues to push on space and radiates far beyond the held form. It is a state of operational tensions that witnesses the movement that proceeded it and promises the trajectory of its completion.

The mimesis of the hon-i of a character, action or emotion in the No is based in what Ortolani terms "the principle of essentialization," which consists of the suppression of individual and nonessential details.[52] The expression of the highest ideals with the simplest means reveals the refining influence of Zen Buddhism. Essentialization is manifested in the pose and the limited use of posturally based gesture. Intense emotional and spiritual energy leads to immobility. In the No, the segmentary and limited movement patterns seek to translate this inner energy into an outer and visible form. It is in the moments of silence between the movements and in the tensions leading up to the "freezing" of gesture, however, that the true essence of the No is born.

THE CODIFIED MOVEMENT
PATTERNS OF THE NO (*Kata*)

All movement in the No consists of kata, which are codified movement patterns or a form in time or in space.[53] The No actor performing one of the character roles uses kata to express the inner mind of the character in an outward and visible form. The term kata, which derives from kami (god) and *ta* (paddy or hand), reveals their source in possession rituals and agricultural rites.[54] There are more than two hundred kata used in the No today. However, most No plays are made up of about thirty basic kata which are combined and repeated within a regular structure. While the kata are the basis of all movement in the No, with every situation having its prescribed position, posture, gesture or action, the No *shimai* (mime-dances), which present a series of kata linked together, are the primary vehicles for conveying the deeply felt attitudes of the shite.

Each kata is composed of a stance or posture (kamae) and a progression or walk (hakobi). Together, these form the basic unit of monomane in the No. Komparu indicates that "the stance and carriage" which comprise the kata "are the bases not of movement but of the acquisition of the technique of non-movement."[55] The kamae is the basic standing position providing a platform for the unfolding of gesture. The torso is held as a unit and transported through space by the legs. The basic form of the kamae is altered by the angle it presents to the audience and by the changing line of the arms, with their long kimono sleeves, which move about the fixed base of the trunk. Gestures in the No unfold from the immobile platform of the basic kneeling or standing kamae. Evolving from stillness, gesture ends in the stillness of a held postural form. The inner tensions of the shite, resulting from the withholding and struggle of emotion for articulation, contributes to gesture which is high in the Effort quality of bound flow. Komparu states, "The basis of No dance lies in stopping each movement just at the moment when the muscles are tensed."[56] It is in the moments of no action when the gesture has become totally bound or frozen that the emotional high point of the kata is most truly expressed.

The progression (hakobi), according to Zeami, expresses "silence in action."[57] It is essentially transported immobility. When the actor is walking, his body is still but continues to radiate inner tension through opposition. The hakobi, or manner of walking, is the most characteristic movement in the No. The walk appears to be partially derived from the slow, circular turning motions made by the miko in primitive kagura as she moved around an altar, striving to become possessed. In the walk, the forward position is usually dominant. The actor looks as though he is being drawn forward by some invisible force. With a slight lean forward and no body rotation, there is a strong frontal focus reminiscent of Zen meditation trance. The feet appear to glide across the smooth, polished wooden surface of the stage, a motion which, according to E.T. Kirby, recalls the movement of ghosts who in Japanese tradition have no feet.[58] In contrast to the moments of no action, where the emotion of the character and the inner spiritual strength of the actor are projected through the energies animating a held posture, the hakobi serves to express the modulations of the inner mental state of the performer through movement of the legs and feet while the torso maintains its immobility. "A few halting steps backwards indicate disappointment, and two or three rapid steps forward show excitement."[59]

The kata, which are the primary vehicles for expressing the attitudes of the shite, were originally derived from the mimesis of concrete phenomena that formed an important element of sarugaku and other performance arts contemporary with the No. Refined by Zeami within the context of the No, the kata are, for the most part, abstract and symbolic renditions of mimetic gesture.

There are three types of kata: realistic (descriptive), symbolic, and abstract.[60] The realistic kata, which are patterns possessing concrete significance, are the most common in the No. While they consist of the portrayal of the characteristic traits of phenomena, they are highly refined and essentialized in form and are often employed symbolically. Realistic kata, which are purely mimetic, include:

> to scoop salt water (shio o kumu): to use special buckets for scooping up seawater for salt; to jump into the bell (kane ni tobikomu): to actually jump into the giant bell property as it falls; to slash with a halberd (naginata de kiru): to brandish a life-size halberd; to thrust with sword (katana de sasu); and to read a book (soshi o yomu): to hold a book or scroll in the hands.[61]

Symbolic kata include:

> to droop (shiori): signifies weeping. One hand . . . or both hands . . . are raised slowly to the eyes and then lowered again; to use the mask (omote o tsakau): to turn the face left and then right, indicating searching or the blowing wind. . . . To view the moon (tsuki no ogi): indicates the moon. The dancer brings the open fan (in the right hand) to the left shoulder and gazes up to the right.[62]

Abstract kata appear to have no inherent meaning and are included in the No mime-dance for their refined beauty as well as choreographic elements, to mark the beginning and end of pieces (sayu), and to provide transitions as well as percussive punctuation by means of foot stamps (ashibyoshi). While it is difficult to trace their origin, the abstract kata are, in all probability, derived from ritual mimetic gestures for exorcism or curing, as well as from the abstract and architectural movements of bugaku.

Bugaku is a dance drama from associated with Buddhist ritual imported from China in the seventh century. It was adapted by the Japanese Buddhist priests and the aristocrats of the Imperial Court. Bugaku often involves abstract renditions of fragmentary mimetic actions—a croquet game, spear dance, or a war dance showing a god symbolically subduing his enemies—by means of architectural and nonrepresentational movements.[63] The geometry, balance, and spiritual calm, devoid of emotion, which characterizes these dances is believed to be connected with Buddhist mandalas of India, Tibet, and China. The kata of the No mime-dance reveal the influence of bugaku in their elaborate symbolism, codification into abstract signs, simplicity, and geometric and architectural grace.

While abstract kata do not have specific denotata, they appear to take on meaning in relation to the kata which precede and follow them, as well as in association with the words in sections of the chanted text. They express the inner attitudes of the shite through a kind of mobile geometry, which is animated by inner tensions or Efforts as well as by the spiritual control of the performer.

THE NO MIME—DANCE AND POETRY

Scholars believe that Japanese poetry, which forms the basis of the No text, began in the shaman's recitation of his spiritual voyage. Nakayama cites the miko's trance utterance as being "the womb of literature."[64] The miko receives the characteristic shamanic gift of poetic inspiration. According to Frank Hoff, it is "possible to view the relation of poetry, that is, song, to significant movement (*fuzei*, to use Zeami's term), as part of a longer continuity in Japan which extends back to song for shaman-related dance."[65]

The No plays are structured in a manner similar to the telling of a story by the possessed shaman; many "are structured very much like an illustrated, acted-out narration of a past event—more like a narrated reenactment than like the apparent presentation of the actual event itself, as is the common practice in kabuki and Western drama."[66] In the No, the kata of the mime-dance serve as semantic equivalents to meanings in the text. As in shamanic enactment, they appear to proceed from and accompany the verbal recitation.

Zeami considered dancing and singing ("The Two Mediums") to be the basis for actor training in the No. The dance, according to Zeami, conveys the meaning of the song, chanted by the shite and chorus, in an outward and visible form:

> The musical element in No appeals to the ear and the posturing appeals to the eye of the audience. Everything in No has its own style, based upon the meaning of the worlds, for it is language by which the profound meaning is conveyed. Song is the substance of No and elegant carriage is its expression.[67]

As the author of many No plays, Zeami offers his advise to other playwrights on how to enable the actor to derive the action naturally from the singing. He suggests that the playwright "must write down the singing passages in his text while always bearing in mind the action that accompanies them."[68] The result is that realistic and symbolic kata tend to be postural and gestural signs for the images in the text. According to Zeami:

> All the various kinds of movement in the No involved in performance depend on the text. Such things as bodily posture and carriage follow from this, as well. Specifically, one must project feelings that are in accord with the words being spoken. For example, when the idea of observing some object is suggested in the text, the actor performs a gesture of looking; if such matters as pointing or pulling are mentioned, then the appropriate gestures must be made; when a sound is to be heard, the actor assumes the attitude of listening.[69]

The more numerous abstract kata, which form the substance of long instrumental dances and have no fixed meaning, appear to take on poetic significance through juxtaposition with images in the chanted text.

The relation between the kata and the text, according to Frank Hoff, seems to be one of equivalence. The kata can be looked upon as "metaphors for certain verbal meanings in the chanted poem, in the No ... movement is not exclusively mimetic, not literal, directly illustrative of the text. Rather it is suggestive."[70] The No texts are essentially poetic language, rich in images and allusions, whose purpose is the lyrical evocation of the most deeply felt attitudes (thoughts and emotions) of the shite. Poetic images in the No are characterized by the density of their symbolism — a word or phrase may contain layer upon layer of meaning. For example, the Japanese word *matsu* (pine tree) is a metaphor which, while denoting a specific tree, encompasses the attitudes of to pine away or longing. According to Ueda, the pine tree carries the additional overtones of "permanence," "constancy in love," and the "eternal God who rules both man and the cosmos."[71] Thus the pine tree condenses cosmic, human and religious levels of meaning into one poetic image. Similarly, the kata rarely function in a purely denotative capacity; rather they tend to serve as metaphors which convey the underlying emotional and spiritual attitudes of the central character.

> It is painful to see an actor who speaks the line "I feel ashamed to see the moon" and then hides his face with his open fan while speaking to the actor facing him, without looking at the moon, all the while stooping and crouching in a realistic manner. Rather, at the words "see the moon," the actor should lift up his open fan high, so as to reveal the fact that his shame concerning the moon forms the basis of his gesture. Then, while glancing at the other actor, he can perform with a slight suggestion of emotion (revealing his embarrassment toward human beings as well). In this way the actor can give rise to a striking artistic effect.[72]

According to Zeami, this kata, if done correctly, combines into one gesture: the moon (which is portrayed by the fan); the action of indicating the moon (through the lifting of the fan); and the action of hiding from the moon (in which the fan serves a double function of shielding the shite from the moon). While expressing these various meanings in a complex symbolic gesture, the kata serves primarily to convey the underlying emotion of shame.

THE TRIPARTITE STRUCTURE
OF THE NO KATA

According to Zeami, the actor's first task in monomane is to grasp a character role in terms of its underlying attitude and to convey this externally through posture. Equally important, he must also discover the essential rhythm of the attitudes expressed through the character's postures and gesture and convey these through the rhythmical structure of *jo-ha-kyu*. According to Masakazu Yamazaki, "The bodily and mental attitude and the rhythm of action (jo-ha-kyu) complement each other in acting; the former is the spacial support of acting, and the latter its chronological axis."[73]

Jo-ha-kyu, which forms the structural principle of all the elements of the No, is originally derived from *gigaku* and meant a "three-part piece played at a gradually increasing tempo."[74] Zeami viewed jo-ha-kyu as the universal rhythm of nature innate, "in all things in the universe, good and bad, large and small, with life and without." It is to be found in such things as "the chirping of birds and the buzzing of insects."[75] The No is based on an animistic mode of perception which derives from the mimesis of the gestic or operational aspects of nature. The No plays take place against an imaginary backdrop of natural surroundings. The texts and songs are interwoven with lines describing, contemplating or enjoying nature, and the attitudes of the characters are frequently expressed by means of poetic metaphors based in natural imagery.

The jo-ha-kyu is similar to the rhythmical structure of the tripartite mimeme (Agent-Agissant-Agi) which Marcel Jousse identifies as forming the basic unit of all actions in the phenomenal world. Like the spoken phrase or poetic image, the structure of the kata is tripartite. Jo means beginning, ha means development in time and space or breaking, and kyu means quick.[76] The dramatic power of the kata is a product of the operational tensions between these three elements. According to Barba:

> The first phase is determined by the opposition between a force which tends to increase and another which holds back (jo = withhold); the second phase (ha = to break) occurs in the moment in which one is liberated from this force, until one arrives at the third phase (kyu = rapidity) in which the action reaches its culmination, using up all of its force to suddenly stop as if face to face with an obstacle, a new resistance.[77]

Zeami states, "The pattern of jo-ha-kyu is visible even in one gesture in a dance, or in the echo of one step."[78] For example, in the kata of standing, jo would be the preparation for movement consisting of the inner mobilization of muscles and energy, as well as a shift of balance or weight. There is an opposing force between the pull downward to remain seated and a movement upwards to stand. Komparu suggests that jo refers to position and is thus a spatial element.[79] Ha consists of the breaking away from the downward force and out of the postural form through a gesture which epitomizes the action of the kata. In the kata of standing this would involve the lifting of the knee off the floor through a visible shift of weight to the rear and the upward progression to the standing position. The kyu is a temporal element characterized by quickness or the increasing tempo of movement leading up to the posture or held pose which summarizes the essence of the kata. In the kata of standing, the left foot is brought quickly to the side of the fight foot as a punctuation while the arms simultaneously assume their final position. While the movement stops, there is a continued momentum in the final posture as if the body were still rising and moving forward.

THE KATA, ATTITUDE, AND NARRATIVE MIMESIS

The tension contained in the posturally based movement patterns of the shite mirrors the deeply felt emotion conveyed by the sung images of the text.

The relationship between kata and the images of the No text can be seen in Hyakuman, which depicts a grief-stricken mother's search for her lost child. It is one of the oldest extant No plays and thus, according to Nakamura, "the mime element in it is strong": "Each kata (movement pattern) of the shite is a movement which illustrates the lyrics of the *utai*. This is especially true of the movement patterns in the ... *kuruma no dan* and *sasa no dan*."[80]

The kuruma no dan is literally the cart pulling scene which reveals Hyakuman's suffering heart and deranged mind. The cart image and related verbs of pulling in the utai (chanted verse) are unifying metaphors which are used throughout both *dan* (scenes) to symbolize the burden of sorrow carried by Hyakuman. The most clearly mimetic gesture which is both realistic and symbolic is the kata of cart pulling in which the shite places the bamboo branch she is carrying in her left hand, turns towards the left and mimes pulling a cart. This kata illustrates the following verses of the utai:

> shite: I tug at my cart, its burden as of seven carriages.
> Chorus: Never yielding to exhaustion.
> shite: I pull its unbearable weight.

The sasa no dan (literally, the bamboo branch scene) depicts Hyakuman's love for her lost child. In this scene, the shite mimes the choral passage, "I am bound to my love from past to present and beyond into the future, yoked like an oxen to a cart" by placing the bamboo branch around her neck and walking a little towards the left and right. This is followed by the kata of cart pulling to the lines, "[chorus] destined to drag my burden/ [shite] dragging this cart."

Many of the abstract kata, which appear to have no meaning when viewed separately from the text, seem to take on significance in relation to such lines as, "I go towards the West," (*sayu*) and "As weeds in wild disarray" (*hiraki*). There are also several indicative gestures as when the shite points with her branch on the lines "a wondrous sight," and to her *eboshi* (hat) on the lines "she wears the ancient eboshi."

The No mime-dance is a pure example in dramatic art of movement held up from going into action. The kata are figurations of mental tensions so profound and intense, that they cause an immobilization of the body. They are not so much a series of movements as they are *tableaux vivants*, which represent the inward struggle of attitudes for expression. The shite appears to be poised between two worlds or two moments of time, seeking to move forward but pulled by the past—a dynamic principle which is conveyed by opposing movement forces which hold the body in check. When the shite finally breaks forth into movement, his gestures appear to engrave the surrounding space—tracing through their bound movements a portrait of his inner landscape of thought and emotion. Gesture in the No begins from immobility and ends in the immobility of a crystallized posture in which the gesture is frozen at its point of greatest emotional intensity.

The No mime-dance is closely connected to ritual. It, therefore, provides evidence of a continuity in creative process and in performance elements between ritual and post-ritual forms of Mime. The creative process of the No actor is analogous to that of the possessed shaman. The actor seeks a state of dissociation comparable to ecstasy in which he strives to bypass the habitual attitudes that comprise his ego in order to become identified with a character image latent within himself. He conveys the essential attitudes of the character both through the assumption of its characteristic posture and Efforts, as well as through gestural images (kata) which serve as metaphors for meanings contained in the accompanying text.

The No actor possesses the shamanic ability of doubling his consciousness. While he performs from a state of unknowing in which his performance seems to flow effortlessly from the realms of subconscious, he is able to remain aware and in control of his body-instrument in order to create the desired effect on his audience. This process contributes to the aesthetics of the marionette, in which the No actor appears to be a piece of sculpture animated by an external force (latent attitudes). In reality his bodily movements are carefully regulated by his controlling mind and will (kokoro), which are analogous to the strings manipulated by a marionettist.

Like the formalized gestural languages of shamanic ritual, the No mime-dance is made up of conventional signs which function as metaphorical equivalents for images in the accompanying text. The verbal and gestural language of the No is closely patterned on the rhythm of nature that underlies all phenomena. As in the *mimeme* of Agent–Acting Upon–Agent which forms the nucleus of all action in the material world, the No kata is a rhythmical tripartite entity consisting of pose–progression–pose. While the kata were originally purely mimetic signs, denoting concrete phenomena within the realm of the viewer's experience, they were refined, abstracted and stylized by Zeami who sought to reduce their mimetic content. The reduction of concrete gesture to its barest traits of line and dynamism in order to create a stylized, symbolic and suggestive language that conveys the inner world of a character is comparable to trends among many of today's mime performers. Indeed, the No has not only had a profound influence on the modern Japanese theatre in such forms a *bhuto*, but has deeply influenced the modern French mime.

Chapter Seven

The Greco-Roman Pantomimes

The Greco-Roman pantomime grew out of a matrix of mime-based performance genres that existed for centuries in Italy and Greece. Prior to the birth of pantomime in 240 B.C., Mime was the most popular form of theatre entertainment in the Roman Republic (509–27 B.C.). The term mime (mimus) was used to designate almost any type of theatrical performance as well as the performer. Pantomime (*pantomimus*) originated in Rome in the third century B.C. and came to rival the mime in popularity. Panto meant "all" and mimus meant "to imitate." Pantomime differed from the mime in that one individual acted a variety of roles in a specially adapted dramatic text (*canticum*) which was chanted and sung by an accompanying actor or chorus. Performers used a language of conventional gesture to translate the verbal images of the canticum into corresponding corporeal images.

The difference between the mime and pantomime is too great to point to a genetic evolution. The Atellan farce continued the satyric style and subject matter of the Dorian mime in group performances characterized by improvisation, stock character-types, dialogue, and burlesque of myth and Roman society. The maskless mimes that existed alongside the Atellan farce also derived from the revels and entertainments associated with Roman fertility rituals, as evidenced by their preference for sexual themes parodying Roman domestic life. The pantomime was more serious in tone. Its subject matter derived wholly from myth and legend, and while adaptations of Greek comedy marked its origins, it quickly took the literature of tragedy for its subject matter. The solo, silent, and narrative style of the pantomime formed a startling contrast to the noisy, group performances of the largely improvised mime plays.

While pantomime undoubtedly incorporated elements of the preexisting mime, its unique characteristics indicate that it arose from an altogether different source than the ribald antics of mimes at Greek and Roman fertility festivals. This source was the Greek dance (*orchesis*). Pantomime was considered an "art of interpretive dancing" and existed among the Greeks in various forms of dance accompanied by song.[1] The earliest known and most influential of these song-dances forms was the *hyporcheme* in which performers mimed the words of a song while they sang it. Hyporchemes were written by the early poets who also composed the music and the dance figures. The schemata (codified postures and gestures) of the hyporchemes were carried over into the choral dances where they continued to illustrate the accompanying chanted and sung verse.[2]

The Romans were well acquainted with the Greek dance and drama. From the middle of the third century B.C., most Roman tragedy and comedy were based on Greek models. Various forms of song and dance genres existed in Rome, but the one from which pantomime arose was that in which one individual would "sing a tragedy" (*cantare tragaediam*) as well as "dance a tragedy" (*saltare tragaediam*) to the accompaniment of music.[3] Legend has it that pantomime was inaugurated with the performance of playwright and actor Livius Andronicus in 260 B.C., who while singing and dancing one of his tragedies before an audience, lost his voice and asked a slave to continue reciting the text while he acted out the verbal images in pantomime. The separation of dance from song, which had heretofore been interpreted by one actor, proved so popular that, by all accounts, in the next two hundred years it lead to the creation of the genre known today as the Greco-Roman pantomime.

THE SHAMANIC ROOTS OF THE PANTOMIME

The technique of singing and mimetically dancing a dramatic narrative is of very ancient Greek origin. It existed among the ancient bards or rhapsoidoi who recreated the myths and heroic legends through spoken and sung recitation accompanied by mime. The bards in turn hold much in common with the shaman and there is evidence that the poetic and narrative function of the bard derived from shamanic performance. While there are strong parallels between the performance of the shaman, the art of the rhapsoidoi, and the unique genre of the Greco-Roman pantomime, there is little historical evidence which shows a direct line of evolution from shamanic techniques to the appearance of Greco-Roman pantomime in the second century A.D.

A tenuous shamanic connection to the pantomime can be traced to the cult of Isis and Astarte in Egypt and Phoenicia, where it seems there reigned a certain form of possession involving ritual pantomime. Libanius in his treatise on the Greco-Roman pantomime refers to Egypt as the "first parent of the pantomimic dance."[4] Lucian traces pantomimic dancing back to the Egyptian Proteus, who was either a king or a Greek sea-divinity possessed of transformational and prophetic powers.[5] Apparently, as accounts go, when seized, Proteus changed into flame, water, and a variety of animals, one after the other; but if his assailant held him fast, he resumed his own shape and foretold the future. Lucian states that the Egyptian Proteus was nothing but a pantomime performing an old ritual dance, perhaps to a sea or river divinity, in which a prominent individual, a priest, or a priest king portrayed mimetically a sequence of ideas such as lion, fire, serpent, water, etc. It is possible that Proteus was a type of trickster shaman who became possessed by various helping spirits while making a ritual voyage and communicated the events of his journey to his audience through corporeal and vocal mime. In addition he seems to have had the shamanic powers of a seer and a prophet which enabled him to foretell future events.

In ancient Greece, shamanism existed in the form of a female medium or *pythia* of Apollo at Delphi. She engaged in a special form of trance combining elements of cataleptic ecstasy and possession in which the god took possession of her immobilized body and used her vocal chords to speak. She did not enact its behavior through mimesis or mimetic dance. There is also no indication that she maintained a lucid trance which enabled her to remember what the god had said.

THE GREEK POETS AND SHAMANISM

The bards, the earliest Greek epic poets, are the most convincing link between shamanism and the origin of pantomime. The arts of poetry and prophesy where closely intertwined in the minds of the Greeks. They were believed to be gifts of the gods which were only available under the influence of possession or divine madness. Plato refers to these two types of inspiration as Prophetic Madness and Poetic Madness. By Prophetic Madness he meant the divinely inspired utterances of the Apollonian pythia.[6] The special creative madness of the poet he attributed to "possession by the Muses." According to Plato, the poet (artist) comes into contact with ideal beauty or the higher realms of existence through a form of divine inspiration in which the gods or muses use him to transmit their messages. Socrates tells Ion the rhapsodist, "A poet is a light and winged and sacred thing, and is unable ever to indite until he has been inspired and put out of his senses, and his mind is no longer in him. . . . For not by art do they utter these things, but by divine influence."[7]

The creative process of the poet, according to Plato, is similar to that of the inspired seers, mediums, and shamans. He alone possesses the divine inspiration to see into past events and embody these images in poetry. According to H.M. and N.K. Chadwick, Indo-European languages had a common term for poet and seer: "It is clear that throughout the ancient languages of northern Europe the ideas of poetry, eloquence, information (especially antiquarian learning) and prophesy are intimately connected."[8]

The earliest Greek poets were the ancient Epic bards (rhapsoidoi) depicted in Homer's *Iliad* and *Odyssey* (1200 to 800 B.C.). The bards were ancient story tellers attached to wealthy men's homes who functioned to instruct and entertain their entourage by recounting the adventures of the Greek gods and heros. The bards mark an historical transition from the shamanic arts of storytelling and prophesy to the art of poetry. In the *Odyssey*, the bard is acknowledged as a man with special knowledge who "sings by grace of gods, knowing delightful epic tales."[9] E. R. Dodds, in summing up the connection between the divine madness of the poet and prophet, states that in ancient Greece

> vision of the past, like insight into the future, remained a mysterious faculty, only partially under its owner's control, and dependent in the last resort on divine grace. By that grace poet and seer alike enjoyed a knowledge denied to other men. In Homer the two professions (poet and seer) are quite distinct; but we have good reason to believe that they had once been united, and the analogy between them was still felt.[10]

The bard's techniques, like that of the shaman, involved bringing alive the great heroic myths of by-gone ages through a narrative accompanied by role playing and vocal and gestural mimesis. As such, the bard may be seen as the prototype of the tragic actor and the Greco-Roman pantomime.[11] According to Michael Walton, in looking at the performances of the bard that are depicted in books one and eight of the Odyssey, we can see three elements that translated directly into the Greek tragedy and subsequently into the pantomime. First, the bard functions as a medium by which images or scenes from recent history or from the myths of the Olympian gods are conjured in the audience's imagination. Secondly, he conveys information and emotion through role playing involving mimesis. In book eight of the Odyssey, when the bard tells the story of Ares and Aphrodite (which was also a standard piece of the Greco-Roman pantomime), he indicates the various characters in the story by adopting elements of their identifying vocal and gestural traits. However, his performance is not truly dramatic because he does not become these characters, which would demand a fuller representation. Thirdly, the bard often performs with a chorus of dancers, who simultaneously translate the spoken and sung narrative into corresponding corporeal images.

PANTOMIME AND GREEK TRAGEDY

In the sixth century B.C., the rhapsodes had spread to all parts of Greece and recited regularly at Athens. The subject matter of their heroic stories was the fantastic exploits, wars, and adventures of god-like, larger than life individuals. According to Else, "The rhapsodes did not merely recite Homer, they acted him, and from this quasi impersonation of Homeric characters it was only a step to full impersonation, from the rhapsode who momentarily spoke in the person of the hero to the 'actor' who presented the hero."[12]

The transition between epic narrative and tragedy was effected in Athens in sixth century B.C. by Thespis, who seems to have been connected in some way with epic singing. Thespis is credited by Else with creating the *direct* impersonation of the epic hero by separating a single actor from the Dithyrambic chorus. This lone actor took to wearing a mask and probably changed character during the tragedy by leaving the stage to don a new mask and costume. While he was offstage, the chorus danced and sang connecting passages. The actor engaged in a dialogue with the chorus or its leader, and when the actor had long speeches, the function of the chorus was to reinforce their meaning through mimetic dance. Embryonic pantomime was present both in the direct impersonation of the actor who became the various characters of the drama and in the technique and function of the choral dance for tragedy.

"The Greeks tended to regard all dancing as 'mimetic,' or expressive, especially in its employment of rhythmical gestures and motions."[13] The purpose of ancient dancing was to represent various objects and events by means of gestures, postures, and attitudes.[14] The dance of the tragic chorus was characterized by symbolic and conventional gestures (cheironomia). This code of gestures was apparently well established by the fifth century and was learned as an art. Readily understood by the spectator, cheironomia appear to have been composed primarily of manual gestures and bodily postures conveying character, action and emotion. Descriptions of the dance indicate that the bottom half of the body moved very little, probably consisting of a walk. The upper half expressed itself in stylized postures and gestures. The ten that are mentioned in ancient sources include muscular tension, rapidity of motion, marked admiration, pointing, mimetic carrying of an imaginary object on the palm of the hand, abandon, deterrence, and caution or stealth. The most common gesture was a tense palm turned upward with fingers open and curved back, used when the chorus reacted to horrible news or events.[15] In time, the dance of the tragic chorus reached a high degree of mimetic clarity enabling it to stand on its own without recourse to the spoken or chanted word. Thus, side by side with the dance of the chorus there arose a separate genre of pure pantomimic dance, which was a forerunner of the Greco-Roman pantomime.[16]

Greek dancing, according to Plato, originated in the instinctive tendency of mankind to accompany speech and song with explanatory movements of the body.[17] Dancing was seen by the Greeks as poetry without words. The close connection between these arts can be seen in the fact that the early dramatic poets, such as Thespis, Phrynichus, Pratinas, and Cratinus, were known as dancers as well as poets. The poets not only composed the schemata or dance figures for the chorus, they also trained their choruses in the art of dancing.[18] Aeschylus personally superintended the training of the chorus and is said to have invented a great number of postures and attitudes to be used in dancing.[19] Sophocles was also an accomplished dancer as well as a choral dance instructor. The dance schemata for tragedy were so mimetically descriptive that Telestes, Aeschylus' principal dancer and choreographer, was able to make the action in Seven Against Thebes clearly understandable solely through pantomimic dance.[20]

The fact that the early dramatists were primarily dancers gives us an idea that literary mimesis was closely linked in its origins with dance and that the essence of Greek drama, especially tragedy, is to be found in mimetic dance. Early poets seem to have first conceived their plays in an internal mimesis of imagery in the muscles and bones of their bodies. Aristotle advises the tragic poet to become in a sense the tragic hero and to conceive of his plays as an internal mimesis of the hero's struggle with destiny.

> In constructing the plot and working it out with the proper diction, the poet should place the scene, as far as possible, before his eyes. . . . The poet should work out his play, to the best of his power with appropriate gestures; for those who feel emotion are most convincing through natural sympathy with the characters they represent.[21]

What is important in this passage is that the poet, during the process of constructing his plots, mimetically identifies with the essential underlying emotion of the characters and conveys it outwardly in gesture and action. It is this internal mimesis that when externalized forms the basis of the art of pantomime. "The mime in essence was the very incarnation, the first ideal of that mimesis on which is based the whole of the peripatetic literary theory . . . [it was] the pure example in dramatic art of Aristotle's theory of mimesis."[22]

Aristotle, along with other early Greek philosophers, did not believe that artistic mimesis was conceived of as a literal replica of nature, concerned solely with the depiction of external traits. An artist should not content himself with a superficial glance at the object, but should attempt to penetrate its inner structure. In the *Poetics,* Aristotle states that the objects of imitation are not things or persons which the arts copy, but human actions mimetically represented. When Aristotle says that poets imitate actions, he does not mean physical activity but a movement of spirit or *energeia.*[23] The ancient concept of mimesis essentially meant the outward expression of deeply felt attitudes by means of verbal and corporeal action. According to Samuel Butcher, it was a reproduction of "an inward process, a psychical energy working outwards; deeds, incidents, events, [and] situations, being included under it so far as these spring from an inward act of will, or elicit some activity of thought or feeling."[24]

The tragic rhythm of the action is based in what Kenneth Burke terms "Purpose to Passion to Perception." Purpose signifies the motivation from which the actions of the tragic hero spring; passion, the suffering or pathos of the tragic hero which both produces and is a product of tragic action; and perception, the contemplation and understanding of the truth of the pattern of action. While Greek tragedy portrays a series of one or more incidents in the hero's life which reveal his fate, according to Else it is more concerned not with what the hero does but with what he suffers (*pathos*). The ultimate outcome of the tragic action, however, was not Dionysian frenzy, but rational and sober contemplation. Greek tragedy concludes with the hero's perception of himself and the chorus' perception of him as a hero and rebel. The logos of the tragic actor, according to Else, is particularly un–Dionysian and even anti–Dionysian. It is founded primarily on the self-perception of the hero. The tragic hero presents himself as an irreducibly separate person. His self-awareness is opposite of the Dionysian abandonment of possession. Like the shaman and the bard, the heroic personage embodied by the actor must be able to both participate in the suffering brought about by his actions and stand at a distance from himself in order to obtain the perception that derives from contemplation of the cause of his suffering.

THE BIRTH OF GRECO-ROMAN PANTOMIME

To recapitulate, there were three important elements present in the early Greek tragedy that needed to unite before pantomime could be born: 1) the poet who creates the dramatic images of the performance; 2) the actor who becomes these images; and 3) the dancer who possesses the technique to embody images. This fusion was effected in the person of Livius Andronicus who is credited with establishing pantomime as a popular performance genre in Rome in 240 B.C.

Like the Greek tragic poets, Livius Andronicus, a freed slave, was a well-known playwright, actor, and dancer. As the legend goes, while performing his first complete dramatic work in verse before an enthusiastic audience, he lost his voice, whereupon he called upon a young slave to declaim the lines of the text while he acted it out in pantomimic dance. Livy states that his performance was even more animated than before, because he was no longer forced to divide himself between gestures and words.[25] It met with instant success and inaugurated a new genre in the performing arts that was to lead to the development of the Greco-Roman pantomime.

Pantomime originated in the separation of word and gesture in which a single dancer/actor would mime the verses of the *cantica* or monodic texts, while they were spoken, chanted and sung by another performer. In Greek tragedy, the mimetic content of the images was expressed by the gestures of the actor(s) and the dance of the chorus. These were now combined in the art of the pantomime, which took over the mimetic dance of the chorus and united it to the mime of the actor. Despite the popularity of the pantomimed narration of the solo performer, the verbal element continued to predominate during the two hundred years that followed Livius Andronicus' performance.

PYLADES AND BATHYLLUS

Pantomime came into its own as a gestural art form in the first century A.D. during the reign of Augustus (63 B.C.–A.D. 14) in the work of two consummate artists: Pylades and Bathyllus. They are credited with downplaying the importance of the canticum in favor of increased spectacle. Pylades replaced the lone actor, who had recited the canticum to the accompaniment of a flute player, with a full orchestra and a choir that chanted at certain intervals, indicating the direction of the plot. In addition, the almost bare stage gave way to elaborate scenery while costumes became more sumptuous. This new form of dance was originally called *Italica orchesis,* or *Italica saltatio,* and its performers were called *pantomimi.*[26]

Pylades, who was probably a freed Sicilian slave of Augustus, was the greatest of the Greco-Roman pantomimes. His style was directly inspired by the solemn dance (emmeleia) of the Greek tragedy, and by all accounts, his performances were dignified and deeply moving.[27] Lucian's dialogue on pantomime "Saltatio," written in the second century A.D., lists an imposing number of pieces in Pylades' repertoire. He excelled in such subjects as "The Angry Hercules," "The Loves of Jupiter and Apollo," "The Feats of Ajax, Prometheus and Hector," and "The Judgment of Paris."

Bathyllus was a freed slave and native of Alexandria whose forte was the performance of comic pieces featuring the amorous exploits of the Olympian society. His most famous piece was "Jupiter and Leda." His quick-paced and light-hearted style was similar to the Greek comic dance kordax. According to Athenaeus, "Pylades' dancing was solemn, expressing passion and variety of character, whereas Bathyllus's was more jolly."[28]

Pylades and Bathyllus went into management together in Rome about 22 B.C., and pantomime flourished as a result. There is evidence that they toured the provinces and opened schools. Their fame was so great that they consorted with emperors and were idolized by nobility as well as the common man. Their effect upon audiences rivaled that of modern film idols and rock stars. Audiences appear to have been mesmerized. Women frequently fainted, and riots broke out at performances between fans of the two artists. Their partnership, however, was soon dissolved due to jealousy and rivalry. In time the tragic style of Pylades prevailed as the norm for pantomime, and the lighter style of Bathyllus disappeared. While the popularity of comic pantomime was short-lived, the tragic pantomime outlived the Roman empire.[29] At the height of the Empire, there were more than six thousand pantomimes throughout the Roman world, and the performances of the best of these outshone all other forms of theatrical entertainment in popularity.

From the first century A.D. to the fourth century, the pantomimes who appeared on the Roman stage and at religious festivals were male. The Greco-Roman pantomimes essentially continued the domination of the male performer that began with the reorganization of the drama in the Athenian state festivals in the fifth century B.C. In the three genres of Greek drama, tragedy, comedy, and satyr plays, all the roles were performed by men, a custom which carried over into the solo performances of the pantomimes. Women pantomimes existed as part of pantomime troupes and were generally slaves who performed minor and sexually stereotyped roles of love goddesses and prostitutes. Prior to the fourth century, female pantomimes were only allowed to perform at aristocratic festivals and wealthy men's banquets, where their highly erotic performances served to arouse their audience sexually. Women pantomimes only appeared on the public stage when decadence began to encroach on Roman society and the arts. By all accounts, they performed semi-nude and portrayed all manner of sexual acts before the public. However, women pantomimes could and did achieve status through their art in the later days of the Empire. In the sixth century A.D., the Byzantine emperor Justinian fell in love with and married a famous female pantomime, Theodora, who was renowned for her beauty and erotic performance style.

CHARACTERISTICS OF THE PANTOMIME

Pantomime was from the first a solo performance in which one masked performer represented all the characters in the play. The classical dance scholar, Lillian Lawler, fleshing out the descriptions provided by ancient authors, describes the performance of the pantomimus as follows:

> After the introductory music, a prologist came forward, and summarized briefly the story which was to be enacted. When he had finished, the chorus, reduced now to an off-stage choir, began to sing; and then, with a flourish, the pantomimus appeared, resplendent in a flowing robe of silk embroidered with gold and jewels, a swirling cloak, and a great mask with closed mouth. Making use of the old Greek art of cheironomia, "speaking gestures," and displaying all the intoxicating grace and suppleness, agility and strength and virtuosity for which he was famous, the great dancer acted, rhythmically, a scene from an ancient myth. In it, he assumed one part, as a rule; but so great was his skill that he suggested other characters, simultaneously. . . . He leaped and crouched, twisted and turned, performed dazzling feats of balance, halted in poses of statuesque beauty. At the end of the scene, the dancer withdrew. During a short musical and choral interlude he changed costume and mask, to reappear as another character in the next scene of the mythological story. This was repeated four or five times, until the whole of the legend was unfolded. The performance closed in a final burst of music, and a tumult of applause.[30]

The above description provides a clue to the key elements that contributed to the unique style of the pantomime. First, the most striking aspect of the pantomime's art was that through vivid role playing and the use of mask and costume he seemed to be the actual incarnation of the super-human gods and heros. Second, his art was based in the corporeal enactment of the great myths and legends of the Greco-Roman world. Third, he dazzled his audience by means of rapid metamorphosis from one character to another. Fourth, his style consisted of rapid movements which contrasted with statuesque poses of the body. Fifth, he used a corporeal language composed of hand gestures, cheironomia, and bodily postures and gestures to make phrases of movement, schemata, that were corporeal equivalents or signs for the verbal images.

While there are many short references by critics and historians of the time to the performances of pantomimes, much of what we know about this genre comes to us from Lucian's treatise on pantomime ("Saltatio"), which many scholars believe may be an adaption of the lost essay by Pylades on pantomime ("Peri Orcheseos"). According to Lucian, the most important qualities that a pantomime needed was a thorough knowledge and memory of all of the recorded myths and legends of the Greco-Roman world. The pantomime should "not be ignorant of anything that is told by Homer and Hesiod the best poets and above all by tragedy...."[31] and

> Like Calchas [the bard] in Homer, the dancer must know "what is, and what shall be, and was of old," so thoroughly that nothing will escape him, but his memory of it all will be prompt. To be sure, it professes in the main to be a science of imitation and portrayal, of revealing what is in the mind and making intelligible what is obscure.[32]

According to Marguerite Bieber, "Boredom with the endlessly repeated subjects of tragedy led to the development of the pantomime."[33] The pantomimes not only performed lesser known stories of the gods and heros for their audiences, but gave fresh life to the old, time-worn subjects of the tragedy.

The pantomime performer was an important repository of these ancient stories and his function was to both instruct and entertain his entourage. Throughout his treatise on pantomime, Lucian stresses that the best pantomime performers were those who could serve the populace as models of learning and humanity.

> In general, the dancer should be perfect in every point, so as to be wholly rhythmical, graceful, symmetrical, consistent, unexceptional, impeccable, not wanting in any way, blessed of the highest qualities, keen in his ideas, profound in his culture, and above all, human in his sentiments. In fact, the praise that he gets from the spectators will be consummate when each of those who behold him recognizes his own traits, or rather sees in the dancer as in a mirror his very self, with his customary feelings and actions. Then people cannot contain themselves for pleasure, and with one accord they burst into applause, each seeing the reflection of his own soul and recognizing himself. Really, that Delphic monition "Know thyself" realizes itself in them from the spectacle, and when they go away from the theatre they have learned what they should choose and what avoid, and have been taught what they did not know before.[34]

Lucian obviously has a high conception of the pantomime's power to serve as a model and a teacher. That the people were hungry for direct, kinaesthetic participation in the underlying gestural impulses from which myths originated can be seen in the immense popularity of this genre, which overshadowed all other types of performance. The orator Libanius, as late as the fourth century A.D., states that the pantomime still continued to educate the people in these ancient stories.[35]

THE HEROIC STYLE

The solo pantomime captivated the popular imagination because he appeared to be a living incarnation of the great epic heros. Like the shaman, he took his audience with him on a voyage to the mythical past, making its images present before his audience. He alone among the artists of his time was able to translate the myths of the Greco-Roman world into heroic images that spoke to the imaginations of the men and women from all classes of society that made up his audience. There seems to have been a great demand on the part of the Roman public for subjects from the heroic age, when the gods and heros commanded the imagination of the Greco-Roman world with their glorious deeds. Pylades and Bathyllus actually made the Greek heros present before their audiences in a way that the tragic and comic actors of the time were unable to. According to Lawler, eye-witnesses repeatedly speak of the dancer "as appearing to be more than human, the actual incarnation of a divinity."[36] The pantomimes seem to have recaptured the original spark that was the essence of the birth of tragedy, when the actor stepped out of the chorus and with the aid of varying costumes and masks, portrayed a series of mythological characters. In eschewing the word, the Greco-Roman pantomime who used posture and gesture as his primary mode of communication approached more closely than the actor the essential archetypal attitudes that were rooted in these myths.

IDENTIFICATION AND METAMORPHOSIS

The ability of the pantomime to actually appear to be the images he enacted lay in the psychophysical technique of identification and metamorphosis that are the essence of mimesis. Lucian suggests that the pantomime's art derived from that of the mythical Proteus, who became what he imitated.[37] In a very real sense the pantomime was possessed by images, a possession he experienced within the muscles and bones of his body and expressed externally in corporeal equivalents. Lucian gives an example of true possession involving a pantomime in the role of Ajax.[38] As the story goes, while the pantomime was performing Ajax's madness on his loss to Odysseus of the arms of Achilles, the pantomime seemed to go actually insane. He tore off the clothes of one of the musicians who beat the time, seized a flute from another, struck Odysseus on the head with it, and would have killed him except that a cap protected his skull. Apparently the audience was infected by his madness and went wild along with him. The pantomime was so distraught by this experience that he refused to perform the dance any more for fear of going mad again.

This lack of control, which resulted in unrefined and exaggerated mimicry, was considered by Roman critics and audience alike to be in bad taste. The pantomime who portrayed the mad Ajax apparently ruined his reputation "upon an ugly bit of acting through exaggerated mimicry."[39] Lucian warns that the pantomime performer must never allow his technique to exceed "the due limit of mimicry" by putting forth "greater effort than they should."[40] The pantomime must not permit the attitudes or energies contained in the portrayal of agents and their actions to take full possession of his body. He must maintain total consciousness of the means of his performance and filter his expression through his mind and thereby shape his mimicry in terms of a subtle and refined technique. When the rival of the pantomime who portrayed the mad Ajax was cast in the same role, Lucian adds, he "enacted his madness so discreetly and sanely as to win praise, since he kept within the bounds of the dance and did not debauch the histrionic art."[41]

The pantomime's identification with imagery manifested itself in a style of performance typified by the corporeal technique of transformation. According to Lucian, the pantomime was able to shape himself and change himself into anything:

> He could imitate even the liquidity of water and the sharpness of fire in the liveliness of his movements; yes, the fierceness of a lion, the rage of a leopard, the quivering of a tree, and in a word whatever he wished. . . . Now just that thing is characteristic of dancers [pantomimes] today, who certainly may be seen changing swiftly at the cue and imitating Proteus himself.[42]

The psychophysical technique of the pantomime was based in an identification with the gestic content of imagery in which the performer embodied the underlying Efforts or energies contained in the gestures and formal shape of phenomena. For example, in the above passage, the pantomime portrays a variety of phenomenon by miming their characteristic gestures: a tree is indicated by its quivering motion; water, in terms of its liquidity (probably an undulation of the body and or hands); and fire by sharpness (perhaps involving quick, direct, light and free-flowing movements).

An essential element of the pantomime's art was the portrayal of all of the characters who made up the story. Like the Greek tragic and comic actors, this included women's roles. Characters were enacted by the pantomime in terms of their characteristic gestures, or in Aristotelian terms, their habitual action. In the above passage, the agents embodied by the pantomime are animals and natural phenomenon, both of whom's characteristic gestures are conceived of in terms of moral and emotional qualities. Thus, the tiger was portrayed as the embodiment of fierceness, and the lion the incarnation of rage. This is an essentially metaphorical process in which characteristic Efforts are selected as they relate to an important attitude which the pantomime wishes to convey to further the plot. The Efforts of the ancient gods and heros were also conceived of in terms of essential attitudes (moral and emotional qualities) rather than merely denotational mimesis. For example, Macrobius relates that Pylades portrayed Agamemnon with the posture of a thinker in profound meditation, because the general was always "preoccupied with weighty matters."[43]

ROLE PLAYING AND THE MASK

The pantomimes adopted the tragic actors' use of mask and multiple role playing within a single tragedy and made it the central feature of their art. The Romans were mesmerized by the rapidity with which the pantomimes could change character. The pantomimes seemed to have conveyed to their audiences the spiritual lightness of the magical hero. Their pliable bodies and flowing capes must have formed a startling contrast to the rigidity of the tragic actor. Like the ancient shaman's and bards, they took spectators on a voyage to the Illud Tempus and enabled them to imaginatively participate in the lives of the gods and heros. So immersed did the audiences become in the unfolding events of the pantomime that Lucian relates they became enraged over the misdeeds of the heros and wept over victims of injustice, and in the process were made better people.[44]

Transformation into characters was facilitated by the pantomime's assumption of one or more facial masks. Unlike the speaking actor who wore masks with large mouth openings, the Roman pantomime wore masks that covered the entire head and had no mouth openings. With the aid of these masks, the performer was able to display the age, sex and appropriate physiognomy of a role. The pantomime performances were generally designated as either "the dance of several masks," or "the dance of one mask."[45] The dance of several masks was made up of a certain number of cantica, which responded to the entrance of an equal number of characters. In these the pantomime underwent a series of rapid transformations offstage where they changed mask and costume.

However, in the dance of one mask, the pantomime portrayed one character and effected transformations through the use of posture, props, and costume. Some of the masks had a different expression painted on each side and depending on the side that was shown to the audience the performer could, for example, portray the character as happy one moment and sad the next by a simple turn of the head. While most performers changed costumes along with masks, others, according to Lawler, "wore a swirling cloak, and by slight rearrangement or handling of it managed to portray vividly all the characters of the story. With a twist of the cloak, say our ancient sources, he could portray a swan's tail, the tresses of Venus, a Fury's scourge."[46]

The pantomime's magical shaping of his cloak allowed him to indicate character, objects and emotion through the technique of imaginative transformation.

POSTURE AND ATTITUDE

De l'Aulnaye writes, "The art of the [Greco-Roman] pantomimes consisted of a series of more or less rapid movements, diverse attitudes [postures] and varied and imitative gestures."[47]

Held postures of the body were an important element of the pantomime's style. Lucian, in quoting Thucydides' statement on Pericles oratorical style, says, "What Thucydides said of Pericles in praising the man would also be the highest possible commendation of a dancer [pantomime], 'to know what is meet and express it;' and by expressing I mean the intelligibility of his postures."[48] The postures of the pantomime were based in part on the schemata of the Greek pantomimic dance. Schemata was a term used by the Greek poets for the figures they created for the choral dance. In its broader applications by the Greeks and Romans, it is used to refer variously to gesture, figure, pose, movement, pattern of motion, or picture, according to the context.[49] However, Plutarch, who was writing one hundred years after Livius Andronicus' performance, uses the term schemata in a narrow sense to refer to the holds or poses "to which the movements lead and in which they end."[50] According to Plutarch "the pose is imitative of shape and outward appearance" of phenomena.[51] Poses, which are held postural forms, seem to have been used in two ways by the pantomime: first, to depict character, actions and emotion through the maintenance of a bodily posture; and secondly, as a momentarily held pose which summarized the essence of a movement phrase. In *The Antique Greek Dance,* Maurice Emmanuel writes, "Sculptors in antiquity studied the poses of dancers [pantomimes], and the dancers, in turn, copied the poses of statues."[52]

The postural nature of the art of pantomime may be seen in the numerous references by Roman historians and critics to the close relationship between pantomime and sculpture. Lucian states that the pantomime "has not kept away from painting and sculpture, but manifestly copies above all else the rhythm that is in them."[53] Libanius tells us that "the pantomimes halted in poses of statuesque beauty"[54] and compares the pantomime to a sculptor or a painter, who creates pictures in the dance by a sudden stopping short of the performer "as if glued" to the spot.[55] Elsewhere, we know that in a particular genre of mime in the first century B.C. (*staticulous saltare*), actors recited verse and danced in place by means of posed attitudes of the body, possibly emulating those of pantomimes.[56]

The enactment of deeply felt attitudes and strong emotion by means of posture is the essence of mimesis. Postural freezing results from strong emotion held up from going into action. The movement phrase, according to Plutarch, "was expressive of some emotion or action or potentiality."[57] Here he seems to indicate that strong emotions are what animated these poses and were actualized in the movement that preceded or followed them. All accounts indicate that the portrayal of agents beset by strong emotion was one of the most popular

features of the pantomime's performances. The pantomime, according to Lucian, set forth the three parts of the soul, "the orgillous part when he exhibits a
man in a rage, the covetous part when he enacts lovers, and the reasoning part
when he bridles and governs each of the different passions."[58] In another passage, he continues, "In general, the dancer undertakes to present and enact
characters and emotions, introducing now a lover and now an angry person,
one man afflicted with madness, another with grief, and all this within fixed
bounds."[59]

Athenaeus states that Pylades' performance was characterized by "passion
and a variety of characters,"[60] and he portrayed heros and heroines in the throes
of strong emotion, such as the maddened Hercules. The articulation of attitudes as they animated character postures and actions formed the basis for
the language of pantomime. The pose distilled a frozen image, conveying the
"emotion, action, or potentiality" of the movement phrase. This stylistic
technique allowed the audience to sense kinesthetically the essence of the attitude that underlay the phrase.

CHEIRONOMIA OR LANGUAGE
OF THE HANDS IN PANTOMIME

In addition to global corporeal postures and gestures, the performer had
a large repertoire of hand signs (cheironomia) which were the primary semantic
vehicles of the pantomime. Cassiodorus spoke of the pantomimes as "Men
whose eloquent hands had a tongue, as it were, on the tip of each finger — men
who spoke while they were silent, and knew how to make a recital without
opening their mouths."[61]

Pylades was a master of cheironomia which indicates that he had probably
studied both the arts of tragedy and dancing. The two careers were distinct at
the time, but the elaborate code of gestures, cheironomia, was common to both.
Cheironomia seems to have been well established by the fifth century B.C. and
taught as an art in special schools.[62]

Hand signs functioned primarily as microcosms of global corporeal schemata. Like these, they involved both a momentarily held position as well as a
gesture. The position or posture of the hand summarizes the essence of the sign
and allows the spectator a moment of readability in what would otherwise be a
rapid flow of movement. These signs were accompanied for the most part by
global corporeal postures and gestures. If the performers had merely translated
the text by means of cheironomia, the pantomime would have quickly waned
in popularity. As indicated in the following description by Cassiodorus, the
pantomime appeared to speak principally by means of the cheironomia, while
he expressed character by means of bodily posture, gesture, and walk:

> The actor appeared on the scene to the acclamations of the spectators.
> A choir of instruments accompanied him. By the sole movement of his

hands, he explained to the eyes the poem that was chanted by the musicians. And by employing gestures composed, as in writing, where one uses letters, he spoke to the vision and rendered sensible even to the slightest nuance of his discourse and showed without speaking all that writing is able to express. The same body presented to us Hercules or Venus, a King or a soldier, a man or a woman, an old man or an adolescent and the illusion was so great that you believed you saw several men in one when the actor varied his posture, his walk and gestures.[63]

Statements that pantomimes seemed to be able to actually speak with their hands indicates that cheironomia was a type of sign language comparable to languages for the hearing imparied. This idea is further reinforced by a story related by Lucian. Pontus, who had come to visit Nero from a neighboring state (where they spoke a different language), witnessed a pantomime performance and, finding it so clear and easy to follow, begged Nero to give him the performer as an interpreter for barbarous neighbors, stating, "This man will interpret everything for me by signs."[64]

By all accounts the Greco-Roman pantomimes developed a series of conventional gestures of great subtlety, constituting a language which was roughly equivalent to the images of the cantica and with which the artist seemed to actually speak in virtual sentences using only his hands and arms. A brief look at how sign languages function will provide an insight into the nature of cheironomia in the pantomime. Wilhelm Wundt, in a discussion of the various gesture languages used by the hearing impaired, Cistercian monks, Native Americans and others, identifies three basic forms of affective gesture—demonstrative, imitative, and symbolic—which are roughly analogous to those that might have been performed by the Roman pantomime.[65]

Demonstrative gestures are the simplest and include pointing to objects which are present, indicating spacial relationships and dimensional concepts, as well as pointing to parts of the body to indicate the various organs and their functions. Plutarch in his discussion of the three elements that make up pantomimic dance states that *deixis* (the pointing) "is something that does not copy the subject-matter, but actually shows it to us. . . . By pointing they [pantomimic dancers] literally indicate objects; the earth, the sky, themselves, or bystanders."[66]

The second class of signs, imitative gestures, are subdivided by Wundt into two types: the plastic and the indicative, which generally occur together. Plastic signs are created by hand postures which are used to depict natural or artificial forms. For example, a horned animal is depicted by extending the index and little finger, with the rest of the hand standing for the head. A bottle is indicated by the up-tilted thumb which stands for the neck of the bottle and the clenched fist for the body.

An indicative gesture involves a rapid sketch in the air. For example the sign for house in language for the hearing impaired, according to Wundt, consists of making an outline of the roof and sides with the index finger. "Smoke" is portrayed by making a spiraling movement with the index finger. These two signs can be placed together to make the sentence "the smoke coming from the house" in which the gesture for smoke is followed by a roof sketch.

Indicative gestures in languages for the hearing impaired generally involve the mimesis of characteristic gestures associated with the phenomenon. For example to communicate bread, the hearing impaired traces a circle to stand for loaf and makes a slicing motion. Imitative gestures can also connote a phenomenon through the depiction of the phenomenon's secondary traits. For example, a goat is depicted by quickly outlining its beard, a man by making the movement of lifting a hat, and a child by a rocking motion.

Evidence that the pantomime used indicative cheironomia can be seen in references by contemporary observers to the performer seeming to write in the air, which probably refers to the use of sketched shapes and characteristic gestures of phenomenon produced by hand. De l'Aulnaye states that the pantomimes of Carthage used indicative gestures consisting of a paraphrase with hand movements of an object that was not on stage and could not be shown to the spectator.[67] Additional evidence of the pantomime's reliance on imitative gesture can be found in Quintilian's advice to orators. Cautioning them not to illustrate what they have to say in the manner of pantomimes, he goes on to say:

> You [the mime/actor] may suggest a sick man by mimicking the gesture of a doctor feeling the pulse, or a harpist by a movement of the hands as though they were plucking the strings. But this is a type of gesture which should be rigorously avoided in pleading.[68]

At first glance, it appears that one of the primary techniques possessed by the Roman pantomime for indicating absent phenomena was descriptive cheironomia. However, like his modern-day counterpart, the Greco-Roman pantomime created the illusion that invisible phenomena were indeed present either through corporeal transformation (assisted by a mask and costume) or by transforming objects which he manipulated, such as his long cloak. It is questionable whether signs, such as those produced by the manipulation of the cloak, were a part of his codified language.

The first-rate pantomime must not only have a prodigious memory, but he must also have an artistic sense. The chanted cantica were essentially second rate imitations of Greek drama and it remained for the pantomime performer to enrich these texts with gestural images derived from his own storehouse of knowledge on mythology. The best pantomimes appear to have been those who were able to create many symbolic schemata made up of cheironomia as well as global corporeal postures and gestures that provided unique nuances and insight into the images of the canticum. Symbolic gestures, according to Wundt, operate through conceptual extension and association, and refer

A pantomimic actor with his masks. Ivory relief in Berlin. Courtesy M. Bieber, Denkmäler zum Theaterwesen in Altertum.

indirectly to the ideas they represent, in contrast to the direct indication of the demonstrative and imitative gestures. That some Greco-Roman pantomimes used extensive symbolic gestures can be found in Athenaeus' description of the pantomime Memphis: "he explains the nature of the Pythagorean system, expounding in silent mimicry all its doctrines to us more clearly than they who profess to teach eloquence."[69]

The learned Memphis was apparently able to demonstrate through symbolic pantomime Pythagorean doctrines concerning the transmigration of the soul and the theory of numbers. According to Athenaeus, Memphis' tragic style was later emulated by Pylades and Bathyllus.

Lucian also indicates that the pantomime did more than merely translate the words of the canticum; he also attempted to find gestural metaphors to express the deeper meanings in the text. The personal choice of gestural images by the performer essentially displayed his mind to the audience and revealed the depths of his artistry. An example of the importance of image selection can be seen in an account of Hylas' and Pylades' differing interpretations of the words "the great Agamemnon." Hylas performed these lines during a pantomime performance with the gestures of a man who measures another greater than himself. Pylades, who was present, stood up and cried, "You make him tall, but not great."[70] When the spectators asked Pylades to perform the same piece, he performed these lines by assuming an attitude of absolute immobility, depicting Agamemnon as plunged into a profound meditation. Whereas Hylas merely translated the words of the text with a demonstrative gesture, Pylades presented a symbolic image of the profound attitude characterizing Agamemnon. Pylades felt that this attitude better designated the monarch, who was constantly occupied with important functions.

PANTOMIME AND POETRY

Plutarch, in his discussion of pantomimic dancing, strongly insists on the intimate union of poetry and the art of gesture, calling pantomime, "silent poetry" and poetry "articulate dance."[71] In his discussion of the three elements of the pantomimic dance (phora, schema, and deixis), he draws a parallel between poetry and pantomime. He suggests that the poet uses concrete words to denote phenomenon such as sky, earth, Odysseus, etc., just as the pantomime uses deixis to point to real objects directly, such as earth sky, and even bystanders. If, however, the poet desires "vivid suggestion" and "imitative representation" he uses onomatopoeia and metaphor, which are similar to the function of phora (the phrase) and schema (the pose). Schema he says is imitative of form (morphe) and outward appearance (idea), while phora is expressive of some feeling or act or power. What Plutarch suggests in this discussion is that poetry and pantomime are alike in their modes of representation and both spring from a common mimetic impulse grounded in the expression of attitudes.

Kenneth Burke states that poetry is a symbolic act that constitutes "the dancing of an attitude."[72] What makes poetry vivid and constitutionally mimetic lies not so much in words as meaning (denotata), but in words as sounds and metaphors that evoke a visceral and emotional response within the listener. Plutarch gives an example of what he means with onomatopoeia and metaphor as used by poets, "They say that broken streams 'splash' and 'babble' and that missiles fly 'longing to take their fill of flesh'...."[73] The sound quality or words (onomatopoeia and metaphor) is basically a spoken manifestation of Effort.

In pantomime, the Efforts or tensions that inform the schemata are analogous to the sounds of words in poetry. While a posture or gesture may denote many things, it is the particular blend of the motion factors that contributes to both its sense and poetic impact. The great power of the pantomime artist did not lie in schemata that merely translated the images of the cantica, but in schemata that portrayed the movement of deeply felt attitudes or energies that underlay the images that constituted the myths and legends. Effort qualities—time, weight, space, and flow—are embodied both in the form that the pantomime assumes (morphe) as well as the phrase (phora), which Plutarch states, "is expressive of some emotion or action or potentiality." The pose in pantomime does not derive its suggestive and evocative power merely from its the outlines of its end shape. The pose is a culmination of the lines of force and Efforts in the gestures that proceed and follow it. In Pylades' depiction of Agamemnon, the posture of a thinker, there are tensional Efforts of bound, direct, heavy, and slow that infuse the pose. The pose in pantomime was never static but in a state of operative tension, either witnessing the gesture that precedes it or promising a plan of action or possible gesture to follow. The pose serves not only to radiate these Efforts to the audience, but also functions as a metaphor which links the qualities of the thinker to the character of Agamemnon.

The pantomimes probably sought to constantly enlarge their vocabularies through variations on the expression of existing signs or through the creation of new signs. The best of these signs (symbolic or otherwise) were probably rapidly incorporated into the stock pantomime vocabulary. There is every indication that Roman pantomimes employed novel transformations as well as newly created signs in an effort to gain popularity by stimulating the spectator's imagination. This would account not only for the continuing popularity of this genre throughout the Roman Empire, but for some of the heated rivalries between many of these performers who attempted to out-do each other by finding the most creative and daring expressions for verbal images in the cantica.

The schemata of the pantomime were closely tied to the recitation of the canticum. According to Plutarch the gestures were intimately associated with the words from moment to moment, as if the words and the parts of the body were connected by strings which the former pulled.[74] Lucian cites one of the primary defects of some performers was the lack of sync between gestures and words.[75] The syntactical and grammatical elements of the language of Roman pantomime were probably roughly analogous to that of languages for the hearing imparied which, according to Wundt, possess certain laws of syntax where postures and gestures performed by the hands are combined to form sentence. These sentences, like verbal language, contain subject, verb, objects, and adjectives. Poetry proceeds by means of images, which likewise possess subjects, verbs and objects. Since the pantomime enacted the phrases of the canticum, the rhythm of his performance would have tended to coincide exactly with the structured images of the sung text, through phrases of movement, which possessed a subject-adjective-verb-object (although not necessarily in that order).

According to Plutarch, one of the main functions of the pose (schema) was that it served as a form of punctuation, clearly separating one phrase from another so that the viewer could grasp and absorb each image as it was articulated. Many pantomimes performed in large arenas in which visibility would have been difficult for those spectators not seated close to the stage. Therefore, the postures, which are an integral part of the expression of attitudes, were probably slightly exaggerated by the performer to clearly delineate one phrase from another.

Apparently, the corporeal language of the pantomime was so clearly readable by the audience that there was no need for a prologue or accompanying canticum. Another story related by Lucian, indicates that the pantomime was able to communicate the story without verbal explanation—prefiguring the silent pantomime performances of the nineteenth and twentieth centuries. Demetrius accused the pantomime of being a parasite that was unable to stand alone without music and choir. According to him, the pantomime's movements were formed by chance and were incomprehensible and lacking in power without the canticum. In answer to this attack, a celebrated pantomime in the time of Nero consented to perform "The Love of Mars and Venus" without music or choir. After his performance, Demetrius cried. "I hear the story you are acting, man, I do not just see it; you seem to me to be talking with your very hands."[76]

Most of the stories that comprised the pantomime's repertoire were probably well known to their audience. As the pantomime gained in popularity and was frequented on a regular basis by all classes of people, the language employed by the performers became familiar to their audience as well. Thus, it is not clear if these performances could truly stand on their own if the spectator did not himself have a thorough knowledge of the myth or legend on which they were based and a ready knowledge of the conventions of the pantomime.

In the preceding discussion, Lucian's example has been followed in an attempt to ascertain the noblest aspects of this performance genre as embodied in its greatest performers. Purposely left out of the discussion was the eventual demise and degradation of pantomime performances that marked the fall of the Empire. It is clear that from its inception pantomime developed away from the symbolic and poetic mime that characterized the Greek orchesis and hyporcheme towards greater realism, eventually resulting in performances of striking brutality and obscenity. However, the essential elements that typified the inception of pantomime—the silence, singularity, and immobility of the corporeal cipher enacting the great heroic myths of the Greco-Roman world—marks this genre neither as an historical aberration or a hybrid art, but a genre in its own right that has an august and ancient lineage with the first pantomimes—the ancient shamans and bards.

Chapter Eight

Romantic and Modern Pantomimes: Deburau and Marceau

BALLET PANTOMIME

The Greco-Roman pantomime passed into oblivion with the crumbling of the Roman empire. Only at the beginning of the Renaissance, in the context of the French court ballets, did the pantomime begin to rise again in popularity. These ballets, which were performed by court nobility, were largely allegorical stories explained by both spoken libretto and pantomime and with elaborate choreographic patterns based upon ballroom dances of the time. French dancers brought the ballet to England at the beginning of the 18th century, delighting their audience with their technical virtuosity in *entr'actes* during dramatic performances. In 1717, Englishman John Weaver arranged the entr'acte ballet dances into a connected story to create the *ballet d'action*. This ballet genre replaced the verses and songs of the court ballets with pantomimic postures and gestures. The largely pantomimic ballets were conceived by Weaver to

> explain Things conceived in the Mind, by Gestures and Motions of the Body, and plainly and intelligibly represents Actions, Manners and Passions; so that the Spectator might perfectly understand the Performer by these motions, tho' he say not a word. . . . And, without the help of an Interpreter, a Spectator shall at a distance, by the lively representation of a just Character, be capable of understanding the Subject of the Story represented, and be able to distinguish the several Passions, Manners, and Actions; as of Love, Anger, and the like.[1]

Weaver created codified postures and gestures for the ballet d'action which he felt to be in accord with ancient tradition. These included both the abstract elements of the court ballet as well as postures and gestures portraying the passions based on the norms for painting and sculpture. An example of purely pantomimic attitudes can be seen in the scenario of his ballet "The

159

Nineteenth century lithograph of Jean-Gaspard Deburau. Billy Rose Theatre Collection, the New York Public Library for the Performing Arts, Astor, Lenox and Tilden Foundations.

Loves of Mars and Venus," which was modeled on a Greek dance of the same name.

> Astonishment: Both hands are thrown up towards the Skies; the Eyes also lifted up, and the Body cast backwards.
> Anger: The left Hand struck suddenly with the right; and sometimes against the Breast.[2]

The tendency in dance from the early seventeenth century through the end of the eighteenth century was towards pictorial poses which resembled painting by portraying a series of instantaneous pictures. The art of posing or posturing has frequently developed into an art within the general body of dance itself and was influenced in large part by tableaux vivants, a predominant element in the staging of European pageants and processionals. The tableaux vivants (living tableaux) generally consisted of a one or more performers who assumed held poses on wagons or stages in which they represented, like a series of silent snap shots, scenes from mythology, legend, or history.

The trend towards instantaneous pictures or frozen postures in ballet culminated in several unique genres which reached their fullest development in the eighteenth century in a unique genre termed Attitudes.[3] Attitudes, a performance genre created by Lady Hamilton and Ida Brun, was primarily an art of posturing based on poses of figures in painting and classical statuary. According to Lorenzo Hammarskold, Attitudes constituted the art of "representing plastic works of art by mimic means, gestures and draping, and transforming their local and existing life into a successive temporal one."[4] Lady Hamilton performed in the middle of a drawing room, dressed in a white tunic and girdle. She hid herself by means of shawls which she would lower to reveal various postures of mythological women copied from classical sculpture and painting. An important aspect of these performances was her ability to depict in rapid succession various emotions such as grief, sadness, joy and fright. Each attitude was characterized by "an intensive instant of immobility carrying within it the seed of a lightening [*sic*] swift movement. The radiation of psychic tension ... was Lady Hamilton's principle artistic means of expression."[5] There is no mention of historical descriptions of dance-like movements as connecting links between the different postures, nor does there seem to have been any musical accompaniment. More importantly this mimoplastic art, embodied in picturesque poses, does not appear to have possessed any dramatic context or plots. It remained for Ida Brun, another performer of this genre, to depict a dramatic sequence of events in Attitudes.

At the same time Weaver was mounting his pantomimic ballets, the genre of the English pantomime was being developed by John Rich (1692–1761). The pantomimes alternated serious plays, based on classical mythology and involving spoken and sung dialogue, with mute, comic episodes centering on the stock types of the Commedia dell'Arte. The comic, pantomimic segments far outshone the serious episodes in popularity. This was due in large part to the magical transformation scenes in which Harlequin would change people and places by a wave of his magic stick. Rich, by all accounts, was an expert pantomime who was able to convey all the elements of a story without the use of the spoken word. A performance by Rich of Harlequin hatching from an egg in "Harlequin a Sorcerer" is described as follows:

This certainly was a masterpiece in dumb show. From the first chipping of the egg, his receiving motion, his feeling the ground, his standing upright, to his quick Harlequin trip around the empty Shell, through the whole progression every limb had its tongue, and every motion a voice, which "spoke with the most miraculous organ" to the understandings and sensations of the observers.[6]

In 1745 English pantomimes were imported to France and met with great popularity. They remained an important part of the theatrical scene for the rest of the century.

Noverre (1727–1810), inspired by the pantomimic acting of Garrick, was one of the first to enrich classical ballet with dramatic content. He began his career as member of the company of the Paris Opera-Comique which was renown for its ballets and ballet pantomime, but because of jealousy and intrigue most of his work was done in companies in major European cities outside Paris. Noverre attempted to reunite action with dancing by placing pantomimic dances (ballets d'action) in a series of dance numbers — much like the recitative in opera. In place of the largely static and courtly postures of earlier ballet, he advocated the concept of *la pantomime heroique*, which he envisioned as a series of shifting or moving pictures endowed with real feeling and life through pantomimic action. Through finely wrought dramatic structure and well-developed characterizations, he attempted to create a flowing narrative composed of mimetic postures and gestures.

> A well-composed ballet is a living picture of the passions, manners, customs and ceremonies of all nations of the globe, consequently, it must be expressive in all its details and speak to the soul through the eyes; if it be devoid of expression, of striking pictures, of strong situations, it becomes a cold and dreary spectacle.[7]

The ballets of Noverre were composed of codified system of postures and gestures which like the letters of the alphabet could be arranged to "explain . . . clearly and simply, the actions which, it [the ballet] represents."[8]

Early in his career, Noverre was interested in the possibilities of a conventional language drawn from the hearing impaired alphabet of Abbé de l'Epée. This was a mimed language, without choreographic or emotional content, which permitted actual dialogue between the dancers. Words were set down in the scenario and translated on stage primarily through gestures of the arms and hands. Certain gestures from "Giselle" and "Swan Lake" could not be deciphered except by specialists. Other pantomimic figures utilized in the classical ballet could be readily understood by spectators unfamiliar with the conventional language of the ballet. For example to say "me" the artists points to himself with the middle finger of both hands. To say "you" he indicates the person with an open right hand, or with the index figure alone if he is angry. To say "love" he presses his hands to his heart. To say "marriage" he mimes placing a ring on the index finger of the right hand. To "call," the two arms are extended horizontally, the right hand above the left hand below. These gestures could be linked together like sentences with subject–verb–object to carry on a dialogue between dancers.

Carlo Blasis, the nineteenth century Italian dancing master who contributed to the codification of dance instruction, believed that "Pantomime is, undoubtedly, the very soul and support of the Ballet."[9] Accordingly, he felt that gesture was the dancer's means of expressing "the inward operation of the mind" through "exterior movements and attitudes of the body." His ballet choreography was often modeled on poses of figures in classical sculpture which he translated into posturally based dance gesture and movement.

DEBURAU AND THE ROMANTIC PANTOMIME BLANCHE

PANTOMIME AT THE FRENCH FAIRS

Side by side with the ballet, which was primarily an affair of the wealthy and aristocracy, the popular form of the pantomime developed among the common people at fairs found at the edge of Paris during the seventeenth century. Because of jealousy and rivalry with the state theatre of the Comédie Française, in 1707 laws were passed against minor acting troupes forbidding them to speak or sing, laws which were enforced sporadically for the next hundred years. The injunction against speech forced the performers to substitute pantomimed speech to carry their plots. This was not difficult because these performers were at once actors, mimes, dancers, and acrobats. When the fair grounds declined in popularity, many of the troupes established companies during the end of the eighteenth century on the Boulevard du Temple. When restrictions against speech were once again lifted pantomime began to add dialogue and musical themes. However, in 1807 when Napoleon reinstituted injunctions against many types of performance and speech, silent pantomime began to flourish. It was at one of these theatres, the Funambules, around 1820 (the exact date is not known) that Jean-Gaspard Deburau (1796–1846) made his debut and immortalized the genre of the pantomime blanche in his silent, white-faced portrayals of Pierrot, whom he called Baptiste.

The pantomime blanche was a genre of mime involving a group of performers, who without recourse to the spoken word, enacted written scripts by means of pantomime interspersed with text. The text was supplied by hand-held cards or sometimes passages of text were suspended above the performers which the audience then sung. Each actor specialized, like the Commedia dell'Arte performers, in a particular role, but they did not wear masks. Their corporeal style consisted of a combination of acrobatics, facial expressions, bodily attitudes, and codified gestures (in which hand signs replaced words), to convey emotion, action and dialogue.

DEBURAU'S PIERROT (BAPTISTE)

For the most part the characters involved in the pantomime were drawn from the Commedia dell'Arte, but were shaped according to French tradition and the personalities of the performers. Pierrot was a French development of the *commedia zanni* Pedrolino, who frequently appeared paired with Harlequin. Prior to Deburau, Pierrot had been portrayed as early as the seventeenth century as the universal fool "who is at once a trickster, dupe, lady killer, pimp, androgyne, catalyst for unlawful sexuality...."[10] With Debureau, Pierrot became the central figure in the pantomime blanche and took on new characteristics which contributed to making him a potent literary and artistic symbol of the age.

Nineteenth century France saw the dawn of the Romantic era, a pivotal age when men and women were on the brink of the modern era. It was characterized by the insecurity of a people who had lived through the revolution, had been buffeted by the rise and fall of Napoleon, and witnessed the overthrow of the French social structure. During this time, the heroic stance gave way to that of the antihero, which was modeled on the carnivalesque image of the fool. According to Louisa Jones:

> The models of the fool show appealed to many young Romantics who felt in themselves a confusion of identity, parallel, in some ways, to the fool's; who felt that their society had undergone a subversion of hierarchy, a confusion of high and low, which was both destructive and liberating and which paralleled, in some ways, the traditional experience of carnival; who could imagine heroic ideals only in terms of irony or parody....[11]

The fool finds its roots in the figure of the trickster-shaman. The appearance of the trickster in different periods of history signals a society in transition. The antiheroic, clown-pantomime is an inversion of the stance of the shaman as hero. He is at once comic and sad — a blend of the comic elements that characterize grotesque realism and a blend of the hero of Greco-Roman pantomime. The clown-hero finds his ultimate mask in the ambivalent type of the Commedia dell'Arte zanni.

The Pierrot of Deburau was a complex character embodying the contradictions of the nineteenth century. He was, according to Gautier,

> imperturbable sang-froid, artful foolishness and foolish finesse, brazen and naive gluttony, blustering cowardice, skeptical credulity, scornful servility, preoccupied insouciance, indolent activity, and all those surprising contrasts that must be expressed by a wink of the eye, by a puckering of the mouth, by a knitting of the brow, by a fleeting gestures.[12]

Deburau's white-floured face, across which flickered subtle expressions, was a mask of impassivity which mirrored the avant-garde fashion of the time.

Frederic Hillemacher. "Deburau as Pierrot with a bottle" (1868). Billy Rose Theatre Collection, the New York Public Library for Performing Arts, Astor, Lenox and Tilden Foundations.

His Pierrot, rendered with finesse and an attitude of cool indifference, embodied the ideal of the nineteenth century courtier. George Sand wrote that Pierrot "is essentially an aristocrat right down to the tips of his long fingers, and thus there is no situation from which he cannot disengage himself politely, in the manner of a courtier."[13] Theodore de Banville believed that Deburau's Pierrot "responded to the need for elegance and splendor that exists in primitive souls, and never a duke or prince knew as well as he how to kiss a hand, touch a woman."[14] His gestures were remarkable for their sobriety and exquisite finesse and while he moved others he himself remained impassive. Of the ideal of the nineteenth century dandy (courtier) Baudelaire writes that his beauty "consists particularly in that cold exterior resulting from the unshakable determination to remain unmoved; one is reminded of a latent fire, whose existence is merely suspected, and which if it wanted to, but it does not, could burst forth in all its brightness."[15] Deburau seems to have possessed the distant and imperturbable calm of an entranced shaman who performs without self-awareness of what he does; this contrasted with dazzling feats of acrobatics and unexpected bursts of action reminiscent of the topsy-turvy behavior and acrobatics of carnivalesque clowns and the Commedia dell'Arte zanni.

The aesthetics of Deburau's performance was one of absence rather than presence. Banville states that "he wandered through the universe with the detachment of an artist and poet."[16] He accentuated the spectral qualities of his character by adopting a long white flowing blouse, baggy white pants, and skull cap. His white-floured mask and costume removed Pierrot from the flesh and blood arena of the comedy and situated him in the beyond—an incarnation from the spirit world and land of dreams—a quality which was enhanced by the changing backdrop of sets against which he moved.

Deburau's Pierrot was also the image of the common man. He created portraits of common laborers and tradespeople in nineteenth century French society, and he wore costume and makeup to fit the role. He carefully studied the gestures of these characters, rending in minute detail the motions of work and the characteristics of their social class. Deburau seems to have been a true actor in the Stanislavski sense, revealing the inner world of the character across his actions. His attention to naturalistic detail and truthfulness was unusual in a time when the style of the grand actor dominated the stage and his fellow pantomimes still resorted to exaggerated and generalized character portraits.

THE LANGUAGE OF THE PANTOMIME BLANCHE

The pantomime blanche was a play performed with scenery, objects, costumes, and music in which action and dialogue between characters was effected by means of gestures substituted for words. Pantomimed words were used primarily as a means of dialogue between characters rather than to create narration as in shamanic performance and the Greco-Roman pantomime. The gestures and attitudes of the pantomime blanche were influenced, in part, by the codified vocabulary of the classical ballet used by Noverre in his pantomime heroique, as well as by the popular nineteenth century theories on attitude expression formulated by Switzerland's Jean-Gaspard Lavater and Germany's J. J. Engels.[17]

The dialogue of the pantomime blanche was based on a system of codified gestures that could be readily understood by spectators unfamiliar with the convention. Like languages for the hearing impaired, it consisted of three types of hand signs—demonstrative, mimed, and symbolic—which were used in conjunction with facial expressions and bodily postures. It had a syntax of subject–adjective–object–verb rather than the subject–verb–object of spoken discourse. For example if the pantomime wanted to say "I love you, if you kiss me, I will marry you" it could be transcribed by the gestures "I you love, you me kiss, I you marry." The hand in conjunction with the face and attitudes of the body conveyed the sense and syntax of the discourse. In the above transcription indicative gestures are used for subject and object; a symbolic gesture for "love" with either a hand placed over the heart or a heart shape formed by the placing together of the thumbs and index fingers of both hands;

and a symbolic gesture for "marry" mimed by placing an imaginary wedding ring on the hand.

The essence and appeal of the pantomime blanche did not lie in the word for word translation of dialogue into gesture. It lay in the radiation of the inner world of the performer outward by means of subtle facial expressions and gestures. As with the Greco-Roman pantomime, audiences would have soon tired of this genre if it were not for the greatness of performers like Deburau. Unlike his predecessors, he was able to express more by the simplicity and quasi-immobility of his pantomime than by grand attitudes and gestures. Like poetry, the evocative power of his performance lay in the emotional and symbolic overtones of minimalist gesture. By paring the gesture to its barest essence, Deburau was able to infuse it with a greater depth of meaning through suggestion. Theodore de Banville relates that "he never emphasized anything, he indicated his intentions by a spiritual gesture."[18] The true discourse of Deburau's pantomime lay in the resonance of the gesture—those Effort qualities that revealed the inner attitudes underlying the denotational meaning of the gesture or attitude and which imparted to them a deeper sense and significance.

Deburau was a performer who possessed years of prodigious corporeal training and performance experience. His achievement was a combination of astute technique, and more importantly, strong inner emotion and sadness acquired through hardship, privation and suffering. This inner tension and feeling was conveyed to his audience through the smallest gesture and even immobility itself. Because he was also an acrobat, Deburau probably knew how to maintain attitudes that were in a precarious equilibrium and witnessed the strong inner emotions from which they sprang. These were enhanced by his flowing white costume which created evanescent sculptural forms that radiated the underlying attitude more fully than hand or facial gestures.

Through his genius, Deburau essentially created the genre of the pantomime blanche. Before his stellar rise as a performer at the Funambules, pantomime had been nothing more than a hodgepodge of preexisting theatrical forms that had an uneasy alliance out of the necessity to bypass the prohibiton against speech. Deburau was able to tap into his society's need for the reincarnation of the romantic hero who takes his audience on an imaginary voyage to the sacred world of the imagination. By all accounts he was the focus of the pantomime, all the other performers seeming to exist in his shadow. He was in essence a solo performer who with his white costume and quasi-immobility stood out in the midst of the spectacle. He was more a force than a presence. His greatness lay in his ability to infuse the hollow system of codified pantomimic gesture with deeper significance and to reinstate the importance of attitude expression as the essential power underlying the pantomime.

After the death of Deburau in 1846, a variety of lesser Pierrots carried on his tradition: Deburau junior; Paul Legrand; Rouffe, who established a school

Marcel Marceau as Bip. Courtesy Columbia Artists Management Inc. Photo Shuhei Iwamoto.

in Marseilles and perfected the language of gesture translating words; and his student Severin. The legacy of Deburau came to an end with the Pierrot of Georges Wague (1874–1958). Wague abandoned the sclerosed language of the pantomime blanche, which he had become the master of early in his career, to develop a modern form of dramatic pantomime in which gesture served primarily to express emotion rather than to tell a story or convey dialogue between characters.

MARCEAU AND THE MODERN PANTOMIME

Marcel Marceau (1923–) carries forward many elements of the style of the Greco-Roman pantomime and the pantomime blanche into the twentieth century. His movement vocabulary contains hand signs that translate words into gestural equivalents; he has largely replaced, however, this convention with another one—the language of illusion. His mode of discourse, like that of the Greco-Roman pantomimic narrative, is made up of bodily attitudes, gestures, and facial expressions which are strung together to tell a story. Marceau's unique style is a consequence of the solo and silent nature of his performance style in which he employs bodily expression in space without recourse to other actors, objects, or scenery. He is at once subject and object of his own art.

Ironically, Marceau would have preferred to create as part of a pantomime troupe. He has even said, "The future of this art is not to be found in solitude, but on the contrary in the collective spirit."[19] In 1947 he founded a company to create mimodramas in the style of the nineteenth century pantomime blanche and continued to work sporadically on mime plays for the next twenty years. By all critical accounts, however, the mimodramas were not a success. Marceau's style, which is based on illusion, did not fit in well with group performances. He needs the empty space of a solo dancer to make his images come alive. The reality of physical actors and tangible objects are antithetical to the aesthetics of his performance. They change its modality to one of presence rather than the absence so necessary for the aesthetics of pantomime.

Marceau's mime is shamanic. He takes his audience on an imaginative voyage into poeticized space which he endows with invisible powers and forces. "The task of the mime is not to show reality, but to recreate reality. . . ."[20] By means of a prodigious technique he condenses space, slows down and speeds up time, and amazes his audience with technical feats of illusion and precarious balance. His style shows a preference for reveries of air and lightness. If Marceau were to have a helping spirit it would be a bird. "My mother was Alsatian; I was born in Strasbourg. My nights were filled with the beating of wings because in Alsace there are swans, and because my father raised pigeons on the roof of our house."[21]

In his drawings and paintings, which have been compared to those of Chagall, Marceau's performance persona, Bip, is almost always depicted with wings and as floating in space. In contrast to his teacher Decroux, who said that objects should appear heavier than in reality, Marceau says, "We must create winged weight. Bip pulled by the wings of the butterfly, then carried by the balloon. When I fight against the wind, one sees the wind, one feels it more than the real wind."[22]

The style and poetic tragedy that characterizes the mime of Marceau lies in this opposition between gravity and lightness. For Marceau it is both a corporeal and a spiritual struggle. It is an opposition which captures the existential human condition of man who has a body which is tied to the earth, but also has a spirit, which in knowing no physical restraints, seeks to be free. Freedom from the laws of gravity is the élan of the dancer, the bound and rooted style is that of the mime. Marceau states, "The mime 'creates, by a succession of attitudes and figures, the anguish of man who lacks wings. Icarus takes wing to approach the sun, his wings melt, he falls back to the earth. I say that it is here that dance finishes and mime begins."[23]

Marceau's style is grounded in the pantomime's defiance of the laws of gravity. The mime, according to Pavis,

> frequently makes us forget the law of gravity, leans forward dangerously without falling, simulates movements while walking on the spot. The

spectator's pleasure is to contemplate himself in this body which always seems to have its own way, free from physical laws, malleable, and capable of shaping and being shaped at will.[24]

The style of Etienne Decroux, Marceau's teacher, is grounded in an acknowledgement of the laws of gravity as the essence of man's moral condition. It seems inevitable that Marceau would break with Decroux, who taught him the essentials techniques which were to shape his style. Decroux's stance as a mime performer is diametrically opposed to that of Marceau. He is a mime of the earth. His reveries are of weight, depth, and crystalline purity. His vision of the Promethean hero is one who exists in a rock hard defiance against the will to transcend his corporeality.

MARCEAU'S PIERROT (BIP)

Marceau has realized the public's need to identify with heroes. To this end, he has felt it necessary to recreate an historical archetype in the tradition of the Commedia dell'Arte and silent pantomimes. He says, "From Pantalone to Pierrot, to Bip, the resemblance with these familiar silhouettes always exists. The mime, the pantomime, the harlequinade have always created archetypes where the public rediscovers typical figures of the times."[25]

Bip is an amalgam of many influences but owes its greatest debt to the Pierrot of Deburau and the Charlot of Chaplin. "Bip is a pale, lunar character," Marceau explains, "the mouth torn with a trace of red, the eyes in circumflex accents, brother of Charlot, little brother of Pierrot."[26]

Bip's costume is a blend of the picaresque comic characters in the sketches by Daumier and the clown. In place of the baggy pantaloons and white blouse of Pierrot, he sports a striped shirt, top hat with a flower and body suit that highlights the linear qualities of his movement. He differs in one fundamental aspect from the creations of Chaplin and Deburau, however, in that he is a universalized and distanced figure of the common man as antihero. His white face with the clown accents, his comic stance with slightly bent knees and turned out legs, and his arms reaching out into space create a clown portrait of the Chaplinesque little man, an eternal victim of absent forces that seek to overwhelm him.

Bip was born after the turmoil and devastation of World War II. The astounding popularity of his performances throughout Europe after the war attest to the potency of the heroic archetype which he had created and which met a deeply felt need in his audience to transcend the war devastation in Europe:

> In a world recovering from the ravages of a cataclysmic war, the presence of a lone figure in white face sporting a top hat with red flower must have given some laughs to audiences who were tired of crying, tired of trying to figure out a world gone mad. Pain and disappointment with the

Marcel Marceau as Bip. Columbia Artists Management Inc.

present can foster nostalgic backward glances to seemingly happier and simpler times.[27]

But Bip in his transcendence also conveys an image of the essential isolation of the existential hero, cut off from contact with the world of things. He exists alone in an imaginary and empty space which is endlessly generating, constantly in flux, filled with unseen forces, but essentially a void.

Existential themes of absence and solitude are the basis for many of Marceau's mime pieces. In "The Mask Maker" (*"Le fabricant de masques"*) the laughing mask becomes stuck to the maker's face; at the moment of his death, he "rips the laughing mask from his face and finds himself naked with the face of his solitude."[28] In "The Cage" (*"La cage"*), "the eye visualizes what does not exist. This cage is of glass, a space where man is prisoner of his solitude, limiting

his liberty. He is condemned in advance and if he happens to leave, it is only
to find himself in another, larger cage. Corridors and labyrinths spring up; he
is enclosed in a Kafkaesque universe."[29]

IDENTIFICATION

Marceau's vocation as a pantomime surfaced in childhood. He had a
tendency towards reverie based in identification with phenomenon.

> As a child, I already identified with a universe that I interiorized: pig-
> eons, plants, fish, butterflies, the world of childhood dreams, that of our
> mythology; not just Charlot who, without a word, made us laugh and
> cry; but also Robin Hood, Robinson Crusoe, William Tell, the Bible, the
> suffering of Christ, the history of France, the tales and the legends.[30]

Marceau recognizes that mime is based in the identification with and
reenactment of the gestures of phenomena which have been recorded by the
body as gestic imagery. "Mime is the art of man identifying with the elements,
people, nature that surrounds us."[31] Mime, according to Marceau, involves "a
creative process which roots in instinct and reminiscence, interior dreams, interior music which are expressed in silence."[32] According to him, the mime
performer's identification with imagery comes close to Zen's complete involvement. The performer "cannot miss the target because he has become the target
himself. When the mime struggles with the wind, he is the wind."[33]

Marceau begins his programs with short movement skits (*pantomimes du
style*) that demonstrate how man does things. The style pantomimes involve
three progressively complex stages. The first are simple exercises involving
identification with the elements — fire, air, water, wind — and simple feats of
illusion such as pulling an invisible rope in "The Tug of War" (*"Les tiereurs
de corde"*) and climbing an imaginary staircase in *"Les escalier."* The second
stage uses the same techniques of illusion to create short skits around universal
human themes in which the emotion of the character is portrayed across his
actions as, for example, in such pieces as "The Cage" (*"La cage"*) and "The
Mask Maker" (*"Le fabricant de masques"*). The third stage involves more abstract and allegoric themes such as "The Creation of the World" (*"La création
du monde"*) which is based on Genesis and performed almost solely with the
hands. The pantomimes du style, which are introduced by an assistant who
strikes a sculptural pose, are almost identical in style and technique to the Bip
pantomimes which form the second half of the programs.

The essence of Marceau's mime is the portrayal of the individual's struggle
with phenomenon in terms of agents acting upon one another. Marceau's
primary means of portraying the human struggle is through illusion involving
conflict with imaginary objects and forces. The techniques used in creating illusion are based on Decroux's early work with objective mime. This is the recreation

of phenomenon from the external world through the use of counterweights, raccourci, and attitude.[34]

Counterweights involve a pushing and pulling of the body as it acts on and reacts to imaginary forces and objects. The mime touches space and endows it with magic qualities and he, in turn, is touched and moved by space. The articulation of space by means of muscular compensations of the body with regard to imaginary phenomenon is the essence of attitude expression in Marceau's work. It reveals dramatic conflict through the deliberate intensification of oppositional forces within the body. For example, the mime of the toreador reconstructs by its corporeal play the alternation of the desire to flee and attack. The mime of the kite, through the action of pulling and being pulled, reveals the movement of the spirit in its desire for freedom and fear of loss. According to Patrice Pavis, the mime creates gestural realism by

> encoding certain relevant traits of behavior and the narrative phases of a story whose steps are always much the same: attack/reconciliation; rivalry/friendship; conflict/pursuit; duel/compromise, etc. The mime expresses with his body how every story is articulated, what opposition it necessitates and how contradictions punctuate it and form it, and what segmentation he follows to organize the mise en scene of his body.[35]

ATTITUDE

Marceau's technique is rooted in attitude expression by means of postures of the body which encapsule the underlying muscular tension signifying an attitude. When Marceau states, as he has on many occasions, that "mime is the art of attitude,"[36] he uses attitude in a double sense; the sense of the inner image that is rooted in identification with phenomenon and which conveys a psychic attitude, and the sense of the outward expression of the image in held postural form or bodily attitude.

Attitudes act as a framing device or punctuation for phrases of movement. They highlight the essence of an action in a series of poses that allow the audience to read the unfolding gestural narrative. Each attitude is a distilled gestural synopsis that embodies several movements in a single form. This is the idea of the *raccourci,* the "condensation of an idea in space and time."[37] The juxtaposition of these bodily attitudes forms the narrative structure of the pantomime. Marceau states, "The mime translates the subject by the sequence of attitudes and corporeal acting, but not with the aid of gestures as in the manner of deaf-mutes."[38]

The attitudes created in space by Marceau's body are based in Decroux's concepts of Mobile Statuary: "mime is most real when, like sculpture, it contains the properties of what it depicts: resistance, breakability, weight and volume."[39] In Decroux's corporeal mime, the dramatic emphasis is on the attitudes projected by the planes and volumes of the torso rather than the extremities. While the torso is important in Marceau's work, especially as it reveals the moral qualities of victory and defeat in the struggle with matter (the convex and concave of pushing and pulling), Marceau's particular talent and style lies in his use of the hands. They accompany the postures of his body like a lyrical melody against a sustained bass. Hands do not have the weight of the body, but they are more capable of magical transformation and descriptive narration.

Marceau uses his hands to create plastic forms that are essentially microcosms of the ensemble. "Through the hands you can create a sort of transposition of elements; snakes, butterflies. You can create love — the touch."[40] In his piece "The Creation of the World," his hands replace the body as the primary mode of discourse in portraying all the characters, emotions, and events in the story. The use of hand signs as a primary narrative device situates Marceau squarely in the tradition of the Greco-Roman pantomimes.

The essence of Marceau's style is in the sketch. This term describes both the nature of his mime pieces and his corporeal style. His narration proceeds by means of quick strokes which summarize the essence of an object, emotion, or action. Marceau's bodily attitudes also lyrically describe. They have the same linear, fluid, and sketched quality of the hands. They serve more to create lines in space, rather than the weight, solidity, and volume of sculptured forms.

The poetic halo which Marceau etches in space around the head of Bip is a typical example of a descriptive hand sketch: "There is one [gesture] which I often make which describes a circle in space and which I call the poetic halo. Like an aura, it envelopes the body in a radiance which awakes lyric resonances."[41] This gesture serves to outline and distance the figure from the audience. It also serves to indicate a halo rather than to express it by an inner tension of the performer, like the No which radiates to the audience and creates the beauty of the performance. Marceau shows rather than reveals. He prepares his audience for many of his actions by providing a preparatory sketch with his body or hand of what he is "intending to do, as if to say 'now look at me, I am about to do. . . .'" He continues, "In the mime, the spectator cannot pick up on the gesture unless one prepares it. Thus, when I go to pick up a wallet, I lift my hand first; one looks at my hand; and it is after this that I go towards the wallet."[42] Gestures like these serve to indicate objects, ideas, and emotions by a quick outline that only captures a few essential traits.

The sketch is the style of the anecdotal. Marceau has not followed Decroux's dictum that less is more. According to Patrice Pavice, "When the body tries to say too much, and with too much wit, the body is 'talkative,' overstated by a precise story and discourse."[43] Marceau's preference for showing how man does things has carried over into all aspects of his work. He is a brilliant technical illusionist who engages his audience in a game of anticipation and guess work: "mime, an art of illusion, makes visible the invisible and concrete the abstract, and the audience identifies with the very trickery of it."[44]

Marceau is a controversial performer primarily because he broke with the modern mime tradition initiated by Decroux. He has melded aspects of corporeal mime technique with elements of romantic pantomime and in the process has reverted to what many feel is the prehistory or dead-end development of mime in silent storytelling.

Marceau both preserves and enlarges the domain of traditional pantomime. He has severed the link between word and gesture and replaced it with a technique of original and non-codified signs which indicate by means of the sketch and illusion. As such, Marceau's mime marks a transitional phase between the codified languages of the classical pantomime and the truly modern, abstract pantomime of Etienne Decroux. Unfortunately, as in all forms of pantomime, the technical vocabulary of signs created by Marceau form the basis of a new system of denotation. The curse of all great pantomimes has been that their styles are copied and not continually enlarged by subsequent performers. Thus, as the audience becomes familiar with the modality of the pantomime's gesture, it begins to play a game of matching which can tend to crowd out metaphorical overtones. While Marceau is seen by many as a prisoner of his own technical genius, he has attempted to bypass this problem by creating pieces of greater abstraction, such as "The Creation of the World," which lie on the hazy borderline between the old pantomime and the new.

Chapter Nine

Etienne Decroux and Corporeal Mime

INFLUENCES ON THE DEVELOPMENT OF CORPOREAL MIME

Etienne Decroux (1898–1991), referred to by some as the father of modern mime, was a philosopher, critic, performer and teacher of mime, who may be credited with having asserted that mime is above all the art of attitude. The system of corporeal mime (*le système du mime corporelle*) created by Decroux marks a divergence from the clichéd poses and realistic mimicry of traditional Western forms of mime such as the Commedia dell'Arte and the nineteenth century pantomime blanche. Influenced by such modernist movements in art as symbolism, abstraction and cubism, corporeal mime is technical grammar of designed postures and movements based in the principles of kinetic architecture and geometry, providing the mime with a technical foundation for expression comparable to that of the ballet dancer.

JACQUES COPEAU AND L'ÉCOLE DU VIEUX-COLOMBIER

Decroux's vocation and the aesthetic principles behind the elaboration of corporeal mime were directly inspired by l'École du Vieux-Colombier, which he attended from 1923 to 1925. Here he was first introduced to mime in a class on corporeal expression called *les jeux masques* which consisted of a series of exercises designed by Copeau to assist the actor in recreating the mimetic impulses, action, and conflict that underlie the drama. The exercises involved the gestural enactment of short scenes by students who wore neutral masks, forcing them to use their bodies as the sole means of communication. Decroux relates, "We mimed modest actions; a man bothered by a fly, attempts to get rid of it; a woman deceived by a fortune-teller, strangles her, actions used in a craft, the sequence of the movement produced by a machine."[1] The pieces developed by the students, according to Decroux, involved the slow execution of gestures "in which many others were synthesized." Of the year-end performance of the

176

class, which he did not participate in but watched, Decroux says, "I had never seen slow-motion movement before. I had never seen prolonged immobilities, or explosive movements followed by sudden petrification."[2] They also experimented with sounds: "We reproduced noises of the town, the house, nature, the cries of animals. All with the mouth, hands and the feet."[3] The techniques exhibited by the students contained the beginnings of what was to form the basis of corporeal mime: the neutral mask, immobility, slow motion, the shock, and the distillation of several movements into one.

THE NŌ DRAMA OF JAPAN

In another course at the Vieux-Colombier, Decroux was introduced to the theories and practices of the No drama. The students were fascinated to discover the similarity between the dramatic laws exemplified by the No and those that were taught in Copeau's theory course, especially the philosophy of discipline and self-abnegation and the performance style with its highly charged, slow-motion, and symbolic, masked action.[4] Decroux was also present at the final rehearsal for a school production of the No play *Kantan,* which, according to witnesses, was one of the greatest achievements of the school.

Decroux never publicly stated that the No had any influence on his work. However, Thomas Leabhart relates that Decroux once confided to Jacques Lecoq (when Decroux took over the school of the Piccolo Teatro in Milan from Lecoq) that "he hoped to make the students there move like Japanese actors."[5] The clearest evidence of Decroux's debt to the No comes from his son Maximilien, who indicates that his father's work is not a continuation of European forms of mime as exemplified in the Commedia dell'Arte,

> but is based in reality on a completely different model, the mime of the extreme Orient. ... A turning point has been made without it being realized or inspired by this model [continuity with the Commedia dell'Arte] but by the contrary model of the Japanese No and new means of expression which came from and were inspired by this pole, this source.[6]

Decroux's corporeal mime training parallels ritually based Oriental models, such as the No, in it transmission of a codified body of theory and techniques. According to Eugenio Barba, Etienne Decroux is

> perhaps the only European master to have elaborated a system of rules comparable to that of an Oriental tradition, [also] seeks to transmit to his students the same rigorous closedness to theatre forms different from his own. In the case of Decroux, as in that of the Oriental masters, it is not a question of narrow-mindedness nor of intolerance. It has to do with the awareness that the bases of an actor's work, his points of departure, must be defended like his most precious possessions, even at the risk of

Etienne Decroux. Photograph by Etienne Bertrand Weill.

isolation, otherwise they will be irremediably polluted and destroyed by syncretism.[7]

The training program at Decroux's school in Boulogne-Bilancourt was similar to a ritually structured initiation into a sacred body of teachings. Decroux called himself a "spiritual materialist" who is "overpowered by the spiritual when it has given its form to the material."[8] While to many, corporeal mime seems more of a rational than a spiritual exercise, for Decroux it was a discipline verging on meditation. The philosophy behind corporeal mime training is that in subjecting the natural expression of the body to a difficult and rigorous anti-natural technique one hones the spirit. The body, purified of the anecdotal and personal, can then become a vessel for the expression of the impersonal symbol.

Corporeal mime training is analogous to spiritually based training, such as the No, in its exclusivity, rigor, demand for self abnegation and in the identification with and imitation of a great model/teacher. As in classical ballet, Decroux's teaching method was based on the method of example and imitation. He, or a select assistant who had achieved a high degree of proficiency, explained and demonstrated the figures and motions that the students then proceeded to imitate through repetition and attention to the most minute detail. In this process, students rigorously suppressed all natural inclination toward expression. This method is exactly the opposite of Lecoq's training, because it demands self-abnegation and the imposition of an acquired technique.

However, as in all major spiritualities, the student must not merely imitate the exterior form, but must penetrate to the interior essence of a figure or movement to discover the impulses from which they spring.

Corporeal mime also reveals many parallels to the techniques of the No and indirectly parallels techniques of shamanic ecstasy, the most important of which are the acquisition of impersonality and of techniques that permit the performer to manipulate his or her body like a marionette. The corporeal mime artist, like the shaman, seeks to acquire the ability to stand at a distance from his body and control its movements with his mind, which is analogous to the strings of a marionette. The mime cannot allow natural expression to possess him and guide his movements. Rather, he imposes a technique upon his body in order to intensify, purify, and channel natural expression into symbolic images.

EDWARD GORDON CRAIG AND THE UBER-MARIONETTE

The concept of the actor-marionette is the primary inspiration behind the formulation of the philosophy of corporeal mime and came to Decroux by way of the Vieux-Colombier. Copeau was one of the first theatrical innovators to adopt Edward Gordon Craig's ideas in France. Many of the theories and exercises at l'École du Vieux-Colombier (including those on the No) had been inspired by Craig's *On the Art of the Theatre* and by his seminal articles in *The Mask*.

Craig envisioned a non-illusionistic theatre based in symbolic movement in which the human actor, as he presently exists, is replaced by a more perfect instrument—one capable of "symbolic gesture."[9] According to Craig, today's actors merely "impersonate and interpret,"[10] and their corporeal expression is little more than a duplication of nature by means of "realistic" gestures. The necessary action in art, according to him, is symbolic movement. Deploring the actor's lack of discipline, predominance of ego and his inability to control corporeal expression under the sway of emotion, Craig stated, "The actor must go, and in his place comes the inanimate figure—the Uber-marionette—we may call him, until he has won for himself a better name."[11]

The *Uber-marionette* is Craig's conception of the perfectly disciplined and controlled actor, capable of using his body as the material of his art. Craig posits it as an antidote to the realistic/naturalistic actor of his day and begins exploring possible models for it in the Oriental theatre. In a series of articles on the No in the 1910 issue of *The Mask*, Craig indicates that the No actor met his ideal of the Uber-marionette. He saw in him a supreme example of the disciplined actor, completely subject to his form, whose acting consists "for the main part of symbolical gesture."[12]

Craig was against the Western actor on two counts: his lack of corporeal and vocal discipline and his egoism — his desire to show himself on stage. He felt strongly that true art necessitated calculation and control. He states:

> The actions of the actor's body, the expression of his face, the sounds of his voice, all are at the mercy of the winds of his emotions: these winds, which must blow forever round the artist, moving without unbalancing him. But with the actor, emotion possesses him; it seizes upon his limbs, moving them wither it will.[13]

The actor, instead of being a master of himself, allowed his emotions to overcome his intelligence and his instincts to overpower his knowledge. This, he felt, resulted in gratuitous and uncontrolled expression.

Craig's conception of acting builds upon Diderot's *Paradox sur le Comédien* (1780s), which was the first serious analysis of the actor's creative process in the West. Diderot had called for the actor to remain cool and disciplined in his approach rather than letting himself be carried away by his passions. The actor, according to him, must be superhuman — that is, shamanic in his control but with the heart and warmth of possession. This could only be accomplished through rigid control and discipline of the body instrument; the actor was to essentially remain unmoved while moving the audience. This is the shamanic essence of the "doubling of consciousness." Just as the sculptor approaches his stone, the painter his canvas, the actor must approach his own instrument from a distance, as it were, separated from himself. He must constantly look at his machine in operation in order to create the desired effect upon the audience.

In a passage remarkably reminiscent of Zeami, Diderot claims that the actor gives all his feelings during the performance to the audience and keeps none for himself, "for the actor is an empty shell, a vessel to be filled with whatever he chooses."[14] Thus the actor creates his characters from nothingness. "Perhaps, it is just because he [the great actor] is nothing that he is before all everything. His own special shape [personality] never interferes with the shape he assumes."[15] In other words, he is able to release his body from the control of the habitual attitudes comprising the ego, which allows for the opening out of a deeper self that lies buried in the subconscious. Therefore, according to Diderot, "A great actor is also a most ingenious puppet, and his strings are held by the poet, who at each line indicates the true form he must take."[16]

Like Diderot, Craig sought to find a compromise between the undisciplined emotionalism of star performers and the vision of a calculated craft. The actor should not show himself but should strive to reveal through the transparency of his art a unique impersonal vision of the world that transcends human limitations. In "The Actor and the Uber-marionette," Craig sets forth his theories on the characteristics of the ideal actor based on the concept of the actor as marionette. The Uber-marionette is the actor who has acquired the essential qualities of the marionette: obedience, impersonality, calculation and symbolism.

According to Craig, if the actor wants to participate in the creative advancement of the theatre, he must annihilate his ego: "The Uber-marionette is the actor plus fire, minus egotism: the fire of the gods and demons, without the smoke and steam of mortality."[17] In order to avail himself of the dictates of his subconscious and to express these to the audience through a controlled technique, he must possess the marionette's obedience and malleability. It is the impersonal quality of the actor-marionette that enables the spectator to see beyond human limitations to vision of a new force.

The distance and control which Craig envisioned for the ideal actor would manifest the trance-like aesthetics of the marionette, that is, "to clothe itself with a death-like beauty while exhaling a living spirit."[18] This involves the actor entering into what Craig terms "a spiritual state of ecstasy" which, according to him,

> is not apparent excitement but apparent calm. It is the white heat of emotion; . . . that is to say, it is almost a trance. . . . You must awaken your imagination and let it possess you entirely. . . . Ecstasy is nothing else than a kind of madness, remember, not any kind of madness. It is all which is Rapid . . . White . . . Glowing . . . Circular . . . Vast . . . Steady.[19]

What Craig meant by ecstasy appears to be a spontaneous liberation of the subconsious or creative imagination, bypassing the inhibiting mechanisms of the ego.

Craig's theories are predicated upon the director as the creative power in the theatre who shapes and controls all of the theatrical elements. The actor is to be a puppet in hands of the director who will manipulate him as one of the elements of the stage design. However, Craig's writings also reveal a vision of the creative possibilities of the actor:

> the ideal actor will be the man who possesses both a rich nature and a powerful brain. . . . It will contain everything. . . . The perfect actor would be he whose brain could conceive and could show us the perfect symbols of all which his nature contains.[20]

The ideal actor envisioned by Craig was one who would be able to create a new language of movement consisting of symbols which are "made mainly from material which lies outside his person."[21]

CORPOREAL MIME AND THE MARIONETTE

Decroux's philosophical conception of corporeal mime is a practical realization of the essential elements of Diderot's and Craig's theories concerning the actor's corporeality—his relation to his body qua instrument. Decroux states, "If the marionette is, at least, the image of the ideal actors, we should, therefore, attempt to acquire the virtues of the ideal marionette."[22] Unlike Diderot, who saw the actor as subordinate to the literary text, and Craig, who envisioned the actor as merely one of the production elements under the control of the director, Decroux sought to reestablish the primacy of the actor as a creator.

The basis for the renovation of the actor's art for Decroux lay in the corporeal mime performer, whose perfectly trained body would be the generating nexus and the focal point of the dramatic event. Ideally, the corporeal mime's controlling will and creative subconscious should command a perfectly articulated instrument in which anarchic spontaneity and naturalistic expression are replaced by a highly technical corporeal grammar. Moreover, this technique would enable the performer to create symbolic representations of emotion, idea and action solely by means of posture and gesture, without the support of words or other theatrical means.

THE MASK OF NEUTRALITY

Like Craig and Diderot before him, Decroux believed that great works of art are not based in the expression of the personal ego of the artist: "The artist must show his work without showing his person."[23] If a work of art is to have lasting value and significance, it should bear the stamp of the impersonal. Decroux was totally against the concept of the star performer. He felt that artist must go beyond expressing the limitations of his ego and, like the unknown builders of the great medieval cathedrals, must dedicate himself to the creation of works which transcend the self.

The corporeal mime achieves impersonality through the vehicle of the neutral or inexpressive mask. "What do I mean by the term neutral or inexpressive mask?" Decroux asks. "The neutral or inexpressive mask has a form that permits the actor to portray all possible sentiments without being ridiculous."[24] According to Decroux, "One may be sublime with a mask, but not with a face. The face has something incurably realistic about it."[25] It subjects the performer to the limitations of physical type, age and sex, and is also prone to fleeting and uncontrolled emotion. Moreover, the audience's attention tends to be drawn to the face if it remains uncovered rather than to the torso, which is the primarily expressive vehicle in corporeal mime.

The concept of the neutral mask originated at the Vieux-Colombier where it was used as a tool to focus attention on the expression of the body. Early in his career, Decroux experimented with various types of neutral masks in his school and performances, but found that the traditional white, rigid, neutral mask distracted the audience—"like a glowing moon"—from attention to the global corporeal ensemble. In its place he used a scarf to veil the face for many of his performances. While Decroux did not use neutral masks in his training program, he advocated neutrality as the basis for all expression — in effect replacing the neutral mask with the neutral expression. Students at his school were required to suppress any tendencies to show fleeting and uncontrolled expressions of thought or emotion in their face while working. This same principle was applied to the movements of the body as well. The neutral mask is a vestige of the blank expression exhibited by individuals as they undergo dissociation in the first phase of possession trance. It is also the characteristic expression of ritual shamans as they make their sacred voyage to the Illud Tempus.

The impersonal style of corporeal mime is based in classicism.[26] Decroux once said, "The classical style does not show things. It has you guess at them. An actor acting in the classical style would have you deduce rather than show you. Classicism in mime is when the body expresses depression — without the face showing it."[27]

What Decroux terms classicism is essentially the concept of the actor who remains unmoved while moving his audience. Decroux states, "One must represent suffering without suffering, effort without effort, pain without pain."[28] The quality of remaining unmoved is emblemized in a neutral attitude that underlies all expression in corporeal mime. Like the shaman and the No performer, the corporeal mime does not allow emotion to overwhelm his instrument. He stands at a distance from his body. Passion is cooled down and channeled through a formidable technique in order to convey universal truths rather than the personal and idiosyncratic.

THE CORPOREAL MIME
CHARACTER ATTITUDES

Corporeal mime training involves the study of four basic character types: the Man of the Drawing Room (*homme de salon*), the Man of Sport (*homme de sport*), the Man of Dreams (*homme de songe*) and the Marionette.

The student acquires a neutral attitude through the imitation of the character/model of the Man of the Drawing Room. The impersonal style of the Man of the Drawing Room was inspired by the figure of the nineteenth century Dandy, who according to Baudelaire, combines the qualities of elegance and forcefulness, but does not show what he is thinking; rather he allows it to be inferred.[29] The Man of the Drawing Room and the figure of the Dandy are Romantic elaborations of the ideal Renaissance court aristocrat. Of the perfect courtier, Baldesar Castiglione writes that he must "... practice in all things a certain sprezzatura (nonchalance), so as to conceal all art and make whatever is done or said appear to be without effort and almost without any thought about it ... much grace comes of this.[30] The Man of the Drawing Room, which forms the basis for the other three characters, as well as applied styles, is a practical realization of the aesthetics and technical mastery of the Uber-marionette. It represents the highest ideals of Western rationalism, which has freed the individual from the necessity for physical labor.

The rationality of corporeal mime is reflected in the hierarchy of the expressive organs and the mathematical segmentation and articulation of the body. In the base posture of the Man of the Drawing Room, the trunk is of first importance, then the arms, hands and legs, and finally, the face. The trunk, which is the performer's primary expressive vehicle, is articulated into three segments—the bust, the waist and the pelvis—which are capable of isolated and independent movement. Of these three, the bust is given highest priority. It represents both the affective emotional organ of the mime's body as well as his eyes (by indicating the direction he is looking). The waist forms a vertical platform for the movement of the bust, while the pelvis tends to remain vertical, rarely inclining forward or backward. The arms move in harmonious resonance with the trunk, and the legs are straight, with the weight installed on one foot and the other foot free and pointed to the back and slightly to the side. The stance of the corporeal mime performer, the use of basic positions for the unfolding of movement, and the geometric paths followed by the body in space reveal the strong influence of the techniques and aesthetics of classical ballet. Decroux states, "I have been walking in a light ... from [a] source ... and that light is classical ballet."[31]

The hierarchy of the elements of the trunk represents the dominance of the will and intellect as the energy and shaping force behind corporeal mime movement. Unlike Eastern theatre where the movement radiates from the diaphragm and is supported by the breath, corporeal mime movement tends to originate in the chest. Breathing, which is an essential element of movement, is rarely, if ever, mentioned by Decroux; and the abdomen, which is the true center of the body, is given little emphasis and is nearly always flat and contained. For this reason, corporeal mime often appears to be more of a rational exercise composed of controlled movements verging on rigidity than a spontaneous, organic expression of the primary nature of the individual. It is truly the embodiment of attitudes expressive of thought and will rather than emotion, as evidenced in Decroux's frequent usage of such words as Promethean, will, mastery, and control in relation to mime.

The Man of Sports was inspired by movements derived from sports, work and crafts. In this character all organs collaborate in harmony with the action being performed. Decroux calls this "inter-organic solidarity," which means that when one organ is engaged all the other organs come to its aid. There is no separate head, neck or bust as in the Man of the Drawing Room, nor can he do several things at once. His attention is directed towards doing one thing at a time and the focus of his energy is directed at his task rather the public.

The study of the Man of Sports entails the exploration of the techniques of the counterweights (*contrepoids*). Counterweights are spasmodic movements of pushing or pulling that constitute the basic actions involved in sports, physical labor, and crafts. They involve an impulse from the stomach which passes from the center of the body down through the legs and feet as the body both releases to and pulls away from gravity. This essentially emotional falling and straightening or straightening to fall culminates in a brief pose which is a complex image epitomizing both the action and the attitude which underlies it.

The Man of Dreams combines the features of the above characters; he is, however, a poetic figure who moves in a dream-like manner. The body is inclined backwards on a vertical with the bust projected towards the sky. The study of the Man of Dreams centers on the technique of the fondue — a slow melting movement similar to cinematic slow motion in which there are no shocks or rapid movements, as there are in the Man of Sports. The most characteristic feature of this figure is the walk, which is similar to the gliding motions of the No. The body moves evenly and slowly across the floor, always maintaining the same level.

The Marionette is studied to help the student achieve spontaneity and quickness. Exercises derived from puppetry train the student in how to achieve effortless articulation of the body through suspension of the will in which there is no sense of "I am doing it." Movements in this figure impart the uncanny aura that the body is animated by an outside force.

The four types of personages outlined above form the basis for the study of corporeal mime technique and are not meant to be seen as character roles per se. Corporeal mime training is more concerned with the attainment of an ideal state of neutrality rather than with exploration of the bases of character. Decroux defines character as "a crystallization of a determined or a dominant sentiment" which is most truly expressed by the walk.[32] While the impersonal and symbolic nature of corporeal mime style is diametrically opposed to the personal and defining nature of characterization, it does not preclude the use of technique to create character.

THE TECHNIQUES OF POSTURE AND THE MARIONETTE

Decroux's model for the actor-marionette was inspired by the acting style of the renowned French actor, Louis Jouvet, who had trained at the Vieux-Colombier. Decroux said, "I felt in his work the beginnings of, a taste for, the marionette ... a certain way of turning the head, of using his neck, a certain way of taking his place on the stage. One sensed in him the articulated man."[33]

The key to corporeal mime lies in the interdependence and articulation of each segment of the body, which allows the performer to play upon it like a keyboard. The trained mime, according to Decroux, should make each part of his body separate from the others, and in so doing, make it capable of obeying the subtlest nuances of emotion and thought.

A student once told Decroux, "The day you said, 'head without neck,' you

Etienne Decroux. "Sport," 1948. Photograph by Etienne Bertrand Weill.

found your whole system."[34] At Decroux's school, the student learned to isolate each organ of the body from the others (i.e., head from neck, neck from chest, etc.) so that the various organs can be commanded singly or in concert. For the mime to move the head, the neck must not move. For every movement that is made there are contingent movements that must be simultaneously suppressed: "One must, therefore, mobilize only that which one wants to mobilize: a single determined organ or several. What is not mobilized must be immobilized."[35]

The immobilization of the body's organs as platforms for the unfolding of movement is the essence of attitude expression by means of the intensification of the postural elements. The decision and mobilization to act produces a contraction and freezing of localized muscle groups which is followed by a release of other muscle groups which discharge crystallized emotion or energy through gesture.

THE PROMETHEAN HERO

In an interview, Decroux once said, "Art is only interesting if it meets difficulties. . . . The idea of difficulty animates us all the time. We don't want man to be an angel, we want him to be a hero. That is to say, a man like us, but who does extraordinary things."[36]

Decroux states that his mime is "Promethean as opposed to religious . . . it is the opposite of dance. It is not accepting."[37] It represents the human struggle to conquer matter by means of the spirit. Corporeal mime is founded upon a moral aesthetic which posits the individual as eternally acting on or against matter. The Promethean quality of corporeal mime is manifested on its most basic level in the mime's struggle to overcome the force of gravity. In the base standing position, a downward force moving through the pelvis, legs, and feet is counterbalanced by a contrary force moving upwards through the waist, chest, neck, and head. Tensional rhythms of thought and emotion are dramatized in the walks of the corporeal mime, which involve a byplay between gravity and freedom from it. In many of the walks, the foot, which is glued to the floor, must be uprooted. There is a struggle between the downward and backward pull through the body into the foot and one exerted upwards and forwards. When the body arrives at a point between these two contrary forces, there is a moment of dramatic suspension. As the body translates itself forward, it arrives by re-rooting the foot in the floor. In a walk reminiscent of the No, *le marche sans accent static* has these same forces operating as the body glides slowly across the floor. Here the tensions are dosed out in each phase of the walk in such a way as to maintain a slow, even movement in which there are no shocks.

The dramatic opposition between stasis and movement, gravity and freedom from gravity are articulated in every aspect of corporeal mime technique. Decroux developed a series of body scales in order to train the student in the articulation and oppositional interdependence of the various organs of the body. The scales involve inclinations, curves, and rotations of the body in space. The simplest of these, the lateral inclination, begins with the head, followed by neck, chest, waist, and pelvis. For the head to incline to the right, the neck must be fixed as a platform. The fixing of the neck demands that an opposing force must be applied to it to counterbalance the pull of the chest and so on.

The counterweights are an extension of the principle of opposition to actions performed by the mime on imaginary objects. The corporeal mime is an individual who is in conflict with matter, his own, and the resistance of material space and objects that surround him. Dorcy defines the counterweights as a visible muscular compensation for an invisible force.[38] The principle of the counterweights are derived from the forces involved in pushing and pulling material objects. Decroux developed a series of exercises involving pistons and extensors in space which the student acts upon using a tripartite execution involving preparation, a spasmodic movement of push or pull, and a relaxation. From these exercises, Decroux created a series of figures based upon abstracts of work and sports: The Carpenter, the Blacksmith, the Hauler, the Reaper, the Discus Thrower, the Spear Thrower, etc. The essence of the counterweights is to capture the contrary tensions that are inherent in any action and to dramatize them within the corpus of the performer. As Eugenio Barba has shown, this involves movement techniques that are contrary to those employed in everyday life:

> He shows, for example, the action of pushing something not by project-ing the chest forward and pressing with the back foot — as occurs in the real action — but by arching the spine concavely, as if instead of pushing he was being pushed, bringing the arms towards the chest and pressing downwards with the front foot and leg. This radical inversion of the forces with respect to how they occur in the real action restores the work — or the effort — which comes into play in the real action.[39]

The deliberate intensification of opposing forces in actions strengthens the dramatic quality of movement and contributes to the Promethean stance that informs corporeal mime.

The singularity of Decroux's system of corporeal mime, and what distin-guishes it from the Nō, is that the techniques of isolation and interdependence of the organs of the body offer an infinite number of combinations which do not limit the student to an acquired system of gesture. Craig, on witnessing a performance by Decroux and his troupe in 1945, stated: "I have travelled far in Europe, visiting many cities in Holland, Germany, Russia, Italy, England and Scotland — but till this day I have never seen anything comparable to this attempt. ... We were present at the creation of an alphabet — an ABC of mime."[40]

In this statement, Craig did not mean that Decroux had created a codified language like the Greco-Roman pantomimes and the nineteenth century pan-tomime blanche. Rather, he recognized in corporeal mime a grammar of designed movement components that enables the performer to communicate using abstract symbols which could be combined like the letters of the alphabet to create meaning.

CORPOREAL MIME AND
THE EXPRESSION OF ATTITUDES

Decroux asserts, "The essential aspect of my art is articulation."[41]

The corporeal mime architects images denoting both his inner world of thought and emotion, as well as actions and events, from the phenomenal world by means of two distinct, but interrelated styles: objective mime and subjective mime.

Objective mime involves the portrayal of phenomena from the surround-ing world, with denotation playing a large role. "In objective mime there is not one movement that does not have a meaning."[42] One aspect of objective mime involves techniques to create illusion in order to make invisible objects appear to be present. It is on such techniques as the stationary walk, climbing an imaginary staircase, touching imaginary walls (elaborated early in Decroux's career) that Marcel Marceau has founded his style.

However, the core of Decroux's philosophy and style of corporeal mime centers on subjective mime, which he defines as "movement of the mind expressed by the body."[43] Decroux states that "when [the mime] wants to be remarkable, [he] makes movements with his body to evoke movements of your soul. What Freud makes you say, the mime makes us do it."[44] This brief and unique allusion to Freud in Decroux's writings suggests that he does not associate the subconscious with the strictly Freudian function of expressing instinctual, sexual or archetypal impulses. Rather, for Decroux, the subconscious expresses movements of the soul that represent a higher manifestation of emotion — in other words, the idealization and universalization of basic instincts, reactions, and desires.

Decroux attributes a rationalizing function, normally associated with the conscious mind, to the subconscious: "It can be either the conscious or subconscious which reasons. The subconscious is the region where we reason logically. We imagine that the subconscious makes mathematical calculations — like an adding machine. We see only the results of its calculations."[45]

The subconscious is the realm of repressed dreams and desires which are expressed in the geometry and dynamic rhythms which characterize the phenomenal world. Reduced to their essential components, the impulses which bubble up from the subconscious appear to have a logic of their own. They vector upwards, stop, turn, descend slowly, veer to the left, and collide. It is this directional and dynamic expression of the subconscious which Decroux seeks to embody in a technique founded on the laws of geometry:

> Decroux believes that the truly expressive attitude [posture], the truly meaningful gestures are exterior manifestations of inner movements which are able to convey the ideal rather than the particular. To achieve this exterior manifestation of inner movement, the entire body must transform itself into a portrait of inner movement.[46]

The inner movements of the subconscious are conveyed in corporeal mime through postures and gestures involving interaction with phenomena. Everything in mime stems from the material world. Decroux noticed that the movements which represent thought and emotion resembled work:

> In looking at the carpenter, you will find all the movements of the mind; struggle, thought, judging. There is finesse of care. We must learn to do all the métiers because a craftsman, worker must think. The thought that makes a straight line on a table, exists as a straight metaphysical thought.[47]

In subjective mime the counterweights are employed to reveal the moral and spiritual strivings of the individual. According to Decroux, everything in the counterweights can be translated with very little change into metaphysical meditation or movement of the spirit. "Emotion and suffering have a manner similar to will and in will there are counterweights—one remembers one's trials in moving things. . . . Danton hitting the table three times—'Audacious: Audacious: and more Audacious!'—is like hitting a forge."[48]

The work of a carpenter making a table involves emotion and thought as translated through the counterweights in the movements of gouging, sanding, and planning. These same movements serve as metaphors for the inner attitudes of the carpenter. What is important in a subjective mime piece like "The Carpenter" is not the recreation of actions from the surrounding world but in the recreation of the inner architecture of the carpenter's mind vis-à-vis his craft. Because the mime uses the impersonal tools of geometrically stylized movement, the portrait of the carpenter becomes a universal expression of the movement of the human psyche.

Corporeal mime is inherently dramatic. It crystallizes the dynamic postures of agents, acting upon one another from the material world, which are the figurative embodiment of attitudes. For Decroux, the mime is not a simple philosopher before the universe; he is an inexhaustible force against the universe. The struggle with phenomena reveals the moral conflict involved in the forces acting in the individual's psyche. The tripartite movement of the counterweights—preparation, action and release—could be seen as an analogue to the Agent-Agissant-Agi or Jo-Ha-Kyu or the conflict between protagonist and antagonist which forms the nucleus of dramatic action.

ATTITUDE AS A PRIMARY STYLISTIC DEVICE IN CORPOREAL MIME

Decroux writes in *Paroles sur le Mime*:

> Might one say that mime is an art of movement in which the attitude is but the punctuation? I have said that I prefer attitude to gesture. I have not said that I prefer attitude to movement. Not yet. Attitude is perhaps more than a punctuation of movement. It is, perhaps the witness, the report. In any case, it is a result. . . . One may conceive of a movement as a succession of attitudes.[49]

The term attitude is used by Etienne Decroux to refer to a designed posture which is either held momentarily or transported through space on a fixed base. It is essentially a product of the fixing of the body or parts of the body in a momentarily held pose. The attitude in corporeal mime is a frozen instant of movement, which serves to punctuate and highlight the essence of a movement phrase through a distilled gestural image: "A successful attitude is like a condensed drama; perfect, complete, it is an image epitomizing identity, origin, destination, and intent. Attitude is the original method of mime and the essence of the Mime."[50]

It is a dynamic symbol which witnesses the movement that precedes it and which promises a plan of action to follow. Decroux has compared the attitude to a snapshot which captures a frozen instant of movement, with the difference that the attitude combines several phases of movement into a postural and gestural image. Dorcy writes, "In the idiom of mime, the attitude as poetic image is the most important element and the movement of translation plays a minor role."[51]

The attitude in corporeal mime is basically a product of a stylistic device created by Decroux, termed raccourci. Similar to the cinematic ellipsis, raccourci involves reducing a simple action to emphasize its primary structural components. For example, the key elements that make up the action of walking are: an internal shift of weight (preparation); the lifting the foot off the floor; the translation of the body through space; and the placement of the foot. Once a movement has been reduced to its constituent features, it is reconstructed with key attitudes which articulate the essence of the original movement. The result is a series of forms that are linked together in time and space but are in actuality, like the individual frames that make up a movie film, a series of arrested moments juxtaposed in such a way that they appear continuous.

The technique of raccourci forms the cornerstone of economy, which is an important stylistic element of corporeal mime. Decroux believes in the philosophical premise that richness of expression arises in direct proportion to the economy of expression. The mime performer, according to Decroux, is like the base of a pyramid, if he does only "one thing at a time," he is able to create highly stylized and simplified images in which the effect is narrowed to "the point of a pyramid pushing at the public."[52] The attitudes which highlight segments of movement are comparable to gestalts. The information of these forms should be simplified and clear enough to allow the memory to store and remember them.

The importance of attitude in corporeal mime is seen most clearly in the crystallized pose called the Fugitive. These are moments of no-action, similar to those in the No drama, in which the movement appears to be totally bound or frozen, but is being animated by the internal tensions within the mime's body held in precarious balance. The Fugitive is based on fragments drawn from memory which have an important accent of significance:

> In memory what stays is things that did not last very long, but last a long time in our memory. Things which have on the surface the sense of being nothing — a modest flower which pushes through the rocks. Memories are little snatches of music, flowers. This is the revenge of the fugitive. You didn't think something was important which passes. Yet it follows us.[53]

Like the image in a poem, the Fugitive is a symbolic posture in which many things are reunited. It is a corporeal attitude which not only condenses several phrases of movement but serves more fully as a gestural symbol.

CORPOREAL MIME AND STATUARY

Decroux often said, "The interior must be expressed on the exterior and this is done through mobile statuary."[54]

The Fugitive, portrayed by a held attitude of the body, is intimately bound up with the aesthetics of the statue, which is a moment of eternity frozen into a fixed form. Decroux defines the art of the mime, in the etymological sense of his corporeality, by analogy with the work of a sculptor: "I would have liked to have been a sculptor. ... Our thought pushes our gestures just as the thumb of the sculptor pushes out forms; and our body, sculpted from the interior, stretches. The mime is at the same time, sculptor and statue."[55]

Posturally based movement and designed attitudes in corporeal mime are elaborated stylistically according to theories and techniques based in mobile statuary (*sculpture mobile*). Decroux states, "We must find postures as crystallized as statuary."[56] Statuary mime involves the creation of attitudes which are either stationary or transported through space. Like the sculptor, the corporeal mime sculpts his body from the interior in order to present designed corporeal forms which are expressive of thought and emotion:

> Statuary mime ... depicts arrested, imaginative, significant movement in silence, like a Rodin statue, motionless yet bursting with potential movement. Instead of breaking forth into facile movement, statuary mime gradually evolves from movement into immobility, seeking to stir the imagination by suggestion.[57]

Like the sculptural postures of the No, the corporeal mime employs a minimum of space and movement to create a maximum of sentiment. Decroux has said that the mime performer "works on a barrel." Rather than filling the performance space like the dancer, the mime creates the semblance of space while working in place (*sur place*). He is like a "Greek statue changing form under a globe."[58] When he moves he should not displace from under his globe—rather, he should move with it. This creates the illusion of what Decroux termed transported immobility. The translational movements (displacement of the mass of the body, primarily by means of the legs) serve to carry a scupltural form (designed attitude) through space creating the aura of an animated statue. Movement in mobile statuary should take place smoothly and almost imperceptibly:

> The actor must change his statue under his transparent glass globe as a sky changes shape and color. One does not notice the sky changing. One notices only that it has changed. Smoothly the clouds move along seeming to keep their formation. Yet little by little the beautiful pattern becomes another pattern, of equal beauty.[59]

As in the moments of non action in the No, when the performer appears to be in a statue-like repose, he is nevertheless projecting energy towards the

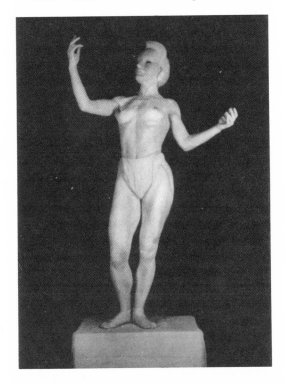

Eliane Guyon. "The Statue." Photography by Etienne Bertrand Weill.

audience; the corporeal mime animates an arrested attitude by projecting its inner dynamism — the tensional oppositions which it contains. Like the No actor, the mime reduces action in space in order to increase it in time. The play of forces between stasis and forward motion are witness to the movements that precede the attitude and indicate the movements, continuation in space. Decroux states, "If a movement stops, if we look closely, we see that something has continued inside.... Like a *serré vie* "bookends." A man pushing against a wall looks like he has stopped but he is pushing like the sap from a tree."[60]

During moments of immobility, the corporeal mime performer keeps her internal motor working. In the lines and forces of the Fugitive form is the promise of the ensuing gesture. The withholding of movement creates a strong kinaesthetic anticipation that the attitude will burst forth into movement.

Decroux's philosophy and aesthetics of mobile statuary shows the influence of canons of classical sculpture, like those manifested in the work of Auguste Rodin. Many of Rodin's ideas on the art of sculpture can be found in Decroux's essays and lectures. In an essay entitled, "Le mouvement dans l'art," Rodin states that he has mostly tried to "accentuate the mime" in such pieces as "The Bourgeois of Calais," "Balzac," and "The Man Who Walks," and that in most of his other works he has always sought to put in some indications of gesture.[61] Rodin, like the great Greek sculptors upon which his work is modeled, deliberately created opposing movements within his figures, imparting to them a sense of animation and vitality.

Rodin relates that an old stone carver taught him to "never consider a surface as anything but the extremity of a volume, the point more or less large it directs towards you."[62] Applying this principle to the execution of sculpted figures, Rodin represents them "as projections of interior volumes": "I endeavored to express every swelling of torso and limbs, the efflorescence of a muscle or bone extending deep under the skin. And so the truth of my figures, instead of being superficial, seems to blossom forth from within like life itself."[63]

This same manner of expressing the inner life of form through the projection of bodily volumes towards the spectator is referred to by Decroux as "pyramid on its point." The mime cannot alter the volumes of his body the way a sculptor can while modeling a figure. Through the isolation and intensification of elements of the torso, however, the corporeal mime can project the energy or tensions contained in the designed attitude outward towards the audience. As Decroux explains, "The point of the pyramid on the chest has a greater force than the bottom of the pyramid (legs). In mime we are trying to have the point of the pyramid go towards the public."[64]

Like Decroux, Rodin conceives of movement as "a transition from one attitude to another."[65] The sculptor creates the illusion of movement through the dynamically charged form, a form which indicates the movement that has been completed and the movement that is just beginning. Similarly, corporeal mime attempts to synthesize and condense several phases of movement into a dynamic postural image.

Decroux states that "we may conceive of a movement as a succession of attitudes" and that corporeal mime "gives the idea of movement by the attitude and the attitude by the movement."[66] According to Rodin, an instantaneous photograph does not express movement, because a photograph arrests movement by immobilizing or paralyzing the subject without any indication of the dynamic line of the movement. The sculptor solves this problem by indicating both the movement that has been completed and the movement that is just beginning and in so doing attempts "to condense several moments into one image."[67] This is essentially the idea of raccourci — the condensation of an idea in time and space that forms the basis of the attitude in corporeal mime.

GEOMETRY AND ABSTRACTION
IN CORPOREAL MIME

Geometry, a primary law of nature, plays an important role in the work of Decroux and Rodin. Rodin states:

I have come to realize that geometry is at the bottom of sentiment or rather that each expression of sentiment is made by a movement governed by geometry. Geometry is everywhere present in Nature. A woman combing her hair goes through a series of rhythmic movements which constitute a beautiful harmony. The entire rhythm of the body is governed by law. ... Nature is the supreme architect. Everything is built in the finest equilibrium; and everything too is enclosed in a triangle or a cube or some modification of them. I have adopted this principle in building up my statuary.[68]

Decroux states that in his school "the accent is on the geometric spirit."[69] Movement in corporeal mime is based on geometric movements of the body in space with regard to paths, planes, intersections, angles and axes:

In space one must mentally set certain lines that one considers to be ideal. Three lines immediately present themselves: the vertical, the horizontal and, between the two, right in the middle, the diagonal. The extension of this principle is quickly grasped: these three lines reappear underneath, to the right, to the left, etc. These are the streets of space. Each of them can be occupied or travelled across.[70]

The laws of geometry in corporeal mime come from the realm of statuary and architecture. The primary illusion of sculpture, according to Susanne Langer, is "virtual space" in the mode of "kinetic volume."[71] Decroux applied architectural geometry to the movement of the human body in a kinetic form, that is, the circle, the straight line, ballistics, etc., as a basis for mobile statuary. Movements in corporeal mime are analyzed and reconstructed according to these geometric principles. The simple task of giving something to someone is reduced to body inclinations, rotations, convex spheres, and arcs in space. All expression is channeled through geometric postures and gestures. Decroux told his students, "Don't just cry, but cry through this fine geometric pipe."[72]

The raccourci, which is conveyed through geometrically stylized attitudes, is the basis for abstraction in corporeal mime. Decroux uses the impersonal elements of geometry to portray emotion and thought through lines, arcs, and tensions in space, as well as to evoke "the concrete by means of the abstract" by presenting the schematization of agents and their actions. Abstraction involves the elimination of the extraneous and particular in order to achieve the essential. In reducing postures and gestures to geometric principles, Decroux sought to find the essential structural elements of phenomena, animated by basic energies or Efforts which fill out their forms. The condensed geometric images created by corporeal mime evoke or suggest reality through ideal movements. They are not a stylization of reality. Their primary aim is to evoke the inner subjective world of the performer by means of postural and gestural metaphors. The images created by the corporeal mime do not point to reality but to ideal and abstract forms which unite the inner world of dream, thought, emotion and memory with the object. The juxtaposition of geometrically designed attitudes in corporeal mime parallels the style of abstract cubism: "The mime passes before the world like a crystal ball."[73] Often the significance of a posture can only be understood in relation to postures which precede and follow it.

CORPOREAL MIME, DANCE, AND PANTOMIME

The influence of classical ballet technique on corporeal mime, coupled with the abstract and geometric nature of its postures and gestures (often having no clear denotational meaning), has led some critics to conclude that corporeal mime is not mime but dance. Decroux provides many arguments as to the basic differences between these genres. The mime, according to him, is a rooted creature subject to the laws of gravity, while the dancer lacks weight and uses the ground primarily as a springboard for movements away from the earth. Moreover, with dance one cannot see the beginnings and ends of movements because they tend to trail off into space, while mime clearly separates phrases from one another through the punctuation of the attitude. Mime, he states, is a series of present actions which are dramatic in nature because they represent the individual's conflict with matter. "Mime is the portrait of work and dance the portrait of dance."[74] The dance translates natural movements into unnatural movements and when it attempts to be dramatic, it becomes mime.

Finally, rhythm, according to Decroux, is the exception in mime, whereas in dance it is the rule and is usually based in a musical accompaniment. The dynamic rhythms that constitute the mime derive from the movement of thought and emotion as metaphorically expressed in terms of agents and their actions. For example, the work of the carpenter is both actual movements of woodworking as well as expressions of thought and emotion, such as the surprise, the question mark, dramatic hesitation, and so forth. Mime is striking in its lack of rhythm; it is characterized more by the abrupt juxtaposition of the dramatic pause, slow fondue, and the shock.

All of Decroux's arguments for distinguishing dance from mime point to the importance of attitude articulation by means of posturally based movement. Corporeal mime, however, constitutes a development of mime articulation in the direction of pantomimic narrative. As Annette Lust explains, "[It] is perhaps better defined as 'pantomime corporelle' in the strictest sense because feelings and ideas were depicted here uniquely through the body and without the help of the spoken word or any other medium."[75] Lust is correct in making a connection between corporeal mime and the solo, silent, and narrative art of pantomime, but her reasons do not go far enough. What situates corporeal mime squarely in the domain of pantomime is that it is so clearly an art of articulation which uses syntactical devices analogous to the diction of spoken language or poetry. Alvin Epstein, a corporeal mime student, teacher, and performer, makes this important connection between corporeal mime and diction:

> It is, indeed, in the spoken word that Decroux's mimetic movement has found its phrasing, rhythm, articulation and even a certain "intonation." . . . It is here that any confusion between the Mime and the Dance is finally dispelled. The articulation and flow of the Mime is directly inspired by the "movement" of the spoken text; its fluctuation, lack of identical repetition, intensity independent of rhythmic structure and *not* by dance movement which is essentially steady flowing, based upon identical repetitions of a rhythmic pattern, and displaying its greatest intensity in moments of speed and complicated rhythmic structure. And the reason for this basic separation is the *dramatic* one: the *psychology* of the dramatic actor opposed to the *elan* of the dancer. The Mime is often most forceful and striking to the eye in near immobility and movement unchoreographic in itself. . . . The mime's virtue is in the faceting of a movement so that each phase is bright and detached to the spectator's gaze. The dancer's virtue is the very opposite, his fluent welding of separate parts into a smooth and indistinguishable effect.[76]

CORPOREAL MIME AND SPOKEN POETRY

Decroux entered the Vieux-Colombier in 1923 with the intention of perfecting his diction for oratory and for the recitation of poetry. He states, "I would have liked to have been a poet."[77] His fascination with the spoken word is revealed in his system of corporeal mime which articulates clearly defined phrases of movement in a manner analogous to diction.

In "The Dosage of Mime for the Speaking Actor," Decroux draws a parallel between diction, which he regards as a type of vocal mime, and corporeal mime: "Because diction . . . is a species of mime — a type of vocal mime, isn't it a good idea to reflect upon it in order to approach the study of mime properly speaking along a similar path."[78]

Decroux outlines four basic elements that constitute diction in speech: inflection, speed, force, and expression. Inflection has to do with the pitch of the voice as it ranges over a scale from low to high and vice versa. Decroux states that "the voice follows a line of inflection. It is a curve, sometimes concave and other times convex."[79] The voice actually appears to be able to sculpt space through variations in range. Speed or rate of the spoken words has to do with the slowness or quickness of the word flow and the duration of silences. Force combines the qualities of volume and intensity in speech with speed, producing a range of expression from a light, slow, sustained quality to an explosion. He explains the concept of force with the example of a child's parachute which is thrown forcibly into the air (explosion/loud/high) and then descends with a light, gliding motion. Decroux does not make clear what he means by expression with regard to diction, but it appears to have something to do with the particular vocal instrument of the actor and the way in which he employs the elements of inflection, speed, and force. It is essentially the ability of one actor to make us cry and the other to make us laugh with the same phrase.

Decroux goes on to say that the principles of diction in speech can be applied to mime. Effort, the four ingredients of movement (time, weight, space, and flow), are analogous to the elements of spoken diction. Laban sometimes refers to these factors as the how, what, when and where of movement: how refers to the way movement flows; what to the weight factor; when to time; and where to space. Similarly, when Decroux reduces a gesture to its primary components, he asks the following questions: What is it that moves? In what direction? With what energy? and In how much time?

The importance of Effort in corporeal mime can be seen in Epstein's discussion of the three basic qualities that characterize mime movement: design, rhythm, and intensity. The design, according to Epstein, is the trajectory through space that a movement follows, beginning at a certain point, passing through others and concluding at still another point.[80] Design is analogous to intonation in diction. It is the spacial element of Effort — the geometric paths and trajectories that a figure travels. Rhythm, is defined by Epstein as "the varying lapses of time between the points" on the path of a movement. In Laban terminology, this would be equivalent to time — the variations of slowness or quickness of a movement combined with stops of varying lengths. Intensity, which is analogous to force in diction, is produced through a combination of weight, the lightness or heaviness of a movement, and flow, the amount of tension in a movement.

Effort qualities underlie all movements in mime; however, it is the combination and dosages of the various Effort qualities, coupled with the particular organs that are utilized, which create the unique meaning of each mime figure. Decroux has often said that mime is plagued by homonyms. Two figures may appear to have the same meaning; however, it is the difference in the Efforts underlying postures and gestures which distinguish them from one another.

Corporeal mime is most clearly an art of diction that finds its phrasing, rhythm, articulation, and even a certain intonation in spoken poetry. Decroux has said, "I prefer rhythmic poetry because it seems that in order to create this rhythm one sculpts the verb. I desire that the actor, accepting the artifice, sculpt the air and make us feel where the verse begins and where it finishes."[81]

Decroux constructed mime pieces from phrases of movement, which like the spoken phrase of subject–verb–object, manifest a tripartite structure. This is seen most clearly in the movement phrase for the counterweights. For example, the verb "to press" is broken down into three broad phases, preparation, movement proper, and attitude. The preparation is the subject; the movement proper, which consists of a gesture, conveys the verb of the action; and the attitude is the object which expresses the sense and significance of the phrase. Decroux includes a fourth element in the counterweight exercises which consists of a relaxation or return to a neutral position following the attitude. Each of the three elements which make up the phrase can be broken down further into similar tripartite units. Within these larger and smaller phrases, the attitude is the punctuation which clearly separates one movement from the next. Corporeal mime is often highly abstract and its meaning may not be readily discernable to a spectator. Meaning is made apparent, however, through the postural articulation of the performer's body as it creates detached images.

The No mime-dance is also an art of diction which traces its roots to shamanic performance. It is built upon a tripartite structure (jo-ha-kyu) which Zeami Motokiyo, the great performer and theorician of the No, states is manifest in every element of the phenomenal world. When Decroux witnessed the performance of the No play *Kantan* at the Vieux-Colombier he exclaimed that it was "the only time in my life when I felt the art of Diction."[82] This is because he recognized in the formalized postures of the No kata a grammatical articulation of the deeply felt attitudes of the shite. These attitudes, moreover, mirror the chanted and sung poetic narration.

While corporeal mime incorporates Effort in a manner analogous to diction in spoken language, it does not seek to create gestural signs which point specifically to concrete phenomena, nor does its substitute gestures for words as in classical and Romantic pantomime. Decroux states, "I renounce all signs, I desire that my spectator be moved by analogy between my mime's action and a certain thing which he remembers. Analogy is not a sign."[83]

Through the use of geometrically stylized postures and gestures, the corporeal mime performer attempts to create images which distill a thought or emotion. The postures and gestures are grounded in the tripartite gestures of phenomena. These images are analogous to word clusters or poetic metaphors, which while they denote concrete phenomena, operate primarily on the meaning created by sounds. The tone produced by the variations of the diction elements (which are contained in the word choice and their juxtaposition) evoke an emotion that exists above and beyond the meaning of the words themselves. In corporeal mime a postural and gestural image operates in a similar manner. While the image may denote concrete phenomena, its primary function is to convey an attitude through the juxtaposition of postures and gestures which project a particular constellation of Effort qualities; in their formal geometric shapes and paths as they move through space; in the tension of their held forms; and in the variation of their design, rate and intensity as they unfold. While corporeal mime may appear to be only a stylization of reality, it is in fact an evocation of both the inner world of the performer as well as a world that lies above and beyond reality. Its true essence lies in the creation of abstract visual metaphors whose suggestiveness does not engage the spectator in matching meanings, but rather, sparked by the postural and gestural images of the performer, triggers his own personal reverie.

The poetic nature of corporeal mime can best be seen in a short exercise from studies in mobile statuary called the Bellringer. While the gestures involve the mimesis of the actions of pulling the rope of a large church bell, these are essentially metaphors for the spiritual awakening of man. The actions of rope pulling (which are counterweights) are presented in three broad phases: the awakening, awake, and sleep. Decroux says of the movement for the Bellringer that it "should not be run together, but should be separated like the facets of a crystal ball."

The piece begins with the mime in a posture prepared to pull the bell's rope. Commencing with a quick up and down movement of the body with the arms extended (which expresses the initial resistance of the rope), the performer begins to pull softy using light, slow, sustained and bound movements. Decroux says of this first phase, "one is asleep, the movements are very slow and lazy. It is not work yet." Throughout the action of pulling, the body retains its attitude of semi-repose, with the head inclined to the side and forward. Each phrase of the piece's awakening segment manifests the movement segments of preparation, attitude of pulling, release and relaxation. The rhythm of this phase is created by the increasing tempo of the initial pull's spasmodic diphthong alternating with the tense, bound continuation of the downward pull and the light upward swing of the body as it is pulled up by the rope. The second phase expresses "work, excitement and activity," characterizing man in his spiritually awakened state. Decroux uses the metaphor of fishing (which is metaphorically embodied in the activity of rope pulling) to describe the significance of this phase, stating that "man fishes god and is fished by him." The awake phase is characterized by increased rapidity of motion and an alteration in the postural tonus of the body, giving the impression of wakefulness, in contrast to the sleepy, relaxed attitude of the preceding phase. The head is inclined backwards with the eyes looking up at the bell. The downward pull is now alternated with an upward pull by the invisible rope. The third and final phase of the piece represents man going slowly back to sleep. It follows the opposite progression from that of the first phase — the rapid energetic movements become increasingly slower until the performer reaches the final posture of sleep. At this point the tolling of the bell is symbolized by slow, evenly spaced vibrating tucks of the head.

Corporeal mime presents a clear example of attitude articulation by means of an intensification of posturally based gesture. By providing a technical grammar based in the isolation and independant movements of organs of the body, it allows the performer to play upon his body to create bodily attitudes and movements. As such, it is a practical realization of Craig's conception of the Uber-marionette—the ideal actor who is at once obedient, impersonal, calculated and symbolic. Unlike classical forms of pantomime, it eschews realism, anecdote, linear narrative, verbal equivalency, and character enactment to concentrate instead on the abstract, universal, and impersonal expression of the inner movements of thought and emotion.

The style of corporeal mime is shamanic. Corporeal mime performers must possess a powerful controlling will, prodigious technique, and the ability to remain unmoved while moving the audience. Their performance is self-reflexive. That is, they must stand at a distance from the self in order to use the body as the impersonal material of their art. The movement style of corporeal mime, which is founded on the principles of diction, places it in the tradition of the art of shamanic narrative and the pantomime. The battle with matter that forms the basis of the corporeal mime style recalls the spiritual voyage of the shaman-hero and the heroic themes of the Greco-Roman pantomime. Decroux has called the art of corporeal mime Promethean because it is not accepting: "it's the body which must pay, it's the body that counts, that proves, that suffers...."[84] Roberta Sklar has observed that when Decroux writes or talks about action he does not use the verb *faire* which means to make, he uses the verb *agir* which means to act.[85] Like the shaman hero who acts upon the spirit world to obtain knowledge and power, the corporeal mime, by deliberately creating oppositions within his body, forges the universal themes of humanity.

NOTES

Introduction

1. Gerald F. Else, "'Imitation' in the Fifth Century," *Classical Philology* 52:2:78.

2. Gloria B. Strauss, "The Aesthetics of Dominance," *Journal of Aesthetics and Art Criticism* 37 (Fall 1978) p. 73.

3. E. G. Chave, "A New Type of Scale for Measuring Attitudes," *Religious Education* 23 (1928): 364.

4. Jane Ellen Harrison, *Ancient Art and Ritual* (New York: Greenwood Press, Publishers, 1969) copyright 1951 (Oxford University Press) p. 28.

Chapter 1

1. Aristotle, *Poetics,* trans. Ingram Bywater. *Introduction to Aristotle,* ed. Richard McKeon (New York: Random House, 1947) p. 627.

2. Marcel Jousse, *L'anthropologie du geste* (Paris: Gallimard, 1974) p. 52.

3. Jousse, p. 142.

4. Jousse, p. 47.

5. Jousse, pp. 51–52.

6. Jousse, p. 128.

7. *Webster's Third New International Dictionary,* s.v. "rite" 1966.

8. Carl Jung, quoted in Joseph Campbell, *Primitive Mythology* (New York: Penguin, 1987) p. 32.

9. Francis Huxley, "The Body and the Play Within the Play," *The Anthropology of the Body,* ed. John Blacking (London: Academic Press, 1977) p. 29.

10. Susanne K. Langer, *Philosophy in a New Key* (Cambridge, MA: Harvard University Press, 1957) p. 153.

11. Jousse, p. 78.

12. John Curtis Gowan, *Trance, Art and Creativity* (Buffalo, N.Y.: Creative Education Foundation, 1975) p. 208.

13. Roger Bastide, *Le rêve, la transe et la folie* (Paris: Flammarion, 1972) p. 49.

14. Vincent Crapanzano and Vivian Garrison, eds., "Introduction," *Case Studies in Spirit Possession* (New York: John Wiley and Sons, 1977) p. 7.

15. David Cole, *The Theatrical Event* (Middletown, CT.: Wesleyan University Press, 1957).

16. Joseph Campbell, *Primitive Mythology* (New York: Penguin, 1976) p. 240.

17. Curt Sachs, *World History of the Dance,* trans. Bessie Schonberg (New York: W. W. Norton, 1937) p. 60.

18. "Trance," *Oxford Universal Dictionary, Illustrated,* 1969 ed.

19. Sachs, p. 60.

20. Arthur S. Reber. "Trance," *Penguin Dictionary of Psychology,* 1986.

21. Jean-Michel Oughourlian, *The Puppet of Desire: The Psychology of Hysteria, Possession, and Hypnosis,* trans. Eugene Webb (Stanford, CA.: Stanford University Press, 1991) p. 127.

22. Michel Leiris, *La possession et ses aspects théâtraux chez les Éthiopiens de Gondar* (Paris: Plon, 1958) p. 8.

23. Huxley, p. 36.

24. Sheila Walker, *Ceremonial Spirit Possession in Africa and Afro-America* (Leiden, Netherlands: E. J. Brill, 1972) p. 152.

25. Walker, p. 155.

26. Walker, p. 157.

27. Walker, P. 157.

28. France Schott-Billmann, *Corps et possession: Le vécu corporel des possédés face à la rationalité occidentale* (Paris: Bordas, 1977) p. 148.

29. Walker, p. 162.

30. T. K. Oesterreich, *Possession, Demonical and Other Among Primitive Races, in Antiquity, the Middle Ages, and Modern Times* (Princeton, N.J.: Princeton University Press, 1966) p. 12.

31. Walter Abell, *The Collective Dream in Art* (Cambridge, MA.: Harvard University Press, 1957) p. 60.

32. Jane Ellen Harrison, *Ancient Art and Ritual* (New York: Henry Holt, 1913) pp. 25–26.

33. E. G. Chave, "A New Type Scale for Measuring Attitudes," *Religious Education* 23 (1928) p. 364.

34. S. L. Rubinstein, "Consciousness in the Light of Dialectical Materialism," *Science and Society* 10 (1946) p. 252.

35. Rudolf Laban, *The Mastery of Movement,* 3rd ed. (Boston: Plays, 1971) p. 13.

36. Joseph Campbell, *Power of Myth,* ed. Betty Sue Flowers (New York: Doubleday, 1988) p. 22.

37. Rudolf Laban, p. 24.

38. Marion North, *Personality Assessment Through Movement* (London: MacDonald & Evans, 1972) pp. 231–32.

39. Charlotte Wolff, *A Psychology of Gesture* (New York: Arno Press, 1972) p. 64.

40. Laban, p. 19.

41. Pierre Verger, "Trance and Convention in Nâgo-Yoruba Spirit Mediumship," *Spirit Mediumship and Society in Africa,* ed. John Beattie and John Middleton (London: Routledge & Kegan Paul, 1969) p. 51.

42. Peter L. McNair, "Kwakiutl Winter Dances: A Reenactment," *Arscanada* 31 (Spring 1974) pp. 94–109.

43. McNair, p. 101.

44. McNair, p. 105.

45. McNair, p. 106.

46. Katherine Dunham, *Dances of Haiti,* rev. ed. "Los Danzas de Haiti" (1947) (Berkeley, CA.: University of California Press, 1983) p. 52.

47. Jean Dorcy, *The Mime,* trans. R. Speller, Jr., and P. de Fontnouvelle (New York: Robert Speller & Sons, 1961) p. 33.

48. "Posture," *Webster's Third.*

49. Alexander Lowen, *Bioenergetics* (New York: Penguin, 1981) p. 55.

50. Wolff, p. 36.

51. Francis J. Huxley, *The Invisibles: Voodoo Gods in Haiti* (New York: McGraw-Hill, 1966) p. 209.

52. F. J. Huxley, "A Discussion on Ritualization of Behavior in Man and Animals," *Philosophical Transactions of the Royal Society of London* 251 (1965) p. 426.

53. Lowen, p. 137.

54. Cecily Dell, *A Primer for Movement Description: Using Effort-Shape and Supplementary Concepts* (New York: Dance Notation Bureau, 1977) p. 82.

55. Huxley, *The Invisibles,* p. 208.

56. Walter Mischel and Frances Mischel, "Psychological Aspects of Spirit Possession," *American Anthropologist* 60 (1958) p. 250.

57. B. W. Lex, "The Neurobiology of Ritual Trance," *The Spectrum of Ritual: A Biogenetic Structural Analysis,* ed. E. d'Aquilli (New York: Columbia University Press, 1979) p. 162.

58. Huxley, "Ritualization," p. 426.

59. Mischel, p. 250.

60. Roger Bastide, *La Candomblé de Bahia: Rite nâgo* (Paris: Mouton, 1958) p. 175.

61. Erika Bourguignon, "Trance Dances," *Dance Perspectives* 35 (1968) p. 13.

62. H. Leurner, *Psychopathy and Pictorial Expression* (Basel: Sandoz, 1974) p. 56.

63. Schott-Billmann, p. 147.

64. Schott-Billmann, p. 120.

65. Alfred Métraux, "A Selection from Voodoo in Haiti," *Anthropology of Folk Religion,* ed. Charles Leslie (New York: Vintage, 1960) p. 415.

66. Pierre Janet, *L'Automatisme psychologique,* Reprint of 4th ed. (Paris: Société Pierre Janet et Laboratoire du Centre National de la Récherche Scientifique [1889], 1973) p. 36.

67. Janet, pp. 36–37.

68. Aristotle, *Movement of Animals,* trans. E. S. Forster, Loeb Classical Library 12 (Cambridge, MA.: Harvard University Press, 1968) p. 1.

69. Nina Bull, *The Body and Its Mind: An Introduction to Attitude Psychology* (New York: Las Americas, 1962) p. 89.

70. C. S. Sherrington, quoted in Bull, p. 15.

71. Moshe Feldenkrais, "Image, Movement, and Actor: Restoration of Potentiality," trans. and ed. Kelly Morris *Tulane Drama Review* 31 (Spring 1966) p. 113.

72. Bull, p. 18.

73. Dell, p. 14.

74. Huxley, *The Invisibles*, p. 209.

75. Jane Belo, *Trance in Bali* (New York: Columbia University Press, 1960) p. 12.

76. Belo, pp. 11–12.

77. Milton H. Erickson, quoted in Belo 4.

78. Leiris, p. 9.

79. Mahadev L. Apte, *Humor and Laughter: An Anthropological Approach* (Ithica, N.Y.: Cornell University Press, 1985) p. 155.

80. Jacques Bourgaux, *Possession et similacres* (Paris: EPI s.a. Éditeurs, 1973) p. 61.

81. Métraux, p. 414.

82. Leiris, p. 51.

83. Leiris, p. 100.

Chapter 2

1. Göran Sörbom, *Mimesis and Art: Studies in the Origin and Early Development of an Aesthetic Vocabulary* (Stockholm: Scandinavian University Books, 1966) p. 12.

2. Gerald F. Else, "'Imitation' in the Fifth Century," *Classical Philology* 53.2: p. 78.

3. E. R. Dodds, *The Greeks and the Irrational* (Berkeley, CA.: University of California Press, 1951) p. 77.

4. Margarete Bieber, *The History of the Greek and Roman Theatre* 2nd ed. (Princeton, N.J.: Princeton University Press, 1961) p. 9.

5. Jane Ellen Harrison, *Prolegomena to the Study of Greek Religion* (New York: Meridian, 1959) p. 568.

6. Dana F. Sutton, *Greek Satyr Play* (Meiselheim am Glan: Hain, 1980) p. 138.

7. H. Jeanmaire, *Dionysus: Histoire du Culte de Bacchus* (Paris: Payot, 1951) p. 280.

8. Jeanmaire, p. 284.

9. M. Charles Magnin, *Les origines du théâtre antique et du théâtre moderne* (Paris: Auguste Eudes, 1868) p. 42.

10. Plato, *Laws* II, trans. R. G. Bury, Loeb Classical Library (Cambridge, MA.: Harvard University Press, 1961) p. 93.

11. Jeanmaire, pp. 287–88.

12. Jeanmaire, pp. 306–7.

13. Mahadev L. Apte, *Humor and Laughter: An Anthropological Approach* (Ithica, N.Y.: Cornell University Press, 1985) p. 155.

14. Sorbom, p. 55.

15. Apte, pp. 164–65.

16. Apte, p. 155.

17. Diomedes, quoted in Allardyce Nicoll, *Masks, Mimes, and Miracles* (New York: Cooper Square, 1963) p. 81.

18. Mikhail Bakhtin, *Rabelais and His World,* trans. Helene Iswolsky (Bloomington: Indiana University Press, 1984) p. 80.

19. Bakhtin, p. 18.

20. Apte, p. 172.

21. Apte, p. 175.

22. Dodds, p. 75–76.

23. Dodds, p. 77.

24. Walter F. Otto, *Dionysus: Myth and Cult,* trans. Robert B. Palmer (Dallas, TX: Spring Publications, 1981) p. 90.

25. Jeanmaire, p. 310.

26. Sir Arthur Pickard-Cambridge *Dithyramb, Tragedy and Comedy* 2nd ed. revised by T.B.L. Webster (Oxford: Clarendon, 1962) p. 135.

27. Francis Macdonald Cornford, *The Origin of Attic Comedy* (Garden City, N.Y.: Doubleday Anchor, 1961) p. 161.

28. Pickard-Cambridge, *Dithyramb,* p. 177.

29. Pickard-Cambridge, *Dithyramb,* pp. 163–64.

30. Jane Burr Carter, "The Masks of Ortheia," *American Journal of Anthropology* 91 (1987) p. 355.

31. Carter, p. 358.

32. Susan Smith, *Masks in Modern Drama* (Berkeley: University of California Press, 1984) p. 47.

33. Bakhtin, p. 26.

34. Sörbom, p. 204.

35. Bakhtin, p. 316.

36. Gisela M. A. Richter, "Grotesques and the Mime," *American Journal of Archaeology* 17 (1913) p. 151.

37. Mario Prosperi, "The Masks of Lipari," *The Drama Review* 26.4 (1982) p. 34.

38. Prosperi, p. 35.

39. Plato, *The Republic,* trans. Desmond Lee (Baltimore: Penguin, 1974) p. 155–56.

40. Nicoll, p. 37.

41. Gaston Baty and René Chavance, *Histoire des Marionnettes* (Paris: Presses Universitaires de France, 1972) p. 14.

42. Charles Magnin, *Histoire des Marionnettes en Europe, depuis l'antiquité jusqu'à nos jours* (Paris: 1852 and 1862) p. 39.

43. Magnin, p. 39.

44. Magnin, p. 25.

45. Nicoll, p. 37.

46. Nicoll, p. 37.

47. Nicoll, p. 126.

48. Xenophon, "The Banquet," *Xenophon's Minor Works* trans. Rev. J. S. Watson (London: George Bell & Sons, 1908) pp. 155–59.

49. Sir Arthur Pickard-Cambridge, *The Dramatic Festivals of Athens,* rev. 2nd ed. (Oxford: Oxford University Press, 1988) pp. 246–47.

50. Else, p. 87.

51. Aristotle, *Poetics,* trans. Ingram Bywater *Introduction to Aristotle,* ed. Richard McKeon (New York: Random House, 1947) pp. 624–25.

52. Lillian B. Lawler, *"Phora, Schêma, Deixis* in Greek Dance," *Transactions of the American Philological Association* 85 (1954) p. 154.

53. A. E. Haigh, *The Attic Theatre,* rev. 3rd ed. (New York: Haskell, 1968) p. 318.

54. Lillian Lawler, *The Dance in Ancient Greece* (Middletown, CT.: Wesleyan University Press, 1964) p. 73.

55. Magnin, p. 51.

56. Lillian Lawler, "Beating Motifs in the Greek Dance," *The Classical Outlook* (1944) p. 60.

57. Bakhtin, p. 370.

58. Lawler, "Beating Motifs," p. 60.

59. Aristophanes. *The Wasps,* trans. Benjamin Bickley Rogers, *Five Comedies of Aristophanes,* ed. Andrew Chiappe (Garden City, N.Y.: Doubleday Anchor, 1955) p. 221.

60. Nicoll, p. 25–26.

61. Lawler, *The Dance in Ancient Greece,* p. 79.

62. Leo Aylen, *The Greek Theatre* (Rutherford, N.J.: Fairleigh Dickenson University Press, 1985) p. 28.

63. Lawler, *The Dance in Ancient Greece,* p. 70.

64. Xenophon, "The Banquet," p. 190.

65. Pickard-Cambridge, *Dithyramb,* p. 174.

66. Pickard-Cambridge, *Dithyramb,* pp. 174–75.

67. Nicoll, p. 59.

68. Cornford, pp. 156–57.

69. Nicoll, p. 83.

70. Nicoll, p. 83.

Chapter 3

1. Paulo Toschi, *Le Origini del Teatro Italiano,* Turin, 1955. Toschi details how the masks of the Commedia dell'Arte developed from the cast of characters that made up the Medieval carnival.

2. Mikhail Bakhtin, *Rabelais and His World,* trans. Helene Iswolsky (Bloomington, IN.: Indiana University Press, 1984) p. 40.

3. Vito Pandolfi, *Histoire du théâtre* 2 (Paris: Marabout Université, 1964) p. 8.

4. Carl G. Jung, *Man and His Symbols* (Garden City, N.Y.: Doubleday, 1972) p. 112.

5. Joseph Campbell, *Primitive Mythology* (New York: Penguin, 1976) p. 274.

6. Yves Lorelle, *L'Expression Corporelle du mime sacré au mime du théâtre* (Paris: La Renaissance du Livre, Collections Dionysos, 1974) p. 65.

7. Allardyce Nicoll, *The World of Harlequin: A Critical Study of the Commedia dell'Arte* (Cambridge, England: Cambridge University Press, 1963) p. 46.

8. Henri Bergson, "Laughter," *Comedy,* intro. and appendix Wylie Sypher (Garden City, N.Y.: Doubleday, 1964) p. 89.

9. Bergson, p. 153.

10. Riccoboni, quoted in Pierre Louis Ducharte, *The Italian Comedy* (New York: Dover, 1966) p. 185.

11. K. M. Lea, *Italian Popular Comedy* 2 vols. (New York: Russell & Russell, 1962) 1: p. 19.

12. Giacomo Oreglia, *The Commedia dell'Arte* (New York: Hill and Wang, 1968) p. 85.

13. Oreglia, p. 86.

14. Anthony Caputi, *Buffo: The Genius of Vulgar Comedy* (Detroit: Wayne State University Press, 1978) p. 62.

15. Lea, p. 54.

16. Caputi, p. 61.

17. Lea, p. 64.

18. Lea, p. 75.

19. Nicoll, *Harlequin*, p. 70.

20. Riccoboni, quoted in Ducharte, p. 125.

21. Quote from *Calendrier historique des théâtres* in Ducharte, p. 133.

22. Ducharte, pp. 37–38.

23. Lea, p. 100.

24. Jung, *Man and His Symbols,* p. 112.

25. Ducharte, p. 215.

26. Nicoll, *Harlequin*, p. 87.

27. Mel Gordon, *Lazzi: The Comic Routines of the Commedia dell'Arte* (New York: Performing Arts Journal Publications, 1983) pp. 4–5. Except where noted, all references to and descriptions of Lazzi are taken from Mel Gordon's book.

28. Lea, p. 69.

29. Nicoll, *Harlequin,* p. 144.

30. Gordon, p. 7.

31. Ducharte, p. 220.

32. Lea, p. 102.

Chapter 4

1. Marie-Hélène Dasté, foreword, "Jacques Copeau's School for Actors," by Barbara Kusler Leigh, *Mime Journal*, nos. 9 and 10: 4.

2. See Mira Felner, *The Apostles of Silence* (Rutherford, N.J.: Fairleigh Dickinson University Press, 1985) for a detailed study of the influence that the Vieux-Colombier had on the mime of Jean Louis Barrault, Etienne Decroux, Marcel Marceau and Jacques Lecoq. See also, "Jacques Copeau's School for Actors" by Barbara Kusler Leigh, *Mime Journal*, nos. 9 and 10.

3. Jacques Lecoq, interview, "La pédagogie du mouvement," *Le théâtre du geste: mimes et acteurs,* Sous la direction de Jacques Lecoq (Paris: Bordas, 1987) p. 108. See this interview for an account of the formative influences on Lecoq's work.

4. Lecoq, interview, "La pédagogie du mouvement," p. 109.

5. Jacques Lecoq, "À propos de la Commedia dell'Arte," *Théâtre du geste,* p. 113.

6. Lecoq, quoted in Bari Rolfe, "The Mime of Jacques Lecoq," *Drama Review*, 16.1 (March 1972) p. 35.

7. Lecoq, interview, "La pédagogie du mouvement," p. 113.

8. See pp. 16–17, Walker.

9. Lecoq, "Le jeu du masque," *Théâtre du geste*, p. 115.

10. Jacques Copeau, "Notes on the Actor," trans. Harold J. Salemson, *Actors on Acting*, eds. Toby Cole and Helen Kritch Chinoy (New York: Crown Publishers, 1970) p. 220.

11. Jacques Lecoq, "L'école Jacques Lecoq," *Théâtre de la Ville*, no. 15 (January 1972) p. 41.

12. Jean Dorcy, *The Mime*, trans. Robert Speller, Jr., and Pierre de Fontnouvelle (New York: Robert Speller & Sons, 1961) p. 12.

13. Lecoq, interview, in Sears Eldredge, "Masks: Their Use and Effectiveness in Actor Training Programs," diss., Michigan State University, 1975, p. 392.

14. Dorcy, *The Mime*, p. 13.

15. Jacques Lecoq, "Mime, Movement, Theatre," *Mimes on Miming*, ed. Bari Rolfe (London: Millington, 1981) p. 153.

16. Sheila Walker, *Ceremonial Spirit Possession in Africa and Afro-America* (Leiden, Netherlands: E.J. Brill, 1972) pp. 152 and 155.

17. Lecoq, interview, "Masks: Their Use and Effectiveness," p. 390.

18. Lecoq, interview, "Masks: Their Use and Effectiveness," p. 390.

19. Lecoq, "Mime, Movement, Theatre," p. 151.

20. Lecoq, "Mime, Movement, Theatre," p. 152.

21. Lecoq, interview, "La pédagogie du mouvement," p. 113.

22. Lecoq, "Mime, Movement, Theatre," p. 153.

23. Lecoq, interview, "La pédagogie du mouvement," p. 114.

24. Lecoq, "Mime, Movement, Theatre," p. 151.

25. Lecoq, interview, "Masks: Their Use and Effectiveness," p. 392.

26. Bari Rolfe, "The Mime of Jacques Lecoq," *Drama REview*, 16.1 (March 1972) p. 36.

27. Russell Graves, "The Psychological Effects of Masks," *Theatre Crafts* (January/February 1971) p. 13.

28. Walker, pp. 153–54.

29. Lecoq, "Mask, Mime, Theatre," p. 152.

30. Rolfe, "The Mime of Jacques Lecoq," p. 38.

31. Lecoq, "Le jeu du masque," *Théâtre du geste*, p. 115.

32. Walker, p. 153.

33. Lecoq, "Le jeu du masque," p. 115.

34. Lecoq, interview, "La pédagogie du mouvement," p. 115.

35. Jacques Copeau, quoted in Nicoll, *Harlequin*, p. 41.

36. Lecoq, "Le jeu du masque," p. 115.

37. Lecoq, "Le jeu du masque," p. 115.

38. Jacques Lecoq, "À propos de la Commedia dell'Arte," *Théâtre du geste*, p. 113.

39. Lecoq, "À propos de la Commedia dell'Arte," p. 113.

40. Lecoq, interview, "La pédagogie du mouvement," p. 113.

41. Lecoq, "Mime, Movement, Theatre," p. 153.

42. Alan Levy, "A Week Avec Lecoq," *Mime, Mask & Marionette* 1 (1978) p. 57.

43. Walker, p. 154.

44. Jacques Lecoq, "Le temps des bouffons," *Théâtre du geste*, p. 119.

45. Lecoq, "Le temps des bouffons," p. 119.

46. Levy, "A Week Avec Lecoq," p. 58.

47. Lecoq, "Le temps des bouffons," p. 119.

48. Lecoq, "Le temps des bouffons," p. 119.

49. Lecoq, "Le temps des bouffons," p. 119.

50. Lecoq, "Mime, Movement, Theatre," p. 153.

51. Graves, pp. 12–13.

52. Laurence Wylie, "À l'école Lecoq j'ai découvert mon propre clown," *Psychologie* (August, 1973) p. 27.

53. Lecoq, "Mime, Movement, Theatre," p. 153.

54. Lecoq, "Le temps des bouffons," p. 119.

55. Jacques Lecoq, "À la recherche de son propre clown," *Théâtre du geste*, p. 117.

56. Levy, p. 57.

57. Walker, p. 154.

58. Roger Bastide, *Le reve, la transe et la folie* (Paris: Flammarion, 1972) p. 97.

59. Jean Perret, "L'explosion du mime," *Le théâtre du geste*, p. 107.

Chapter 5

1. For a discussion of the origins of shamanism and possession rites see Joseph Campbell, *Primitive Mythology*, (New York: Viking Penguin, 1956) Vol. 1 of *The Masks of the Gods*.

2. E. T. Kirby, "The Shamanistic Origins of Popular Entertainments," *The Drama Review*, 18:1 (March 1974) p. 6.

3. Michael Harner, *The Way of the Shaman: A Guide to Power and Healing* (New York: Bantam, 1982) p. 26.

4. Johan Reinhard, "Shamanism and Spirit Possession: The Definition Problem," *Spirit Possession in the Nepal Himalayas*, ed. J. T. Hitchcock and Rex L. Jones (New Dehli, India: Vikas, 1976) p. 16.

5. Mircea Eliade, *Shamanism: Archaic Techniques of Ecstasy*, trans. Willard R. Trask, Bollingen Series 76 (Princeton, N.J.: Princeton University Press, 1964) p. 5.

6. Gilbert Rouget, *La musique et la transe* (Paris: Gallimard, 1980) p. 36.

7. Erika Bourguignon, *Possession* (San Francisco: Chandler & Sharp, 1976) pp. 42–49.

8. Rouget, p. 195.

9. Eliade, p. 5.

10. Jacques Bourgaux, *Possessions et Simulacres* (Paris: EPI s.a. Éditeurs, 1973) p. 71.

11. Andreas Lommel, *Shamanism; The Beginnings of Art*, trans. Michael Bullock (New York and Toronto: McGraw-Hill, 1967) p. 138.

12. Lommel, p. 137.

13. Roger Bastide, preface, *Les Dieux d'Afrique*, by Pierre Verger (Paris: Paul Hartmann, 1954).

14. Harner, p. 27.

15. Evaline Lot-Falck, "Le chamanisme en Sibérie: Essai de mise au point," *Asie du Sud-Est et Monde Insulindien* (Chamanisme et possession, fasc. 2) (Paris: Mouton, 1973) Vol. 4, 3: p. 9.

16. Lot-Falck, p. 9.

17. A. P. Elkin, *Aboriginal Men of High Degree* (Sydney, Australia: The John Murtagh Macrossan Memorial Lectures for 1944, University of Queensland: Australasian Publishing, 1945) pp. 74–75.

18. Lot-Falck, p. 9.

19. N. Kershaw Chadwick, *Poetry and Prophecy* (London: Cambridge University Press, 1952) pp. 77 and 88.

20. Rouget, p. 192.

21. Bourgaux, p. 72.

22. Lommel, p. 137.

23. Stephen Larsen, *The Shaman's Doorway: Opening the Mythic Imagination to Contemporary Consciousness* (New York: Harper and Row, 1976) p. 87.

24. Lucile H. Charles, "Drama in Shaman Exorcism," *Journal of American Folklore* 66 (April-June 1953) p. 96.

25. Waldemar Bogoras, "Ideas of Space and Time in the Conception of Primitive Religion," *American Anthropologist* 27.2 (April 1925) p. 216.

26. Shirokogoroff, quoted in I. M. Lewis, *Ecstatic Religion: An Anthropological Study of Spirit Possession and Shamanism* (Baltimore: Penguin, 1971) p. 53.

27. Shirokogoroff, quoted in *Ecstatic Religion*, p. 53.

28. Bourgaux, p. 71.

29. Campbell, p. 254.

30. Knut Rasmussen, quoted in Peter Furst, "The Roots and Continuities of Shamanism," *Arscanada* 31 (Spring 1974) pp. 34–35.

31. Francis Huxley, *The Way of the Sacred* (Garden City, N.Y.: Doubleday, 1974) p. 257.

32. Francis Huxley, "The Body and the Play Within the Play," *The Anthropology of the Body,* ed. John Blacking (London: Academic Press, 1977) p. 37.

33. Carl G. Jung, *Man and His Symbols* (Garden City, N.Y.: Doubleday, 1972) pp. 110 and 112.

34. Rudolf Laban, *The Mastery of Movement,* 3rd ed. (Boston: Plays, 1971) p. 11.

35. Bourguignon, p. 48.

36. Anna-Leena Siikala, "The Rite Technique of the Siberian Shaman," *F. F. Communications* 93 (1978): 52–53.

37. Chadwick, p. 78.

38. Lommel, p. 137.

39. Campbell, p. 257.

40. Rouget, p. 196.

41. Gananath Obeyesekere, "The Ritual Drama of the Sanni Demons: Collective Representations of Disease in Ceylon," *Comparative Studies in Society and History* 11:2 (April 1969): 174–216.

42. Campbell, p. 274.

43. Campbell, p. 274.

44. Campbell, p. 238.

45. Bourgaux, p. 69.

46. Rouget, p. 37.

47. Rouget, p. 187.

48. Chadwick, pp. 93–94.

49. Lommel, p. 140.

50. Rouget, p. 188.

51. Radlov, quoted in Eliade, *Shamanism*, pp. 191–92.

52. Wilhelm Wundt, quoted in André Veinstein, *La Mise en Scène Théâtrale et sa Condition Esthétique* (Paris: Flammarion, 1955) p. 95.

53. Rouget, p. 192.

54. Ivor Richards, quoted in Archibald MacLeish, *Poetry and Experience* (Baltimore: Penguin, 1960) p. 75.

55. Susanne K. Langer, *Philosophy in a New Key* (Cambridge, MA.: Harvard University Press, 1957) pp. 152–53.

Chapter 6

1. *Shite* refers both to the central character in the *No* as well as to the actor performing this role.

2. Benito Ortolani, "Shamanism in the Origins of the Nō Theatre," *Asian Theatre Journal* 1:2 (Fall 1984) p. 177.

3. Ortolani, "Shamanism in the Nō," p. 180.

4. Zeami, *Kadensho,* trans. Chūichi Sakurai et al. (Kyoto: Sumiya-Shinobe Publishing Institute, 1968) p. 54.

5. Ortolani, "Shamanism in the Nō," p. 174.

6. Carmen Blacker, *The Catalpa Bow: A Study of Shamanic Practices in Japan* (London: George Allen & Unwin, 1975) pp. 21–22.

7. Blacker, p. 22.

8. René Sieffert, "Les Dances Sacrées au Japon," *Les Danses Sacrées,* ed. René Sieffert (Paris: Éditions du Seuil, 1963) p. 459.

9. Kunio Komparu, *The Noh Theatre: Principles and Perspectives*, trans. Jane Corddry (New York and Tokyo: John Weatherhill, 1983) p. 45.

10. Chifumi Shimazaki, *God Noh* (Tokyo: Hinoki Shoten, 1972) pp. 22–27 Vol. 1 of *The Noh.*

11. Blacker, p. 34.

12. Blacker, p. 36.

13. Blacker, p. 37.

14. Komparu, pp. 47–48.

15. Zeami, "Fūshikaden," *On the Art of the Nō* Drama: The Major Treatises of Zeami, ed. and trans. J. Thomas Rimer and Masakazu Yamazaki (Princeton, NJ: Princeton University Press, 1984) p. 10.

16. Benito Ortolani, "Zeami's Aesthetics of the Nō and Audience Participation," *Educational Theatre Journal* 24 (1972) p. 111.

17. Zeami, "Kakyō," *On the Art of the Nō* Drama, p. 77.

18. D. T. Suzuki, *Zen Buddhism,* ed. William Barrett (Garden City, NY: Doubleday, 1956) p. 290.

19. D. T. Suzuki, introduction, *Zen and the Art of Archery,* by Eugen Herrigel, trans. R. F. C. Hull (New York: Vintage, 1971) p. vi.

20. Zeami, "Fūshikaden," p. 55.

21. Komparu, p. 126.

22. Zeami, "Shikadō," *On the Art of the Nō Drama*, p. 65.

23. Masakazu Yamazaki, "The Aesthetics of Ambiguity: The Artistic Theories of Zeami," *On the Art of the Nō Drama* pp. xlii–xliii.

24. Carl Woltz, "The Spirit of Zen in Noh Dance," in *CORD Dance Research Annual 8: Asian and Pacific Dance: Selected Papers from the 1975 CORD-SEM Conference,* ed. Adrienne Kaeppler, Carl Woltz, and Judy Van Zile (New York: CORD, 1977) pp. 55–56.

25. Yamazaki, "The Aesthetics of Ambiguity," p. xliii.

26. Yasuo Nakamura, *Noh: The Classical Theatre,* trans. Don Kenny (New York & Tokyo: Walker/Weatherhill, 1971) p. 228.

27. Zeami, "Kakyō," p. 77.

28. R. G. O'Neill, *Early Nō* Drama (London: Lund Humphries, 1958) p. 140.

29. Ananda K. Coomaraswamy, *The Transformation of Nature in Art* (New York: Dover, 1956) p. 11.

30. George Rowley, *Principles of Chinese Painting* (Princeton, N.J.: Princeton University Press, 1959) p. 35.

31. Rudolf Laban, *The Mastery of Movement* 3rd ed. (Boston: Plays, 1971) p. 20.

32. Richard N. McKinnon, "Zeami on the Art of Training," *Harvard Journal of Asiatic Studies* 16 (June 1953) pp. 220–21.

33. Zeami, "Shikadō," p. 65.

34. Zeami, "Fūshikaden," p. 13.

35. Nakamura, p. 161.

36. Makoto Ueda, *Zeami, Basho, Yeats, Pound* (The Hague: Mouton, 1965) p. 29.

37. Komparu, p. 229.

38. Komparu, p. 229.

39. Nakamura, p. 161.

40. Komparu, p. 7.

41. Zeami, "Kakyō" quoted in Komparu p. 16. Also see passage in "Kakyō," *On the Art of the Nō Drama*, p. 81.

42. Richard Pilgrim, "Some Aspects of kokoro in Zeami," *Monumenta Nipponica* 24:4 (1969) p. 394.

43. Pilgrim, p. 396.

44. Zeami, "Kakyō," pp. 97–98.

45. Kotaro Takayama, quoted in Makoto Ueda, *Zeami, Basho, Yeats, Pound*, p. 28.

46. Hideo Kanze, quoted in Eugenio Barba, "Theatre Anthropology," *The Drama Review* 26.2 (Summer 1982) p. 12.

47. Nomura, quoted in Barba, p. 12.

48. Zeami, "Kakyō," p. 75.

49. Zeami, "Kakyō," p. 75.

50. Zeami, "Kakyō," p. 97.

51. Komparu, p. 216.

52. Ortolani, "Zeami's Aesthetics of the No and Audience Participation," p. 111.

53. Woltz, p. 56.

54. Komparu, p. 221.

55. Komparu, p. 216.

56. Komparu, p. 216.

57. Zeami, quoted in Nakamura, p. 228.

58. E. T. Kirby, "The Origins of No Drama," *Educational Theatre Journal* 25 (1973) p. 275.

59. Komparu, p. 221.

60. Komparu, p. 217.

61. Komparu, p. 217.

62. Komparu, pp. 217–18.

63. Faubion Bowers, *Japanese Theatre* (Rutland, VT., and Tokyo: Charles E. Tuttle, 1977) p. 9.

64. Nakayama Taro, quoted in Blacker pp. 293–94.

65. Frank Hoff, "Dance to Song in Japan," *Dance Research Journal of CORD* 9/1 (Fall/Winter 1976–77) p. 7.

66. Ortolani, "Shamanism in the No," p. 177.

67. Zeami, *Kadensho,* p. 72.

68. Zeami, *Kadensho,* p. 72.

69. Zeami, "Fūshikaden," p. 27.

70. Hoff, p. 1.

71. Ueda, pp. 27–28.

72. Zeami, "Sarugaku dangi," *On the Art of the No Drama,* p. 185.

73. Yamazaki, xliv.

74. Komparu, pp. 24–25.

75. Zeami, "Shūgyoku tokka," *On the Art of the No Drama*, p. 137.

76. Shimazaki, I:42.

77. Barba, p. 22.

78. Zeami, "Shūgyoku tokka," p. 138.

79. Komparu, p. 25.

80. Nakamura, pp. 225–26.

Chapter 7

1. Allardyce Nicoll, *Masks, Mimes, and Miracles* (New York: Cooper Square, 1963) p. 131.

2. Athenaeus, *Deipnosophistae,* trans. Charles Barton Gulik, Loeb Classical Library (Cambridge, MA.: Harvard University Press, 1927) 14, pp. 389–93.

3. M. Charles Magnin, *Les origins du théâtre antique et du moderne* (Paris: Auguste Eudes, 1868) p. 488.

4. Libanius, "Hyper ton Orcheston," quoted in, Lillian Lawler, "Portrait of a Dancer," *Classical Journal* 41.6 (March 1946) p. 247.

5. Lucian, "The dance (Saltatio)," trans. A. M. Harmon, Loeb Classical Library (Cambridge, MA.: Harvard University Press, 1962) V, pp. 231–33.

6. Plato. *Phaedrus,* trans. Harold North Fowler, Loeb Classical Library (Cambridge, MA.: Harvard University Press, 1950) pp. 465–67.

7. Plato, *Ion,* trans. W. R. M. Lamb Loeb Classical Library (Cambridge, MA.: Harvard University Press, 1962) III, p. 423.

8. H. M. and N. K. Chadwick, *The Growth of Literature* (Cambridge, England: Cambridge University Press, 1968) p. 637.

9. Odyssey 17:518, quoted in Dodds, *The Greeks & the Irrational,* 117, p. 100.

10. E. R. Dodds, *The Greeks and the Irrational* (Berkeley, CA.: University of California Press, 1951) p. 81.

11. J. Michael Walton, *Greek Theatre Practice* (Westport, CT.: Greenwood Press, 1980) pp. 49–50.

12. Gerald F. Else, *The Origin and Early Form of Greek Tragedy* (Cambridge, MA.: Harvard University Press, 1965) p. 69.

13. Sir Arthur Pickard-Cambridge, *The Dramatic Festivals of Athens,* rev. 2nd ed. (Oxford: Oxford University Press, 1988) pp. 246–47.

14. A. E. Haigh, *The Attic Theatre,* 3rd ed. (New York: Haskell House, 1968) p. 313.

15. Lillian Lawler, *The Dance of the Ancient Greek Theatre* (Iowa City, Iowa: The University of Iowa Press, 1964) pp. 36–37.

16. Magnin, p. 55.

17. Plato, *Laws,* trans. R. G. Bury, Loeb Classical Library (Cambridge, MA.: Harvard University Press, 1961) 2, p. 95.

18. Athenaeus, *Deipnosophistae,* I.22: 95.

19. Athenaeus, *Deipnosophistae,* I.21: 95.

20. Athenaeus, *Deipnosophistae,* I.22: 95.

21. Aristotle. *Poetics* XVII trans. S. H. Butcher (New York: Hill and Wang, 1961) p. 87.

22. Nicoll, pp. 81–82.

23. Francis Fergusson, *Literary Landmarks: Essays on the Theory and Practice of Literature* (New Brunswick, N.J.: Rutgers University Press, 1975) p. 5.

24. S. H. Butcher, *Aristotle's Theory of Poetry and Fine Art* (New York: Dover, 1951) p. 123.

25. *Livy,* trans. B. O. Foster, Loeb Classical Library (Cambridge, MA.: Harvard University Press, 1924) 3, pp. 359–65.

26. Lawler, "Portrait of a Dancer," p. 242.

27. Athenaeus, *Deipnosophistae,* I.20:91. See also Plutarch, *Moralia* 7: 81.

28. Athenaeus, *Deipnosophistae* I.20: 91.

29. A. M. Nagler, *A Source Book in Theatrical History* (New York: Dover, 1952) p. 28.

30. Lawler, "Portrait of a Dancer," pp. 242–43.

31. Lucian, p. 263.

32. Lucian, p. 247.

33. Margarete Bieber, *History of the Greek and Roman Theatre,* 2nd ed. (Princeton, N.J.: Princeton University Press, 1961) p. 165.

34. Lucian, p. 283.

35. Libanius, *Against Aristedes* 3:391.

36. Lawler, "Portrait of a Dancer," *Classical Journal,* 41.6 (March 1946) p. 243.

37. Lucian, p. 233.

38. Lucian, p. 285.

39. Lucian, p. 285.

40. Lucian, p. 285.

41. Lucian, pp. 287–89.
42. Lucian, p. 233.
43. Macrobius *Sat.* 2.7 quoted in Lawler, "Portrait of a Dancer," p. 245.
44. Lucian, p. 277.
45. Magnin, pp. 497–98.
46. Lawler, "Portrait of a Dancer," p. 243.
47. De l'Aulnaye, *De la Saltation Théâtrale: Récherches sur l'origin, les progrés, & les effets de la pantomime chez les anciens* (Paris: Chez Barrois l'Aine, 1790), p. 84.
48. Lucian, p. 249.
49. Lillian Lawler, "Phora, Schéma, Deixis in Greek Dance," *Transactions of the American Philological Association* 85 (1954) p. 154.
50. Plutarch, *Moralia* IX, trans. Edward L. Minar, et al., Loeb Classical Library (Cambridge, MA.: Harvard University Press, 1961) 15, p. 291.
51. Plutarch, p. 293.
52. Maurice Emmanuel, *The Antique Greek Dance,* trans. Harriet Jean Beauley (New York, N.Y.: John Lance, 1916) p. xiv.
53. Lucian, p. 247.
54. Libanius, quoted in Lawler, "Portrait of a Dancer," p. 243.
55. Libanius, quoted in Lawler, "Phora, Schéma, Deixis," p. 154.
56. Magnin, pp. 339–40.
57. Plutarch, p. 293.
58. Lucian, p. 273.
59. Lucian, p. 271.
60. Athenaeus, *Deipnosophistae,* 1.20–21: p. 91.
61. Cassiodorus, quoted in R. J. Broadbent, *A History of Pantomime* (New York, N.Y.: Benjamin Blom, 1901) p. 67.
62. De l'Aulnaye, p. 25.
63. Cassiodorus, quoted in De l'Aulnaye, *De la Saltation Théâtrale* 87.
64. Lucian, p. 269.
65. Wilhelm Wundt, *The Language of Gesture* (Paris: Mouton, 1973) pp. 72–101.
66. Plutarch, 291–93.
67. De l'Aulnaye, p. 89.
68. Quintilian, *Institutio Oratoria,* trans. H. E. Butler, Loeb Classical Library (Cambridge, MA.: Harvard University Press, 1958) 4, pp. 291–93.
69. Athenaeus, *Deipnosophistae,* I.20: p. 89.
70. Macrobius, quoted in Lawler, "Portrait of a Dancer," p. 245.
71. Plutarch, p. 295.
72. Kenneth Burke, *The Philosophy of Literary Form: Studies in Symbolic Action* (Baton Rouge: Louisiana State University Press, 1941) p. 9.
73. Plutarch, p. 291.
74. Plutarch, p. 297.
75. Lucian, p. 281.
76. Lucian, p. 267.

Chapter 8

1. John Weaver, *An Essay Towards a History of Dancing* (London: John Tonfon, 1712) pp. 160–61.

2. John Weaver, quoted in Selma Jeanne Cohen, ed. *Dance as a Theatre Art: Source Readings in Dance History from 1581 to the Present* (New York: Dodd, Mead, 1974) p. 54.

3. See Kirsten Gram Holmstrom, *Monodrama, Attitudes, Tableaux Vivants* (Stockholm: Almquist & Wiksell, 1967).

4. Holmstrom, p. 119.

5. Holmstrom, p. 120.

6. John Jackson, *The History of the Scottish Stage* (Edinburgh, 1793) pp. 367–68.

7. Jean Georges Noverre, *Letters on Dancing and Ballet,* trans. Cyril W. Beaumont (New York: Dance Horizons, 1968) p. 16.

8. Noverre, p. 20.

9. Carlo Blasis, *The Art of Dancing,* trans. R. Barton (London: Edward Bull, 1831) p. 111.

10. Louisa E. Jones, *Sad Clowns and Pale Pierrots: Literature and the Popular Comic Arts in 19th-Century France* (Lexington, KY.: French Forum, 1984) p. 42.

11. Jones, p. 12.

12. Theophile Gautier, quoted in Robert Storey *Pierrots on the Stage of Desire: Nineteenth-Century French Literary Artists and the Comic Pantomime* (Princeton, N.J.: Princeton University Press, 1985) p. 30.

13. George Sand, quoted in Jaroslav Svehla, "Jean Gaspard Deburau: The Immortal Pierrot," *Mime Journal* 5 (1977) p. 23.

14. Theodore de Banville, *Mes Souvenirs.* (Paris: G. Charpentier, 1882) p. 215.

15. Charles Baudelaire, *Selected Writings on Art and Artists,* trans. P. E. Charvet (Baltimore: Penguin, 1972) p. 422.

16. Banville, p. 216.

17. Marian Hannah Winter. *The Theatre of Marvels.* (New York: Benjamin Blom, 1964) p. 64.

18. Banville, p. 216.

19. Marcel Marceau, *Marcel Marceau ou l'Aventure du silence,* interview et textes Guy et Jeanne Verriest-Lefert (Paris: Desclée De Brouwer, 1974) p. 35.

20. Marceau, *Marcel Marceau,* p. 37.

21. Marceau, *Marcel Marceau,* p. 8.

22. Marceau, *Marcel Marceau,* p. 51.

23. Marceau, *Marcel Marceau,* p. 68.

24. Patrice Pavis, *Languages of the Stage: Essays in the Semiology of Theatre* (New York: Performing Arts Journal Publications, 1982) p. 62.

25. Marceau, quoted in Yves Lorelle, *L'Expression corporelle du mime sacré au mime du théâtre* (Paris: La Renaissance du Livre, Collections Dionysos, 1974) p. 129.

26. Marceau, *Marcel Marceau,* p. 41.

27. Thomas Leabhart, *Modern and Post-Modern Mime* (New York: St. Martin's Press, 1989) p. 78.

28. Marceau, *Marcel Marceau,* p. 39.

29. Marceau, *Marcel Marceau,* p. 39.

30. Marceau, *Marcel Marceau,* pp. 8–9.

31. Marceau, lecture/demonstration on mime, videotape, Brooklyn College, 1976.

32. Marceau, quoted in Norma McLain Stoop (ed.), "The Interior Music of Marcel Marceau," interview *Dance Magazine* 49 (July 1975) p. 36.

33. Marceau, videotape lecture/demonstration, 1976.

34. See Chapter Nine pp. 189–91 for a fuller discussion.

35. Pavis, p. 64.

36. Marceau, videotape lecture/demonstration, 1976.

37. Jean Dorcy, *À la rencontre de mime et des mimes* (Neuilly sur Seine: Les Cahiers de Danse et de Culture, 1958) p. 66.

38. Marceau, *Marcel Marceau,* p. 44.

39. Decroux, *Paroles sur le Mime* (Paris: Gallimard, 1963) p. 180.

40. Marcel Marceau quoted in Alan Bunce "French Emissary of Mime," *The Christian Science Monitor,* 8 May 1970.

41. Marceau, *Marcel Marceau,* p. 54.

42. Marceau, *Marcel Marceau,* p. 47.

43. Pavis, p. 56.

44. Marceau, quoted in Bari Rolfe, "Mime-Paradigm of Paradox," *Impulse,* (1969–70) p. 37.

Chapter 9

1. Etienne Decroux, *Paroles sur le mime* (Paris: Gallimard, 1963) p. 18.

2. Decroux, "Etienne Decroux Eightieth Birthday Interview," *Mime Journal,* nos. 7 and 8, p. 39.

3. Decroux, *Paroles,* p. 18.

4. Barbara Kusler Leigh, "Jacques Copeau's School for Actors," *Mime Journal,* nos. 9 and 10, p. 47.

5. Thomas Leabhart, *Modern and Post-Modern Mime* (New York: St. Martin's Press, 1989) pp. 31–32.

6. Maximilien Decroux quoted in Pinok et Matho, *Écrits sur pantomime, mime, expression corporelle* (Paris: Publication du Temp, 1975) p. 25.

7. Eugenio Barba, "Theatre Anthropology," *The Drama Review* 26.2 (Summer 1982) p. 6.

8. Decroux, "80th Birthday Interview," p. 8.

9. Edward Gordon Craig, *On the Art of the Theatre* (New York: Theatre Arts, 1956) p. 61.

10. Craig, p. 61.

11. Craig, p. 81.

12. Edward Gordon Craig, rev. of *The Japanese Dance,* by M. A. Hinckes. *The Mask* 2 (October 1910) p. 90.

13. Craig, *On the Art of the Theatre,* p. 56.

14. Denis Diderot, *The Paradox of Acting,* trans. Walker Herries Pollock (London: Chatto & Windus, 1883) p. 53.

15. Diderot, p. 53.

16. Diderot, p. 62.

17. Craig, *On the Art of the Theatre*, pp. ix–x.

18. Craig, *On the Art of the Theatre*, p. 85.

19. Edward Gordon Craig, "Hamlet in Moscow: Notes for a Short Address to Actors of the Moscow Art Theatre," *The Mask* 7.2 (May 1915) p. 109–10.

20. Craig, *On the Art of the Theatre*, p. 11.

21. Craig, *On the Art of the Theatre*, p. 11.

22. Decroux, *Paroles*, p. 21.

23. Decroux, *Paroles*, p. 118.

24. Decroux, "80th Birthday Interview," p. 31.

25. Decroux, "80th Birthday Interview," p. 34.

26. Decroux, 1975 class lecture, Boulogne Bilancourt, France.

27. Decroux, 1975 class lecture.

28. Decroux, 1975 class lecture.

29. Charles Baudelaire, *Selected Writings on Art and Artists,* trans. P. E. Charvet (Baltimore: Penguin, 1972) p. 422.

30. Baldesar Castiglione, *The Book of the Courtier,* trans. Charles S. Singleton (Garden City, N.Y.: Doubleday, 1959) p. 43.

31. Decroux, "80th Birthday Interview," p. 40.

32. Decroux, "80th Birthday Interview," p. 31.

33. Decroux, "80th Birthday Interview," p. 14.

34. Decroux, "80th Birthday Interview," pp. 14–15.

35. Decroux, *Paroles,* p. 105.

36. Decroux, "80th Birthday Interview," p. 47.

37. Decroux, "80th Birthday Interview," p. 51.

38. Dorcy, *The Mime,* p. 47.

39. Barba, p. 20.

40. Edward Gordon Craig, "Enfin un Créateur au Théâtre," *Arts* August 3, 1945: 1.

41. Decroux, quoted in Annette Lust, "Etienne Decroux and the French School of Mime," *The Quarterly Journal of Speech* 57 (October 1971) p. 294.

42. Decroux, 1975 class lecture.

43. Decroux, 1975 class lecture.

44. Decroux, *Paroles*, p. 155.

45. Decroux, 1975 class lecture.

46. Lust, p. 18.

47. Decroux, 1975 class lecture.

48. Decroux, 1975 class lecture.

49. Decroux, *Paroles*, pp. 124–25.

50. Dorcy, *The Mime,* p. 33.

51. Dorcy, p. 36.

52. Decroux, 1975 class lecture.

53. Decroux, 1975 class lecture.

54. Decroux, 1976 class lecture.

55. Decroux, *Paroles,* pp. 29–30.

56. Decroux, 1976 class lecture.

57. Annette Lust, "Etienne Decroux: The Father of Modern Mime," *The Mime Journal* 1 (1974) p. 20.

58. Decroux, *Paroles,* p. 58.

59. Decroux, *Paroles*, p. 58–59.

60. Decroux, 1975 class lecture.

61. August Rodin, *L'Art: entretiens réunis par Paul Gsell* (Paris: Gallimard, 1967) p. 41.

62. Rodin, *L'Art*, pp. 36–38.

63. Rodin, *L'Art*, pp. 38–39.

64. Decroux, 1976 class lecture.

65. Rodin, *L'Art,* p. 43.

66. Decroux, *Paroles* pp. 46 and 125.

67. Rodin, *L'Art*, p. 55.

68. Rodin interviewed in Ionel Jianou, *Rodin,* trans. Kathleen Muston and Geofrey Skelding (Paris: Arted, Éditions d'Art, 1970) p. 23.

69. Decroux, "80th Birthday Interview," p. 60.

70. Etienne Decroux, *Words on Mime,* trans. Mark Piper *Mime Journal* (1985) pp. 77–78.

71. Susanne Langer, *Feeling and Form: A Theory of Art* (New York: Charles Scribner's Sons, 1953) p. 89.

72. Decroux, "80th Birthday Interview," p. 61.

73. Decroux, class lecture 1975.

74. Decroux, *Paroles*, p. 76.

75. Lust, "Decroux and the French School of Mime," p. 293.

76. Alvin Epstein, "The Mime Theatre of Etienne Decroux," *Chrysalis* 11. 1–2 (1958) p. 11.

77. Decroux, *Paroles,* p. 29.

78. Decroux, *Paroles,* p. 55.

79. Decroux, *Paroles,* p. 52.

80. Epstein, p. 9.

81. Decroux, *Paroles*, p. 29.

82. Decroux, quoted in Leigh, p. 48.

83. Decroux, quoted in Lust, "Decroux: Father of Modern Mime," p. 17.

84. Decroux, "80th Birthday Interview," p. 10.

85. Roberta Sklar, "Etienne Decroux's Promethean Mime," *The Drama Review* 29.4 (Winter 1985) p. 66.

SOURCES

Abell, Walter. *The Collective Dream in Art*. Cambridge, MA.: Harvard University Press, 1957.

Apte, Mahadev L. *Humor and Laughter: An Anthropological Approach*. Ithica, N.Y.: Cornell University Press, 1985.

Aristophanes. *The Wasps*. Trans. Benjamin Bickley Rogers. *Five Comedies of Aristophanes*. Ed. Andrew Chiappe. Garden City, N.Y.: Doubleday, 1955.

Aristotle. *Introduction to Aristotle*. Trans. and ed. Richard McKeon. New York: Random House, 1947.

_____. *Movement of Animals*. Trans. E. S. Forster. Loeb Classical Library 12. Cambridge, MA.: Harvard University Press, 1968.

Athenaeus. *Deipnosophistae*. Trans. Charles Barton Gulik. Loeb Classical Library 14. Cambridge, MA.: Harvard University Press, 1927.

Aylen, Leo. *The Greek Theatre*. Rutherford, N.J.: Fairleigh Dickenson University Press, 1985.

Bakhtin, Mikhail. *Rabelais and His World*. Trans. Helene Iswolsky. Bloomington: Indiana University Press, 1984.

Theodore de Banville. *Mes Souvenirs*. Paris: G. Charpentier, 1882.

Barba, Eugenio. "Theatre Anthropology." *The Drama Review* 26.2 (Summer 1982): 5–32.

Bastide, Roger. *La Candomblé de Bahia*. Paris: Mouton, 1958.

_____. *Le rêve, la transe et la folie*. Paris: Flammarion, 1972.

Baty, Gaston, and Rene Chavance. *Histoire des Marionnettes*. Paris: Presses Universitaires de France, 1972.

Baudelaire, Charles. *Selected Writings on Art and Artists*. Trans. P. E. Charvet. Baltimore: Penguin, 1972.

Belo, Jane. *Trance in Bali*. New York: Columbia University Press, 1960.

Bentley, Eric. "The Pretensions of Pantomime." *Theatre Arts* (Feb. 1951): 26–30.

Berberich, Junko Sakaba. "Some Observations on Movement in No." *Asian Theatre Journal* 1.2 (Fall 1984): 207–216.

Bergson, Henri. "Laughter." *Comedy*. Intro and appen. Wylie Sypher. Garden City, N.Y.: Doubleday, 1964.

Bertrand, Monique, and Mathilde Dumont. (Pinok et Matho). *Écrits sur pantomime, mime, expression corporelle*. Paris: Publication du Temp, 1975.

Bieber, Margarete. *History of the Greek and Roman Theatre*. 2nd ed. Princeton, N.Y.: Princeton University Press, 1961.

Blacker, Carmen. *The Catalpa Bow: A Study of Shamanic Practices in Japan.* London: Allen and Unwin, 1975.

Blasis, Carlo. *The Art of Dancing.* Trans. R. Barton. London: Edward Bull, 1831.

Bogoras, Waldemar. "Ideas of Space and Time in the Conception of Primitive Religion." *American Anthropologist* 27.2 (April 1925): 205–266.

Bourgaux, Jacques. *Possessions et Simulacres.* Paris: EPI s.a. Éditeurs, 1973.

Bourguignon, Erika. *Possession.* San Francisco: Chandler & Sharp, 1976.

_____. "Trance Dances," *Dance Perspectives* 35 (1968): 10–62.

Bowers, Faubion. *Japanese Theatre.* Rutland, VT, and Tokyo: Charles E. Tuttle, 1977.

Broadbent, R. J. *A History of Pantomime.* New York: Benjamin Blom, 1901.

Bull, Nina. *The Body and Its Mind: An Introduction to Attitude Psychology.* New York: Las Americas Publishing Co., 1962.

Burke, Kenneth. *The Philosophy of Literary Form: Studies in Symbolic Action* Baton Rouge: Louisiana State University Press, 1941.

Butcher, S. H. *Aristotle's Theory of Poetry and Fine Art.* New York: Dover, 1951.

Campbell, Joseph. *Primitive Mythology.* New York: Viking Penguin, 1959. Vol. 1 of *The Masks of God.* 5 vols. 1959–68.

Caputi, Anthony. *Buffo: The Genius of Vulgar Comedy.* Detroit: Wayne State University Press, 1978.

Carter, Jane Burr. "The Masks of Ortheia." *American Journal of Anthropology* 91 (July 1987): 355–383.

Cassirer, Ernst. *Myth and Language.* Trans. Susanne K. Langer. New York: Dover, 1953.

Castiglione, Baldesar. *The Book of the Courtier.* Trans. Charles S. Singleton Garden City, N.Y.: Doubleday, 1959.

Chadwick, H. M., and N. K. Chadwick *The Growth of Literature.* Cambridge: Cambridge University Press, 1968.

Chadwick, N. Kershaw. *Poetry and Prophecy.* London: Cambridge University Press, 1952.

Charles, Lucile Hoerr. "Drama in Shaman Exorcism." *Journal of American Folklore* 66 (April-June 1953): 95–122.

Chave, E. G. "A New Type Scale for Measuring Attitudes," *Religious Education* 23 (1928): 354–69.

Cohen, Selma Jeanne, ed. *Dance as a Theatre Art: Source Readings in Dance History from 1581 to the Present.* New York: Dodd, 1974.

Cole, David. *The Theatrical Event.* Connecticut: Wesleyan University Press, 1957.

Coomaraswamy, Ananda K. *The Transformation of Nature in Art.* New York: Dover, 1956.

Copeau, Jacques. "Notes on the Actor." Trans. Harold J. Salemson. In *Actors On Acting.* Eds. Toby Cole and Helen Kritch Chinoy. New York: Crown, 1970: 216–25.

Cornford, Francis Macdonald. *The Origin of Attic Comedy.* Garden City, N.Y.: Doubleday, 1961.

Craig, Edward Gordon. Book review. *The Japanese Dance,* by M. A. Hinckes. *The Mask* 3.4–6 (October 1910): 90–91.

_____. "Enfin un Créateur au Théâtre." *Arts.* August 3, 1945: 1–3.

_____. "Hamlet in Moscow: Notes for a Short Address to the Actors of the Moscow Art Theatre." *The Mask* 7.2 (May 1915): 109–115.

_____. *On the Art of the Theatre*. New York: Theatre Arts Books, 1956.

Crapanzano, Vincent, and Vivian Garrison, eds. *Case Studies in Spirit Possession*. New York: John Wiley and Sons, 1977.

Dasté, Marie-Hélène. Forward. "Jacques Copeau's School for Actors." By Barbara Kusler Leigh. *Mime Journal* Nos. 9 & 10: 4–6.

Decroux, Etienne. *Paroles sur le mime*. Paris: Gallimard, 1963.

_____. *Words on Mime*. Trans. Mark Piper. Claremont: Mime Journal, 1985.

De l'Aulnaye, *De la Saltation Théâtrale: Rêcherches sur l'origin, les progrès, & les effets de la pantomime chez les anciens*. Paris: Chez Barrois l'aine, 1790.

Dell, Cecily. *A Primer for Movement Description: Using Effort-Shape and Supplementary Concepts*. New York: Dance Notation Bureau Press, 1977.

Deren, Maya. *Divine Horsemen: The Living Gods of Haiti*. New Paltz, NY: McPherson, 1983. (Originally published London and New York, Thames and Hudson, 1953.)

Diderot, Denis. *The Paradox of Acting*. Trans. Walker Herries Pollock. London: Chatto & Windus, 1883.

Dodds, E. R. *The Greeks and the Irrational*. Berkeley, CA.: University of California Press, 1951.

Dorcy, Jean. *À la rencontre de la mime*. Neuilly-sur-Seine: Les Cahiers du Danse et Culture, 1958.

_____. *J'aime la mime*. Lausanne: Éditions Rencontre, 1962.

_____. *The Mime*. Trans. Robert Speller, Jr., and Pierre de Fontnouvelle. New York: Robert Speller & Sons, 1961.

Ducharte, Pierre Louis. *The Italian Comedy*. New York: Dover, 1966.

Dunham, Katherine. *Dances of Haiti,* rev. ed. "Los Danzas de Haiti" (1947). Berkeley, CA.: University of California Press, 1983.

Eldredge, Sears Atwood. "Masks: Their Use and Effectiveness in Actor Training Programs." Diss. Michigan State University, 1975.

_____, and Hollis Huston. "Actor Training in the Neutral Mask." *Drama Review* 22.4 Dec. 1978: 19–28.

Eliade, Mircea. *Shamanism: Archaic Techniques of Ecstasy*. Trans. Willard R. Trask. Bollingen Series 76. Princeton, N.J.: Princeton University Press, 1964.

Elkin, A. P. *Aboriginal Men of High Degree*. Sydney, Australia: The John Murtagh Macrossan Memorial Lectures for 1944. University of Queensland: Australasian, 1945.

Else, Gerald F. "'Imitation' in the Fifth Century." *Classical Philology* 53.2: 73–90.

_____. *The Origin and Early Form of Greek Tragedy*. Cambridge, MA.: Harvard University Press, 1965.

Emmanuel, Maurice. *The Antique Greek Dance*. Trans. Harriet Jean Beauley. New York: John Lance, 1916.

Epstein, Alvin. "The Mime Theatre of Etienne Decroux." *Chrysalis* 11.1–2 (1958): 3–13.

Feldinkrais, Moshe. "Image, Movement, and Actor: Restoration of Potentiality." Trans. and ed. Kelly Morris. *Tulane Drama Review* 31, Spring 1966: 112–25.

Felner, Mira. *Apostles of Silence*. Rutherford, N.J.: Fairleigh Dickinson University Press, 1985.

Fergusson, Francis. *Literary Landmarks: Essays on the Theory and Practice of Literature*. New Brunswick: Rutgers University Press, 1975.

Furst, Peter. "The Roots and Continuities of Shamanism." *Arscanada* 31 (Spring 1974): 34–45.

Goodman, Felicitas D. "Body Posture and the Religious Altered State of Consciousness: An Experimental Investigation." *Journal of Humanistic Psychology* 26: 81–118.

Gordon, Mel. *Lazzi: The Comic Routines of the Commedia dell'Arte*. New York: Performing Arts Journal Publications, 1983.

Gowan, John Curtis. *Trance, Art, and Creativity*. Buffalo, N.Y.: Creative Education Foundation, 1975.

Graves, Russell. "The Psychological Effects of Masks." *Theatre Crafts* Jan.-Feb. 1971: 12–13 & 33.

Haigh, A. E. *The Attic Theatre*. 3rd ed. New York: Haskell House, 1968.

Harner, Michael. *The Way of the Shaman: A Guide to Power and Healing*. New York: Bantam Books, 1982.

Harrison, Jane Ellen. *Ancient Art and Ritual*. New York: Greenwood Press, 1969. (Copyright 1951, Oxford University Press.)

————. *Prolegomena to the Study of Greek Religion*. New York: Meridian, 1959.

Hastings, Lily, and Baird Hastings. "The New Mime of Etienne Decroux." *Dance Magazine* (Sept. 1951).

Hoaas, Solrun. "The Legacy of Possession." *Drama Review* 28.4 (Winter 1982): 82–86.

Hoff, Frank. "Dance to Song in Japan," *Dance Research Journal of CORD* 9/1 (Fall/Winter 1976-77): 1–15.

Holmstrom, Kirsten Gram. *Monodrama, Attitudes, Tableaux Vivants*. Stockholm: Almquist & Wiksell, 1967.

Homer. *The Odyssey* 17: 518.

Huxley, Francis. "The Body and the Play Within the Play." *The Anthropology of the Body*. Ed. John Blacking. London: Academic Press, 1977.

————. "A Discussion on Ritualization of Behavior in Man and Animals." *Philosophical Transactions of the Royal Society of London* 251, 1965.

————. *The Invisibles: Voodoo Gods in Haiti*. New York: McGraw-Hill, 1966.

————. *The Way of the Sacred*. Garden City, N.Y.: Doubleday, 1974.

Inoura, Yoshinobu. *A History of Japanese Theatre 1: Noh and Kyogen*. Tokyo: Kokusai Bunka Shinkokai (Japan Cultural Society), 1971.

Jackson, John. *The History of the Scottish Stage*. Edinburgh, 1793.

Janet, Pierre. *L'Automatisme psychologique*. Reprint of 4th ed. Paris: Société Pierre Janet et Laboratoire du Centre National de la Récherche Scientifique, (1889) 1973.

Jeanmaire, H. *Dionysus: Histoire du Culte de Bacchus*. Paris: Payot, 1951.

Jianou, Ionel. *Rodin*. Trans. Kathleen Muston and Geofrey Skelding. Paris: Arted, 1970.

Jones, Louisa E. *Sad Clowns and Pale Pierrots: Literature and the Popular Comic Arts in 19th-Century France*. Lexington: French Forum, 1984.

Jousse, Marcel. *L'anthropologie du geste*. Paris: Gallimard, 1974.

Jung, Carl G. *Man and His Symbols.* Garden City, N.Y.: Doubleday, 1972.

————. *Psychology and Religion.* Terry Lectures, 1937. New Haven, CT.: Yale University Press, 1938.

Keene, Donald. *No: The Classical Theatre of Japan.* Tokyo, New York, San Francisco: Kodansha, 1966.

Kirby, E. T. "The Origin of No Drama," *Educational Theatre Journal* 25.3 (1973): 269–284.

————. "The Shamanistic Origins of Popular Entertainments." *The Drama Review* 18:1 (March 1974): 5–15.

Komparu, Kunio. *The Noh Theatre: Principles and Perspectives.* Trans. Jane Corddry. New York and Tokyo: John Weatherhill, 1983.

Laban, Rudolf. *The Mastery of Movement.* 3rd ed. Boston: Plays Inc., 1971.

Langer, Susanne. *Feeling and Form: A Theory of Art.* New York: Charles Scribner's Sons, 1953.

————. *Philosophy in a New Key.* Cambridge, MA.: Harvard University Press, 1957.

Larsen, Stephen. *The Shaman's Doorway: Opening the Mythic Imagination to Contemporary Consciousness.* New York: Harper and Row, 1976.

Lawler, Lillian. "Beating Motifs in the Greek Dance." *The Classical Outlook* (1944): 59–61.

————. *The Dance in Ancient Greece.* Middletown: Wesleyan University Press, 1964.

————. *The Dance of the Ancient Greek Theatre.* Iowa City, IA: The University of Iowa Press, 1964.

————. "Phora, Schêma, Deixis in Greek Dance." *Transactions of the American Philological Association* 85 (1954): 148–159.

————. "Portrait of a Dancer." *Classical Journal,* 41.6 (March 1946): 241–47.

Lea, K. M. *Italian Popular Comedy.* New York: Russell & Russell, 1962.

Leabhart, Thomas, ed. "Etienne Decroux Eightieth Birthday Issue." *Mime Journal* Nos. 7 & 8.

————. *Modern and Post-Modern Mime.* New York: St. Martin's Press, 1989.

Lecoq, Jacques. Interview in *Masks: Their Use and Effectiveness in Actor Training Programs.* By Sears Eldredge. Diss. Michigan State University, 1975.

————. "La Pédagogie du Mouvement." Interview with Jean Perret. *Le théâtre du geste: mimes et acteurs,* Sous la direction de Jacques Lecoq. Paris: Bordas, 1987.

————. "Mime, Movement, Theatre." *Mimes on Miming.* Ed. Bari Rolfe. London: Millington, 1981.

Leigh, Barbara Kusler. "Jacques Copeau's School for Actors." *Mime Journal,* nos. 9 and 10.

Leiris, Michael. *La possession et ses aspects théâtraux chez les Éthiopiens de Gondar.* Paris: Plon, 1958.

Leurner, H. *Psychopathy and Pictorial Expression.* Basel: Sandoz, 1974.

Lewis, I. M. *Ecstatic Religion: An Anthropological Study of Spirit Possession and Shamanism.* Baltimore: Penguin, 1971.

Levy, Alan. "A Week Avec Lecoq," *Mime, Mask & Marionette* 1 (1978): 45–61.

Lex, B. W. "The Neurobiology of Ritual Trance." In *The Spectrum of Ritual: A*

Biogenetic Structural Analysis. E. d'Aquilli, ed. New York: Columbia University Press, 1979.

Livy. Trans. B. O. Foster. The Loeb Classical Library 3. Cambridge, MA.: Harvard University Press, 1924.

Lommel, Andreas. *Shamanism: The Beginnings of Art.* Trans. Michael Bullock. New York: McGraw-Hill, 1967.

Lorelle, Yves. *L'Expression corporelle du mime sacré au mime du théâtre.* Paris: La Renaissance du Livre, Collections Dionysos, 1974.

Lot-Falck, Evaline. "Le chamanisme en Sibérie: Essai de mise au point." *Asie du Sud-Est et Monde Insulindien.* Vol. 4,3. Chamanisme et possession, fasc. 2. Paris: Mouton, 1973: 1–10.

Lowen, Alexander. *Bioenergetics.* New York: Penguin, 1981.

Lucian. "The Dance (Saltatio)." Trans. A. M. Harmon. Loeb Classical Library 5. Cambridge: Harvard University Press, 1962.

Lust, Annette. "Etienne Decroux: Father of Modern Mime." *Mime Journal* No. 1 (1974): 14–23.

————. "Etienne Decroux and the French School of Mime." *The Quarterly Journal of Speech* 57.2 (Oct. 1971): 291–297.

McKinnon, Richard N. "Zeami on the Art of Training." *Harvard Journal of Asiatic Studies* 16 (June 1953): 200–225.

MacLeish, Archibald. *Poetry and Experience.* Baltimore: Penguin, 1960.

McNair, Peter L. "Kwakiutl Winter Dances: A Reenactment." *Arscanada* 31 (Spring 1974): 94–109.

Magnin, M. Charles. *Histoire des Marionnettes en Europe, depuis l'antiquité jusqu'à nos jours.* Paris: 1852 and 1862.

————. *Les origines du théâtre antique et du théâtre modern.* Paris: Auguste Eudes, 1868.

Marceau, Marcel. "The Language of the Heart." *Theatre Arts* (March 1958): 58–59, 70.

————. "Lecture/Demonstration on Mime," Videotape, Brooklyn College, 1978.

————. *Marcel Marceau ou l'Aventure du silence,* interview et textes Guy et Jeanne Verriest-Lefert. Paris: Desclée De Brouwer 1974.

————. "Marcel Marceau Speaks." Interview with Rebecca Cox and Sally Boxer. *Prompt* No. 11 (1968): 9–11.

————. "Un qui se tait," *Arts,* April 1950.

————. "Who Am I." *Dance Magazine* (Nov. 1965): 49–51.

Martin, Ben. *Marcel Marceau Master of Mime.* New York: Paddington, 1978.

Métraux, Alfred. "A Selection of Voodoo in Haiti." *Anthropology of Folk Religions.* Ed. Charles Leslie. New York: Vintage, 1960.

Mischel, Walter, and Frances Mischel. "Psychological Aspects of Spirit Possession." *American Anthropologist* 60 (1958): 233–260.

Nagler, A. M. *A Source Book in Theatrical History.* New York: Dover, 1952.

Nakamura, Yasuo. *Noh: The Classical Theatre.* Trans. Don Kenny. New York & Tokyo: Walker/Weatherhill, 1971.

Nearman, Mark. "Feeling in Relation to Acting: An Outline of Zeami's Views." *Asian Theatre Journal* 1.1 (Spring 1984): 40–51.

Nicoll, Allardyce. *Masks, Mimes, and Miracles*. New York: Cooper Square, 1963.

_____. *The World of Harlequin: A Critical Study of the Commedia dell'Arte*. Cambridge, MA.: Cambridge University Press, 1963.

North, Marion. *Personality Assessment Through Movement*. London: MacDonald & Evans, 1972.

Noverre, Jean Georges. *Letters on Dancing and Ballet*. Trans. Cyril W. Beaumont. New York: Dance Horizons, 1968.

Obeyesekere, Gananath. "The Ritual Drama of the Sanni Demons: Collective Representations of Disease in Ceylon," *Comparative Studies in Society and History* 11:2 (April 1969): 174–216.

Oesterreich, T. K. *Possession, Demonical and Other Among Primitive Races, in Antiquity, the Middle Ages, and Modern Times*. Princeton, N.J.: Princeton University Press, 1966.

O'Neill, R. G. *Early No Drama: Its Background, Character and Development*. London: Lund Humphries, 1958.

Oreglia, Giacomo. *The Commedia dell'Arte*. New York: Hill and Wang, 1968.

Ortolani, Benito. "Shamanism in the Origins of the No Theatre." *Asian Theatre Journal* 1:2 (Fall 1984): 166–190.

_____. "Zeami's Aesthetics of the No and Audience Participation," *Educational Theatre Journal* 24 (1972): 109–117.

Otto, Walter F. *Dionysus: Myth and Cult*. Trans. Robert B. Palmer. Dallas, TX: Spring Publications. 1981.

Oughourlian, Jean-Michel. *The Puppet of Desire: The Psychology of Hysteria, Possession and Hypnosis*. Trans. Eugene Webb. Stanford, CA.: Stanford University Press, 1991.

Pandolfi, Vito. *Histoire du théâtre*. Vol. 2. Paris: Marabout Université, 1964.

Pavis, Patrice. *Languages of the Stage: Essays in the Semiology of Theatre*. New York: Performing Arts Journal Publications, 1982.

Perret, Jean. "L'explosion du mime." *Théâtre du geste*. Sous la Direction de Jacques Lecoq. Paris: Bordas, 1987.

Peters, Larry G., and Douglas Price-Williams. "A Phenomenological Overview of Trance." *Transcultural Psychiatric Research Review* 20: 5–39.

Pickard-Cambridge, Sir Arthur. *Dithyramb, Tragedy and Comedy*. 2nd ed. Revised by T. B. L. Webster. Oxford: Clarendon, 1962.

_____. *The Dramatic Festivals of Athens*. Rev. 2nd ed. Oxford: Oxford University Press, 1988.

Pilgrim, Richard. "Some Aspects of Kokoro in Zeami,'" *Monumenta Nipponica* 24:4 (1969): 393–401.

Plato. *Ion*. Trans. W. R. Lamb. Loeb Classical Library 3. Cambridge, MA.: Harvard University Press, 1962.

_____. *Laws*. Trans. R. G. Bury. Loeb Classical Library. Cambridge, MA.: Harvard University Press, 1961.

_____. *Phaedrus*. Trans. Harold North Fowler. Loeb Classical Library. Cambridge, MA.: Harvard University Press, 1950.

_____. *The Republic*. Trans. Desmond Lee. Baltimore: Penguin, 1974.

Plutarch. *Moralia*. Trans. Edward L. Minar, et al. Loeb Classical Library 15. Cambridge, MA.: Harvard University Press, 1961.

Prosperi, Mario. "The Masks of Lipari." *The Drama Review* 26.4 (1982): 25–66.

Quintilian. *Institutio Oratoria*. Trans. H. E. Butler. Loeb Classical Library 4. Cambridge, MA.: Harvard University Press, 1958.

Reinhard, Johan. "Shamanism and Spirit Possession: The Definition Problem." In *Spirit Possession in the Nepal Himalayas*. Eds. J. T. Hitchcock and Rex L. Jones. New Dehli, India: Vikas, 1976.

Richter, Gisela, M.A. "Grotesques and the Mime." *American Journal of Archaeology* 17 (1913): 149–155.

Rodin, Auguste. *L'Art: entretiens réunis par Paul Gsell*. Paris: Gallimard, 1967.

Rolfe, Bari. "The Mime of Jacques Lecoq." *Drama Review* 16.1 (March 1972): 34–38.

_____. "Mime-Paradigm of Paradox," *Impulse*, (1969–70): 36–38.

Rouget, Gilbert. *La musique et la transe*. Paris: Gallimard, 1980.

Rowley, George. *Principles of Chinese Painting*. Princeton, N.J.: Princeton University Press, 1947.

Rubinstein, S. L. "Consciousness in the Light of Dialectical Materialism," *Science and Society* 10 (1946), p. 252.

Sachs, Curt. *World History of the Dance*. Trans. Bessie Schonberg. New York: W. W. Norton & Co., 1937.

Schott-Billmann, France. *Corps et possession: Le vécu corporel des possédés face à la rationalité occidentale*. Paris: Bordas, 1977.

Shimazaki, Chifumi. *The Noh: Vol. 1 God Noh*. Tokyo: Hinoki Shoten, 1972.

Sieffert, René. "Les Dances Sacrées au Japon." *Les Danses Sacrees*. Ed. René Sieffert. Paris: Éditions du Seuil, 1963.

Siikala, Anna-Leena. "The Rite Technique of the Siberian Shaman." *F. F. Communications* (Finland) 93 (1978): 79–212.

Sklar, Roberta. "Etienne Decroux's Promethean Mime," *The Drama Review* 29.4 (Winter 1985): 66.

Smith, Susan Harris. *Masks in Modern Drama*. Berkeley, CA.: University of California Press, 1984.

Sorbom, Goran. *Mimesis and Art: Studies in the Origin and Early Development of an Aesthetic Vocabulary*. Stockholm: Scandinavian University Press, 1966.

Stoop, Norma McLain. "The Interior Music of Marcel Marceau." Interview *Dance Magazine* 49 (July 1975): 34– 36.

Storey, Robert. *Pierrots on the Stage of Desire: Nineteenth-Century French Literary Artists and the Comic Pantomime*. Princeton, N.J.: Princeton University Press, 1985.

Strauss, Gloria B. "The Aesthetics of Dominance," *Journal of Aesthetics and Art Criticism* 37 (Fall 1978): 73.

Sutton, Dana F. *Greek Satyr Play*. Meisenheim am Glan: Hain, 1980.

Suzuki, D. T. Introduction. *Zen and the Art of Archery*. By Eugen Herrigel. Trans. R. F. C. Hull. New York: Vintage, 1971.

_____. *Zen Buddhism*. Ed. William Barret. Garden City, N.Y.: Doubleday, 1956.

Svehla, Jaroslav. "Jean Gaspard Deburau: The Immortal Pierrot." *Mime Journal* No. 5 (1977): 1–39.

Toschi, Paulo. *Le Origini del Teatro Italiano*. Turin, 1955.

Ueda, Makoto. *Zeami, Basho, Yeats, Pound.* The Hague: Mouton & Co., 1965.

Veinstein, Andre. *La Mise en Scène Théâtrale et sa Condition Esthétique.* Paris: Flammarion, 1955.

Verger, Pierre. *Les Dieux d'Afrique.* Preface Roger Bastide. Paris: Paul Hartmann, 1954.

————. "Trance and Convention in Nâgo-Yoruba Spirit Mediumship." *Spirit Mediumship and Society in Africa.* Ed. John Beattie and John Middleton. London: Routledge & Kegan Paul, 1969.

Walker, Sheila. *Ceremonial Spirit Possession in Africa and Afro-America.* Leiden, Netherlands: E. J. Brill, 1972.

Walton, J. Michael. *Greek Theatre Practice.* Westport, CT.: Greenwood Press, 1980.

Weaver, John. *An Essay Towards a History of Dancing.* London: John Tonfon, 1712.

Winter, Marian Hannah. *The Theatre of Marvels.* New York: Benjamin Blom, 1964.

Wolff, Charlotte. *A Psychology of Gesture.* New York: Arno Press, 1972.

Woltz, Carl. "The Spirit of Zen in Noh Dance." *CORD Dance Research Annual 8: Asian and Pacific Dance: Selected Papers from the 1975 CORD-SEM Conference.* Ed. Adrienne Kaeppler, Carl Woltz, and Judy Van Zile. New York: CORD, 1977: 55–64.

Wundt, Wilhelm. *The Language of Gesture.* Paris: Mouton, 1973.

Wylie, Lawrence. "À l'école Lecoq j'ai découvert mon propre clown." *Psychologie* (Aug. 1973): 17–27.

Xenophon. *Xenophon's Minor Works.* Trans. and ed. Rev. J. S. Watson. London: George Bell & Sons, 1908.

Yamazaki, Masakazu. "The Aesthetics of Ambiguity: The Artistic Theories of Zeami." In *On the Art of the No Drama.* Ed. J. Thomas Rimer and Masakazu Yamazaki. Princeton: Princeton University Press, 1984.

Zeami Motokiyo. *On the Art of the No Drama: The Major Treatises of Zeami.* Ed. and trans. J. Thomas Rimer and Masakazu Yamazaki. Princeton, N.J.: Princeton University Press, 1984.

————. *Ze-ami: Kadensho.* Trans. Chuichi Sakurai, et. al. Kyoto: Sumiya-Shinobe, 1968.

ANNOTATED BIBLIOGRAPHY

This annotated bibliography includes works in French and English dealing specifically with mime and its related forms for the scholar and general reader.

HISTORIES OF THE MIME

BOOKS

Lecoq, Jacques, ed. *Le théâtre du geste: mimes et acteurs.* Paris: Bordas, 1987. A rich offering of essays and interviews by French scholars and theatre artists which approaches mime from historical, anthropological, aesthetic, and philosophical perspectives. Foremost among its subjects are: the concepts of imitation, mimesis, and mimetism; mimetic gestures in everyday life; a history of mime from the Greeks to the present day; mixed performance genres which include theatre, mime and dance; interviews and essays by Jacques Lecoq on his pedagogy and views on mime; the mime of the actor and the place of gesture in the spoken theatre; and the gesture of the Japanese theatre. It particularly emphasizes the French mime tradition and the contributions of pioneering French mimes, such as Marcel Marceau, Etienne Decroux, and Jacques Lecoq, as well as theatre practitioners who use mime in their work, such as Ariane Mnouchkine. Includes extensive black and white and color illustrations. Oversized "coffee table" book. (150 pages)

Lorelle, Yves. *L'Expression corporelle du mime sacré au mime du théâtre.* Paris: La Renaissance du Livre, Collections Dionysos, 1974. Lorelle seeks to enlarge the notion of mime beyond that presented by its various and diverse performance genres by linking mime to a discussion of other disciplines. In tracing mime from its earliest manifestations in ritual (*mime sacré*) up through a discussion of modern French mime, he seeks to underscore the importance of mime in its biological, social, ethnic, psychological, linguistic, and philosophical aspects. The first half of the book is devoted to a discussion of biological mimetism and mime in its ritual manifestations. Here he touches upon: the role or model in imitation; identification; the power of the imagination; the rapport between mask and gesture; ritual corporeal techniques; and the complexity and richness of gestural signs. Next he applies his findings to brief discussions of Greek and Roman mime, the *Commedia dell'Arte* and finally, the work of Barrault, Decroux, and Marceau. In his discussion of

233

modern mime he focuses on the linguistic function of gestural signs and broaches the problem of schism between word and gesture. Many black and white illustrations. (142 pages)

Magnin, M. Charles. *Les Origines du Théâtre Antique et du Théâtre Modern.* Paris: Auguste Eudes, 1868. Includes a lengthy scholarly history of mime in the context of the origins and development of the Western theatre up to the sixteenth century. Magnin gives an in depth discussion of the numerous diverse forms of Greek and Roman mime by analyzing the many, often fragmentary, accounts left by writers of the time. No illustrations. (550 pages)

Nicoll, Allardyce. *Masks, Mimes, and Miracles.* New York: Cooper Square, 1963. An excellent source on the origins and development of mime for the scholar as well as the general reader. Chapter I: The Mimes—Dorian, Epicharmus, Phlyakes, Atellan Farce. Chapter II: Heyday of Mimic Drama—Greek and Roman mime and pantomime. Chapter III: The Fate of the Mimes in the Dark Ages—secular and religious drama of the Middle Ages. Chapter IV: Commedia dell'Arte—scenarios, stock types, companies. Appendices on the Commedia dell'Arte. Over two hundred black and white illustrations. (408 pages)

Rolfe, Bari, ed. *Mimes on Miming: Writings on the Art of Mime.* London: Millington, 1979. A book for the general reader. Includes a wide variety of writings by mime performers, teachers of mime, writers of mime sketches, critics, and historians. The 66 essays, many of them short snippets from longer works, are compiled in a chronological sequence from the Greeks up through contemporary twentieth century mime. A good book for the general reader seeking primary sources on mime performers, clowns, dancers, and silent film actors, but the offerings are too short to do little more than whet the appetite. Probably best used as a supplement to histories on the mime. Black and white illustrations. (232 pages)

ARTICLES

Rolfe, Bari. "Mime in America." *The Mime Journal* 1 (1974): 2–12. A brief historical survey of mime in America and the artists associated with it from the 1700s to the present and underscores the influence of French mime tradition.

_____. "Queens of Mime." *Dance Magazine* (December 1976): 68–73. Short essay on Theodora (Empress of Byzantiaum), Isabella Andreini, La Belle Otero, Collette, Angna Enters, and Lotte Goslar. Bibliography and list of additional source materials.

HISTORIES OF THE PANTOMIME

BOOKS

Broadbent, R. J. *A History of Pantomime.* New York: Benjamin Blom, 1901. A rather dated, superficial history. Not of much use to the general reader or scholar.

Weaver, John. *A History of Mimes and Pantomimes.* London, 1728. This is the earliest treatise on pantomime by one of its originators.

Willson-Disher, Maurice. *Clowns and Pantomimes.* London: Constable, 1925.

A useful and generally reliable history of pantomime from its origins to its twentieth century forms. Some illustrations. For the general reader and the cautious scholar.

Wilson, Albert E. *King Panto: The Story of Pantomime.* London: E. P. Dutton, 1933. A readable and popular history of pantomime for the general reader which should be used with caution by the scholar. Illustrated.

Winter, Marian Hannah. *The Theatre of Marvels.* New York: Benjamin Blom, 1964. A good history which deals primarily with the theatre of the marvelous in France from 1789 to 1860. Also includes a chapter on America. Covers the three styles of the marvelous: exotic, troubadour, and supernatural. Also examined are the forerunners of mime — Noverre, Jacques-Louis David, and Pixerecourt — techniques, pantomime, Romantic ballet, choreographers, and performing animals. Chiefly for the scholar.

CLASSICAL GREEK AND ROMAN DANCE/PANTOMIME

BOOKS

Emmanuel, Maurice. *The Antique Greek Dance.* Trans. Harriet Jean Beauley. New York: John Lance, 1916. An authoritative but somewhat dated book on the Greek Dance which makes little mention of the pantomime. Primarily for the scholar.

Lawler, Lillian. *The Dance in Ancient Greece.* Middletown: Wesleyan University Press, 1963. Lawler offers the non-specialist and scholar the fruits of her considerable research on ancient Greek dance. Includes chapters on: introduction to Greek dance; dance of prehistoric Crete; dance in Mycenaean and pre-classical Greece; animal dances; dance and drama; orgiastic and mystery dances, dances at shrines and festivals; the dance and the people; and dance as a profession. Sixty-two black and white illustrations. (160 pages)

_____. *The Dance of the Ancient Greek Theatre.* Iowa City: The University of Iowa Press, 1964. A work for the serious scholar of Greek drama and dance. Surveys and interprets what is known of the dramatic and cyclic performances in the Greek theatre, particularly in Athens. Includes chapters on the dance of: the dithyramb, tragedy, comedy, and satyr play. Does not enter into a discussion of the origins of Greek drama, rather attempts to isolate dance from drama as a whole. No bibliography. Footnotes. (135 pages)

ARTICLES

Lawler, Lillian. "Portrait of a Dancer." *Classical Journal* 41.6 (March 1946): 241–47. A short article on the Greco-Roman pantomime Pylades, supported by quotations from contemporary observers. For the general reader.

_____. "Phora, Schêma, Deixis in Greek Dance." *Transactions of the American Philological Association* 85 (1954): 148–58. An analysis of the meaning of the dance terms *phora, schema* and *deixis* as used by classical authors. For the scholar.

Lucian. "The Dance ('Saltatio')." Trans. A. M. Harmon. Loeb Classical Library 5.

Cambridge, MA.: Harvard University Press, 1962: 209–91. The best extant
contemporary account of the Greco-Roman pantomime.

CLASSICAL BALLET AND PANTOMIME

BOOKS

Christout, Marie Françoise. *Le Merveilleux et le Théâtre du Silence*. Paris: Mouton,
1965. A scholarly work which analyzes the role of the marvelous in the ballet
and its allied arts (including pantomime) from the seventeenth century to the
1960s. The book is divided into two parts: the techniques of the academic
ballet and related arts and themes of the marvelous—gods, heros, exotism,
and feerie. Many beautiful color and black and white illustrations. (447 pages)

Winter, Marian Hannah. *The Pre-Romantic Ballet*. London: Sir Isaac Pitman and
Sons, 1974. An important and useful analysis of the influence of John
Weaver, John Rich, Noverre and the acrobatic dancers of the Parisian fairs on
the development of pantomime. Good illustrations. This book is chiefly for
the scholar.

NINETEENTH CENTURY ENGLISH PANTOMIME

BOOKS

Mayer, David, III. *Annotated Bibliography of Pantomime and Guide to Study
Sources*. London: Commission for a British Theatre Institute, 1975: 1–11. An
annotated bibliography and study guide of the English pantomime by a well
known scholar in the field. Contains eight sections with suggested readings
for the scholar as well as the layman. Includes sections on: memoirs and
bibliographies of pantomimists; articles in periodicals; bibliographies and
catalogues of manuscript collections; collections of pantomime libretti; collections of pantomime music; and sources of illustrations. The annotated
bibliography and additional information on pantomime can be obtained
from the British Pantomime Association, 170 Clarence Gate Gardens, London
NW1 6AR, which also publishes a journal entitled PANTO.

————. *Harlequin in His Element: The English Pantomime, 1806–1836*. Cambridge, MA.: Harvard University Press, 1969. An intensive and scholarly
study of the pantomime in the "age of Grimaldi" and its intimate relationship
to the times. Brief postscript on later pantomime; appendices on music,
trickwork, and available pantomime libretti. Extensive illustrations. For the
general reader as well as the scholar.

NINETEENTH CENTURY PANTOMIME BLANCHE

BOOKS

Hugounet, Paul. *Mimes et Pierrots*. Paris: Librairie Fischbacher, 1889. Traces the
development of Pierrot from Greece and Rome through the Middle Ages to
the French pantomimes of the Boulevard du Temple and the Funambules.
Includes chapters on Charles Deburau, Paul Legrand, Alexandre Guyon, the
pantomime at Marseille, the last French Pierrots, the British pantomime, and
Pierrot in literature and art. (253 pages)

Janin, Jules. *Deburau, histoire du Théâtre à Quatre Sous pour faire suite a l'histoire du Théâtre-Français*. 1832; rpt. in 1 vol., Paris: Librairie de Bibliophiles, 1881. The critic Jules Janin's purpose in writing this book as he explains in the preface is to "summarize the History of the Dramatic Art considered under its ignoble aspect, the only aspect under which it can be regarded." His work eulogizes Deburau as a "King" of the common people and surrounds the events of Deburau's life with the fabulous air of a folk tale. The picture of Deburau takes on the dimensions of myth, but does disservice to those who want a clear understanding of the nature of his art.

Jones, Louisa E. *Sad Clowns and Pale Pierrots: Literature and the Popular Comic Arts in 19th-Century France*. Lexington, Kentucky: French Forum, 1984. Examines the history of pantomime and circus arts and the legends created around them by the world of literature in nineteenth century France. Chapter one, Antiheroics, examines the Romantics' preference for the grotesque which was most clearly exemplified in the idiom of the Commedia dell'Arte whose tradition was continued in the pantomime plays of the Funambules and was emblemized in Deburau's Pierrot. A scholarly study devoted to modern variants of the sad clown iconography; it shows how and why these arose and what exchanges between popular and avant-garde art produced them. Reveals the iconography of the sad clown as a creation of the projection of the personal preoccupations of the audience, the myths of the time, and the general patterns of archetypes. Covers Pierrot, the pantomime tradition, and clowns in literature and art.

Kozik, Francis. *The Great Deburau*. Trans. Dora Round. New York and Toronto: Farrar & Rinehart, 1940. A biographical novel of Deburau which embroiders the romantic myth and legend surrounding the great pantomime. Much is made of his humble beginnings and suffering as a member of his family's troupe of traveling circus performers and of his subsequent exploitation at the Funambules in order to depict Deburau as the embodiment of the spirit of *le peuple* of nineteenth century France. The book makes fun reading but contains more fiction than fact. (376 pages)

Storey, Robert. *Pierrots on the Stage of Desire: Nineteenth-Century French Literary Artists and the Comic Pantomime*. Princeton: Princeton University Press, 1985. A scholarly study that attempts in the first chapter to clear away the myth surrounding Deburau and present a clear picture of the varied roles he performed and the diversity of the pantomimic forms in which he appeared. Storey develops the argument that pantomime at the Funambules was based in regressive fantasy. It was a forum in which the audience played out its fears and desires. Includes chapters on nineteenth century French literature, history and criticism, psychoanalysis, and literature.

ARTICLES

Carlson, Marvin. "The Golden Age of Boulevard." *Drama Review* 18.1 (1974): 25–33. A good general background of the origins and diverse theatrical fare offered by the nineteenth century Parisian "boulevard" theatres.

Rolfe, Bari. "Magic Century of French Mime." *Mime, Mask & Marionette*. 1.3 (Fall 1978): 135–58. An excellent essay on the French pantomimists who carried on the tradition of the pantomime blanche after the death of Deburau. Briefly covers the careers of Charles Deburau (1829–1883), Paul Legrand (1816–1898), the Marseilles Mimes (Louis Rouffe [?–1885] and Severin [1863–1930]), the Cercle Funambulesque; the women mimes of the Belle Epoque (1890–1914), and Georges Wague (1874–1965). Bibliography and several black and white photos. For the general reader.

Svehla, Jaroslav. "Jean-Gaspard Deburau: The Immortal Pierrot." Trans. Paul Wilson. *Mime Journal* 5 (1977): 1–43. This fine article for the general reader is a translated condensation of Svehla's book-length study *Deburau, nesmrtelny Pierot* (Prague: Melantrich, 1976). In addition to providing a brief history of Deburau's childhood, travels through Europe as a member of his family's acrobatic troupe, and his rise to stardom at the Funambules in Paris, it also includes a description of the Funambules and the pantomimes performed there as well as a discussion of the essence of Deburau's Pierrot and mime style. Many fine nineteenth century drawings and engravings of Deburau in his various roles.

TWENTIETH CENTURY FRENCH MIME

BOOKS

Dorcy, Jean. *The Mime.* Trans. Robert Speller, Jr., and Pierre de Fontnouvelle. New York: Robert Speller & Sons, 1961. An anecdotal book of eleven short chapters written by a student and teacher at the Vieux-Colombier School. The first half of the book, devoted to "The Mime of the Actor," summarizes the contributions of the school and the companies and individuals it spawned, to the development of mime: the Comédiens Routiers, the Compagnie des Quinze, Jean Dasté, Gilles and Julien, and Proscenium. The second half of the book, devoted to "The Mime of the Mime," contains chapters on mime, Etienne Decroux, Jean-Louis Barrault, and Marcel Marceau. Also includes essays by Decroux ("For Better and Worse"), Marceau ("The Poetic Halo"), and Barrault ("The Tragic Mime"). (116 pages)

Felner, Mira. *Apostles of Silence.* Rutherford, N.J.: Fairleigh Dickinson University Press, 1985. An in-depth critical comparison of the work of Etienne Decroux, Jean-Louis Barrault, Marcel Marceau, and Jacques Lecoq which attempts to analyze their individual contributions towards defining a new mime aesthetic. The introduction provides a brief discussion of the mime definition problem and a short history of the mime, culminating in the nineteenth century French pantomime blanche. The book includes an important first chapter on the formative influence of Jacques Copeau's l'École du Vieux-Colombier on the work of these four mimes. In separate chapters devoted to each mime, Felner cites numerous examples of their work and backs up her discussion with quotations from contemporary critics and mimes. Her comprehensive bibliography includes an extensive list of theatre reviews and articles on these mimes. Felner, who studied with Lecoq, skews her discussion somewhat in his favor and repeats many of the arguments accusing Decroux of formalism.

Leabhart, Thomas. *Modern and Post-Modern Mime.* New York: St. Martin's Press, 1989. A very readable and much needed addition to the literature on mime for the general reader. It provides an historical introduction which goes beyond the pantomime blanche to include important formative influences on modern mime, such as the photographer Eadweard Muybridge, the French philosopher Paul Souriau, François Delsarte, and gymnastics. The book includes separate chapters on Jacques Copeau, Etienne Decroux, Jean Louis Barrault, Marcel Marceau, and Lecoq/Mummenschantz. The chapters provide an excellent overview of the development of their mime philosophies and styles. The book fills an important lacuna in mime literature by providing chapters on the development of post-modern mime out of modern mime. Leabhart discusses post-modern mime in the context of the movement in the fine arts, dance, and theatre and attempts to arrive at a definition. He cites the San Francisco Mime Troupe as one of the earliest proponents of this eclectic and synthetic style which had a seminal influence on the rise of New Vaudevillians and New Mimes (the subject of the final chapter). Short discussions are devoted to the work of contemporary mimes in the United States, Canada, and Europe. Leabhart, the originator and editor of the *Mime Journal*, studied and taught with Decroux for many years and is a mime performer and teacher based at Scripts College in California. As such, he is eminently knowledgeable and qualified to speak on his subject.

See also in Histories of the Mime: *Le théâtre du geste: mimes et acteurs,* Sous la direction de Jacques Lecoq. Paris: Bordas, 1987.

DECROUX

BOOKS

Decroux, Etienne. *Words on Mime.* Trans. Mark Piper. Claremont, CA.: Mime Journal, 1985. (*Paroles sur le mime.* Paris: Gallimard, 1963.) The book consists of a series of notes, essays and articles, both published and unpublished, by Decroux. The chapters include: Sources, historical and formative origins of corporeal mime, Theatre and Mime, a philosophical inquiry into mime's place in the speaking theatre; Dance and Mime, which distinguishes the elements proper to each; Mime and Mime, a theoretical discussion of the aesthetics and style of corporeal mime; Specific Means and Effects of Mime, program notes and commentaries by Decroux on his productions; Teaching, the purpose of his school; and Related Subjects. The book also includes excellent photographs of Decroux's mime pieces.

Much of the writing is idiosyncratic, employing images and metaphors that demand more than a casual acquaintance with the idiom of corporeal mime. However, this book is unique in providing an important body of writings on the historical, philosophical, and theoretical foundations of modern mime, written by an individual who many consider the force behind the renovation of the art of mime in this century. Moreover, it situates mime within the larger context of its place within the theatre and has much to say on its possibilities for the renovation of the theatre and the art of the actor in particular.

Mark Piper, who was a student of Decroux's for three years, provides an excellent translation. (160 pages)

ARTICLES

Decroux, Etienne. "An Interview with Decroux." *The Mime Journal* No. 1 (1974): 26–37. Decroux discusses: how he began corporeal mime; the influence of Copeau, Dullin and Jouvet on his work; and muses on the future of the theatre.

————. "Etienne Decroux Eightieth Birthday Interview." *Mime Journal* Nos. 7 & 8. (1978): 1–77. An "improvisational" and meandering interview in which Decroux muses on: the origin of corporeal mime; the use of the mask and marionette as pedagogic and performance devices; and a wide variety of topics such as the qualities necessary to become a great mime, the geometric spirit of the school and the difference between corporeal mime and pantomime. There is also an excellent series of photographs by Etienne Bertrand Weill of Decroux performing.

Also includes a highly technical Design Lecture covering the movement possibilities involved in the fixing of one or more straight elements. Provides an explanation of the corporeal mime terms inclination, translation, *piston, rateau* (rake), *rateau-piston* and *piston-absolu.*

————. "Etienne Decroux on Masks." (Interview) *The Mime Journal* No. 2 (1975): 55–62. Talks about: the inexpressive mask at the Vieux-Colombier; the development and use of the neutral mask in his work; the expressive or character mask; and the aesthetics of the mask.

Epstein, Alvin. "The Mime Theatre of Etienne Decroux." *Chrysalis* 11, nos. 1–2 (1958): 3–12. Epstein provides a brief overview of Decroux's career, and passes rapidly over how Decroux used the analysis of the movement qualities of design, rhythm, and intensity to create theatrical movement that led from the literal to the abstract. While the article has been surpassed by more indepth discussions of the same material, Epstein cleaves to the heart of corporeal mime and what distinguishes it from the dance in his explanation of the statement "the articulation and flow of the Mime is directly inspired by the 'movement' of the spoken text."

Lust, Annette. "Etienne Decroux and the French School of Mime." *The Quarterly Journal of Speech* 57.3 (October 1971): 291–97. An excellent article by a one-time student of Decroux. Lust defines corporeal mime by comparing it with the Oriental theatre and by contrasting it with the nineteenth century pantomime blanche. The article ends with a brief discussion of the similarities and differences between the mime of Marceau and Decroux.

————. "Etienne Decroux, Father of Modern Mime." *The Mime Journal* No. 1 (1974): 14–45. Covers the same material as "Etienne Decroux and the French School of Mime."

Sklar, Deidre. "Etienne Decroux's Promethean Mime." *The Drama Review* 29.4 (Winter 1985): 64–75. Sklar examines Decroux's statement that "mime is political or Promethean as opposed to religious." She sees Prometheus as a "summarizing key symbol" for Decroux's corporeal mime philosophy and technique. She asserts the corporeal mime is a technique of oppositions based in the mime's struggle with the resistance of his own body with gravity and is the embodiment of the opposition between aspiration and limitation inherent in the Promethean myth. She supports her argument with photographs and examples of technical exercises and improvisations. Like Eugenio Barba, she compares Decroux's school to that of a "strict holy order" and offers some valuable description of the ritual aspects of his pedagogical style drawn from her experiences as a student at the school.

_____. "Movement Sequences from Corporeal Mime." *Journal of Association of Graduate Dance Ethnologists* 7 (Spring 1983): 45–53. Laban notation of specific corporeal sequences including the rope, the horse walk, the sea horse, annalee, and statuaire mobile.

LECOQ

ARTICLES

Lecoq, Jacques. "La Pédagogie du Mouvement." (Interview) *Le théâtre du geste: mimes et acteurs.* Sous la direction de Jacques Lecoq. Paris: Bordas, 1987. (See above)

_____. "Mime, Movement, Theatre." *Mimes on Miming.* Ed. Bari Rolfe. London: Millington Books, 1981: 150–53. A reprint of an article that appeared in *yale/theatre* (now *Theatre*) 4.1 (Winter 1973). Provides a brief overview of Lecoq's training program.

Levy, Alan. "A Week Avec Lecoq." *Mime, Mask & Marionette* 1 (1978): 45–62. A breezy and anecdotal article which includes a brief discussion of the evolution of Lecoq's career and descriptions of class sessions at Lecoq's school during a one-week visit by the author in 1976.

Rolfe, Bari. "The Mime of Jacques LeCoq." *Drama Review* 16.1 (March 1972): 34–38. A brief discussion of Lecoq's mime philosophy and basic principles of his methodology—observation, analysis and improvisation—by a former student.

Wylie, Laurence. "À L'école Lecoq j'ai découvert mon propre clown." *Psychologie* August 3, 1973: 17–27. Wylie is a Harvard psychologist who spent a year at Lecoq's school. In this article, he discusses the stages of the two-year training program and Lecoq's teaching method from his perspective as a psychologist, with special reference to the cultural differences in body movement exhibited by the diverse group of international students.

MARCEAU

BOOKS

Marceau, Marcel. *Marcel Marceau ou l'Aventure du silence.* Interview et textes Guy et Jeanne Verriest-Lefert. Paris: Desclée De Brouwer 1974. The best source available on Marceau's mime philosophy.

Martin, Ben. *Marcel Marceau Master of Mime.* New York: Paddington Press, 1978. A photojournalist's view of Marceau. Introductory background of Marceau's life and career and extensive black and white photos of Marceau rehearsing, performing, and relaxing with his family at his home in the French country-tryside.

Pawlikowski-Cholewa, Harald von. *Le Mime, Marcel Marceau* 2 vols. Hampburg-Volksdorf: Verlag Hans Hoeppner, 1961. Black and white photographs of pieces performed by Marceau and his troupe. Volume One contains: The

Animal Trainer (*Le Dompteur*) Duel in the Darkness (*Le Duel dans l'Obscurité*), and The Coat (*Le Manteau*). Volume Two contains solo pieces: The Butterfly (*Le Papillon*) and The Strolling Musician (*Le Musicien Ambulant*).

ARTICLES

Marceau, Marcel. "The Language of the Heart." *Theatre Arts* (March 1958): 58 & 70. A short article which covers material previously published in the interview with Guy and Jeanne Verriest-Lefert. Includes: how he discovered his advocation for mime in Chaplin's silent films; a brief résumé of his training; the creation of Bip; and the universality of the art of pantomime.
————. "Marcel Marceau Speaks," (Interview) *Prompt* No. 11 (1968): 9–11. Brief interview chiefly covering: the difference between dance and mime, attitude, Bip, and mime and film.

COMMEDIA DELL'ARTE

BOOKS

Ducharte, Pierre-Louis. *The Italian Comedy*. Trans. Randolph T. Weaver. New York: Dover, 1966. A translation from the French of *La commedie italienne* (1929). An important work on Commedia dell'Arte for the general reader and serious scholar. Includes chapters on the: origins; techniques of improvisation; the masks; scenarios; theatres, stages, and staging; the actors and the troupes; the Italian comedy in France; eighteenth century revivals; the ancestry of the masks and their families; and the women of the Commedia dell'Arte. Also includes important appendices, extensive bibliography, and black and white illustrations. (367 pages)
Gordon, Mel. *Lazzi: The Comic Routines of the Commedia dell'Arte*. New York: Performing Arts Journal Publications, 1983. Presents over 250 Commedia dell'Arte routines used by performers in Europe from 1550 to 1750. It also features an introduction by the author, two complete commedia scenarios, and a glossary of commedia characters. (92 pages)
Green, Martin, and John Swan. *The Triumph of Pierrot: The Commedia dell'Arte and the Modern Imagination*. New York: Macmillan, 1986. The influence of the Italian Commedia dell'Arte on the work of many major artists of the late nineteenth and early twentieth centuries and on Western art and culture to this day. Beginning wth Diaghilev's Ballet Russes, the saltimbanque paintings of Picasso, and Schoenberg's musical experiments, the authors show how commedia sensibility penetrated and shaped the Modernist consciousness and with it the plot and mood in painting, literature, theatre, ballet, opera, music, and film. Illustrations and extensive bibliography. (297 pages)
Lea, K. M. *Italian Popular Comedy*. 2 vols. New York: Russell & Russell, Inc., 1962. Excellent scholarly study of the Commedia dell'Arte. Volume I covers the forms, masks, scenarios, and development of commedia. Volume II covers contacts and comparisons with Elizabethan drama. Appendices. (685 pages)
Nicoll, Allardyce. *The World of Harlequin: A Critical Study of the Commedia*

dell'Arte. Cambridge, MA.: Cambridge University Press, 1963. Explores why the Commedia dell'Arte remained so vital for more than two centuries. Draws an interesting comparison between Hamlet and Harlequin. Uses pictorial evidence where available and accounts from the time period. Does not cover the origins of the Commedia dell'Arte or its characters. (235 pages)

    See also Masks, Mimes and Miracles by Allardyce Nicoll.

Niklaus, Thelma. *Harlequin: or the Rise and Fall of a Bergamask Rogue*. London: Oxford University Press, 1965. Provides a well written background of the development and spread of the Commedia dell'Arte across Europe. Illustrations.

Richards, Kenneth, and Laura Richards. *The Commedia dell'Arte: A Documentary History*. Oxford, England, and Cambridge, MA. Published by Basil Blackwell for Shakespeare Head Press, 1990. A survey of the important documentary accounts of the activities of the Commedia dell'Arte players and companies from 1550 to 1750. For the general reader and the specialist.

Sand, Maurice. *The History of the Harlequinade*. 2 vols. London: J. B. Lippincott, 1915. A translation from the French of *Masques et Buffons* (Paris: Michel Levy Freres, 1860.) Makes interesting reading for the general reader but is not a reliable source for scholars. Primarily deals with the characters of the Commedia dell'Arte and the actors who shaped them. (622 pages)

Smith, Winifred. *The Commedia dell'Arte*. New York: B. Blom, 1964. A history for the general reader, covering: origins, typical scenarios, commedia in foreign countries in the sixteenth and seventeenth centuries, and transformation of the commedia. Appendices include: scenarios, relations with English drama. Bibliography. Index. Illustrations. (291 pages)

Toschi, Paulo. *Le origini del Teatro Italiano*. Turin, 1955. Toschi details how the masks of the Commedia dell'Arte developed from the cast of characters that made up the Medieval carnival. Excellent scholarly work.

ARTICLES

Mazzone-Clementi, Carlo. "Commedia and the Actor." *The Drama Review* 18.1 (March 1974): 59–64. Mazzone-Climenti, the director of the dell'Arte Troupe and School, discusses the influence of Lecoq and Marceau on his work and his approach to teaching commedia acting. The article includes some techniques and exercises.

ANTHROPOLOGY OF MIME AND GESTURE

BOOKS

Fleshman, Bob: ed. *Theatrical Movement: A Bibliographical Anthology*. New York: Scarecrow Press, 1986. Guide for those working in theatre, dance, and related movement forms who are seeking a basic understanding of various areas of human movement beyond their own particular discipline. Each section is written by an expert in the area. Includes an essay which orients the reader to the subject area and a basic bibliography which lists published materials on the subject. The section on mime is written by Bari Rolfe. Also includes theatrical movement in Asia, Africa, Oceania, and the Americas.

Jousse, Marcel. *L'antropologie du geste*. Paris: Gallimard, 1974. An anthropological study for the serious scholar which traces the origin of human expression to a "language of gestures." The book is divided into three large chapters; rhythmism, bilateralism, and formalism. Jousse's point of departure is the law of human mimesis—that human beings have a spontaneous tendency to imitate or mime all the actions both human and inanimate from the world which surround them. His basic premise is that the universe performs an immense mimodrama made up of myriad tri-phased actions. These actions are intussuscepted by man and form the basis of his memory, thoughts, dreams, and hence his language. In chapter two—Bilateralism—Jousse traces logic as well as parallelism in oral recitation to human bilateralism. In chapter three—Formalism—he discusses human's biological tendency to stereotype the originally spontaneous gesture as the social, religious, liturgic and artistic forms that are the basis of culture. A fascinating and unique study. (411 pages)

Lorelle, Yves. *L'expression corporelle du mime sacré au mime du théâtre*. Paris: La Renaissance du Livre, Collections Dionysos, 1974. (*See* under Histories of Mime.)

Royce, Anya Peterson. *Movement and Meaning: Creativity and Interpretation in Ballet and Mime*. Bloomington: Indiana University Press, 1984. For the knowledgeable reader and specialist. Written by an anthropologist and a dancer with a strong interest in mime. Argues that the meaning ballet and mime convey have been affected not only by their form and structure but also by the context of their performances, i.e., time in history, location, political and legal pressures, and level of audience sophistication. References to Marceau, Decroux, and special chapter on Commedia dell'Arte. (234 pages)

ARTICLES

Barba, Eugenio. "Theatre Anthropology." *The Drama Review* 26.2 (Summer 1982): 5–32. The task of theatre anthropology, according to Barba, is to trace "recurrent principles" that might be useful to theatre practice. This article analyzes the special techniques possessed by Oriental actors that contribute to their powerful stage presence. Barba attributes the actor's presence in the Noh, Kabuki, Balinese and Indian traditions to techniques of balance in action, the play of oppositions, and simplification. Applies findings to the mime of Decroux and Marceau.

THE NO

BOOKS

Blacker, Carmen. *The Catalpa Bow: A Study of Shamanic Practices in Japan*. London: Allen and Unwin, 1975. An excellent, authoritative study of shamanism in Japan which includes references to shamanic influence on the No. The study begins and ends with episodes from No plays. For the general reader as well as the scholar.

Inoura, Yoshinobu. *A History of Japanese Theatre 1: Noh and Kyogen*. Tokyo: Kokusai Bunka Shinkoki (Japan Cultural Society), 1971. One of the most authoritative studies in the field on the history of Japanese theatre from ancient and medieval periods up to A.D. 1600. Gives a detailed account of the origins, history, prototypes and actuality of the various genres of the performing arts, especially the No. Includes chapters on Kagura, bugaku, new Sarugaku, prototypes of the No, Ennen Noh, Sarugaku Noh, Dengaku Noh, Shugen Noh, Nohgaku, and relation with chinese drama. For the serious scholar only. Appendices. No illustrations. (163 pages)

Keene, Donald. *No: The Classical Theatre of Japan.* Tokyo, New York, and San Francisco: Kodansha, 1966. An elaborate book on all aspects of No and Kyogen intended for the sophisticated enthusiast but not the serious scholar. Chapters include: the pleasures of the No; history of No; No and Kyogen as literature; background of the performances (actor training, schools, masks, and costumes); music and dance; No stage and its properties. The text by Keene is richly illustrated with 398 gorgeous color plates and black and white photos with extensive explanatory captions. Also includes an excerpt and phono sheet from the No play *Funa Benki.* Oversized book. (400 + pages)

Komparu, Kunio. *The Noh Theatre: Principles and Perspectives.* Trans. Jane Corddry. New York, Tokyo, and Kyoto: Weatherhill/Tankosha, 1983. Probably the best and most lucid book available in English on No for the general reader as well as the scholar. Written by a No drum (taiko) player who is also a journalist specializing in architecture, it focuses on the No as an art of time and space. The book is divided into three parts: principles and perspectives, elements and patterns, structure and performance. Under these headings, thirteen chapters cover individual elements of the No. Includes glossary, index and illustrations. (376 pages)

Ortolani, Benito. *The Japanese Theatre: From Shamanistic Ritual to Contemporary Pluralism.* Leiden, The Netherlands: E. J. Brill, 1990. A book for the scholar which draws upon all the important international scholarship on the origins of the Japanese theatre arts. It is of special importance because it includes current scholarship which throws new light on the influence of shamanic practices on the development of the theatre and dance, especially with regard to the Nō. Chapters include: The Beginnings; Kagura; Gigaku; Bugaku; Theatrical Arts from the ninth to the thirteenth century: Nogaku (Theories on origins of Nō, History of Founders, Zeami's Writings, Basic Concepts of Zeami's Aesthetics, Zenchiku's Theories on the No, No play classification, and No performance); Kabuki; The Puppet Theatre; The Modern Theatre: Shimpa; Shingeki: The New Drama; Modern Music and Dance Theatre; and History of Western Research on Japanese Theatre. Also includes a glossary, extensive bibliography, and index. (368 pages)

Zeami, Motokiyo. *Ze-ami: Kadensho* (Writings on the tradition of [creative] flowering, ca. 1404). Trans. Chuichi Sakurai et al. Kyoto: Sumiya-Shinobe, (1968) 1969. The teaching of Kan-ami as recorded by his son. Includes: the ages of training for the No actor, discussion of monomane, origin of the No, and some of its secrets. (109 pages, 8 color plates)

_____. *On the Art of the Nō Drama: The Major Treatises of Zeami.* Trans. Thomas Rimer and Masakazu Yamazaki. Princeton, N.J.: Princeton University Press, 1984. Includes nine of Zeami's treatises on the secrets of the No.

Introductory Essays by Thomas Rimer and Masakazu Yamazaki. Glossaries. Selected bibliography in western languages and index. Color and black and white illustrations. (300 pages)

ARTICLES

Berberich, Junko Sakaba. "Some Observations of Movement in No." *Asian Theatre Journal* 1.2 (Fall 1984): 207–215. Based on Berberich's participation in a two week workshop on the No taught by Nomura Shiro, a No actor of the Kanze school. Describes basic posture kamae, slide walk (hakobi); jo-ha-kyu; movement phrase; and the three dimensionality of No movement. Includes drawings.

Bethe, Monica, and Karen Brazell. "Dance in the No Theatre." *Cornell University East Asia Papers* 1.29 (1982). A lengthy scholarly analysis and classification of No dance patterns from the standpoint of ground patterns and design patterns. Develops the thesis that abstract ground patterns predominate and create the structure of the dance, while design patterns evoke the meaning of the text.

Gillespie, John K. "Interior Action: the Impact of Noh on Jean-Louis Barrault." *Comparative Drama.* Winter 1982/83: 325–44. Discusses the influence of the No on Barrault via his relationship with Charles Dullin, Etienne Decroux, Antonin Artaud, and Paul Claudel.

Hoaas, Solrun. "The Legacy of Possession." *The Drama Review* 26.4 (Winter 1982): 82–86. An excellent short article that explores the transition of the No mask from religious object to artistic object.

Hoff, Frank. "Dance to Song in Japan," *Dance Research Journal of CORD* 9/1 (Fall/Winter 1976-77): 1–15. An important essay which relates movement (*fuzei*) in the No to the meaning of the words in the chanted text. Hoff finds that there is a metaphorical equivalency between significant movement and verbal meaning which originated in shamanic song and dance.

Ito, Sachiyo. "Some Characteristics of Japanese Expression as They Appear in Dance." *CORD Dance Research Annual* (1979): 75–80. An article for the general reader on traditional Japanese dance (No, Kabuki, Kamigata Mai, and Shin Buyo). Includes definitions and classification of mai and odori; the relationship of calligraphy to Japanese dance quality; and the emotional and spiritual nature of Japanese dance.

Kirby, Ernest Theodore. "The Origin of No Drama." *Educational Theatre Journal* 25.3 (October 1973): 269–84. An interesting article for the general reader. Is not considered to be authoritative because of inaccuracies and lack of knowledge of the primary sources in Japanese.

Lamarque, Peter. "Expression and the Mask: The Dissolution of Personality in Noh." *The Journal of Aesthetics and Art Criticism* 47.2 (Spring 1989): 157–167. Drawing primarily on the writings of Zeami Motokiyo, Lamarque explores characterization in the No, as exhibited in performances, from the standpoint of individuality without personality.

McKinnon, Richard N. "Zeami on the Art of Training." *Harvard Journal of Asiatic Studies* 16 (June 1953): 206–25. Discusses Zeami's three major requisites for an ideal No actor: technical mastery of an exhaustive repertoire; cultivation of the aesthetic quality of yugen, or gracefulness, and; the acquisition of intuitive perceptiveness about the No. Also includes Zeami's procedures for actor training: the importance of the three roles (santai), and the technical mastery of chant and dance.

Ortolani, Benito. "Shamanism in the Origins of the No Theatre." *Asian Theatre Journal* 1:2 (Fall 1984): 166–90. An article for the serious scholar which discusses the nature and variety of theories concerning the No and then focuses upon current research which connects the No to shamanic rituals.

———. "Zeami's Aesthetics of the No and Audience Participation," *Educational Theatre Journal* 24 (1972): 109–17. An article for the general reader which explores the concepts of monomane (imitation), hana (flower), and yugen (profound and mysterious beauty) in Zeami's theoretical writings as they relate to audience participation.

Pilgrim, Richard. "Some Aspects of Kokoro in Zeami," *Monumenta Nipponica* 24:4 (1969): 393–401. Discusses four layers of meaning and usage of the term kokoro and its compounds in the writings of Zeami. The kokoro of emotion, of conscious self, of unconscious self, and of spirituality.

Sieffert, René. "Les Danses Sacrées au Japon." *Les dances sacrées*. Ed. René Sieffert. Paris: Le Seuil, 1963: 454–86. A scholarly essay that is devoted to the classification of Japanese ritual dances according to their origins. Includes a discussion of kagura, ta-mai, dengaku, gigaku, bugaku, sangaku, and sarugaku.

HOW-TO BOOKS ON MIME

Avital, Samuel. *Le Centre du Silence Mime Workbook*. Venice, CA.: Wisdom Garden Books, 1977. A how-to mime workbook with basic techniques and exercises.

Hamblin, Kay. *Mime: The Playbook of Silent Fantasy*. Garden City, N.Y.: Doubleday, 1978. Not designed to be a course in mime. Emphasis is on the exploration of mime from the standpoint of play. Each section contains a short description of specific techniques followed by games involving object illusion that can be played with partners or groups. A lot of wasted page space and a plethora of black and white photos comprise the bulk of the book. Of possible use to the creative dramatics teacher. (192 pages)

Kipnis, Claude. *The Mime Book*. New York: Harper and Row, 1974. One of the best how-to books on mime available. Provides exercises in the isolation and articulation of the various organs of the body and explains how these can be used to create mime illusions and mime pieces. Includes a glossary, photographs illustrating techniques, and six moving "flip" sequences of mime illusions.

Chisman, Isabel, and Gladys Wiles. *Mimes and Miming*. London: Thomas Nelson, 1934. Stories, songs, and ballads for simple mime plays such as "Sleeping Beauty," and "The Three Kings." Very dated.

Loeschke, Maravene Sheppard. *All About Mime: Understanding and Performing the Expressive Silence*. Englewood Cliffs, N.J.: Prentice Hall, 1982. A book for general readers—especially grade school mime teachers. Provides a superficial discussion of the history, and various schools of mime. Emphasizes the difference between literal and abstract mime. Provides some how-to on gestures and mime walks. Black and white photos. (184 pages)

Nobleman, Roberta. *Mime and Masks*. Rowayton, CT.: New Plays Books, 1979. Simple mime improvisations and mask making for the grade school creative dramatics teacher. Black and white illustrations. (151 pages)

Pecknold, Adrian. *Mime: The Step Beyond Words*. NC Press, Ltd., 1982. Written by a Canadian mime and directed to theatre students, theatre and dance professionals, and mime teachers. Designed to be used as a one semester mime course. Offers an introduction to the basic concepts of mime, neutral body attitude, tumbling routines, techniques of manipulation and illusion, and a selection of mime pieces written by the author for the Canadian Mime Theatre. Lots of fun mime exercises and good accompanying descriptive photos but, as with most how-to books on mime, it is of little value to the serious student.

Shephard, Richmond. *Mime: The Technique of Silence*. New York: Drama Book Specialists, 1971. Thirty chapters illustrated with line drawings provide a one semester introductory course on mime. Each chapter offers techniques based upon a simplified version of Decroux's scales (inclination, rotation, translations, etc.) as well as elements of illusionary mime (the walk, manipulation of imaginary objects). Also includes improvisations and homework assignments. The author does his best to try to make complex techniques and exercises understandable for the layman. (142 pages)

HOW-TO MIME BOOKS WITH
A FOCUS ON CLASSICAL BALLET

Lawson, Joan. *Mime: The Theory and Practice of Expressive Gesture with a Description of Its Historical Development*. Brooklyn: Dance Horizons, 1973 (1957). A book intended for the general reader and student of mime in its many forms. Focuses primarily on the three types of mime found in classical ballet: natural emotional expression, characterization, and occupational gesture.

Walker, Katherine S. *Eyes on Mime*. New York: John Day Co., 1969. A book for the general reader which primarily focuses on mime in classical ballet. Chapters include: character of mime, chronology of mime East and West, excursions into technique, mime in daily life, contemporary mime. Selected bibliography and filmography. Black and white photos. (190 pages)

INDEX